THE ANNALS OF
QUINTUS ENNIUS

T0382368

THE ANNALS OF
QUINTUS ENNIUS

EDITED BY

ETHEL MARY STEUART

CLASS. TRIP. CAMB.
M.A.LOND., D.LITT.EDIN.

Ottilie Hancock Fellow of Girton College,
Cambridge, Lecturer in Latin
in the University of
Edinburgh

CAMBRIDGE
AT THE UNIVERSITY PRESS
MCMXXV

CAMBRIDGE
UNIVERSITY PRESS

University Printing House, Cambridge CB2 8BS, United Kingdom

Published in the United States of America by Cambridge University Press, New York

Cambridge University Press is part of the University of Cambridge.

It furthers the University's mission by disseminating knowledge in the pursuit of
education, learning and research at the highest international levels of excellence.

www.cambridge.org
Information on this title: www.cambridge.org/9781107426870

First published 1925
First paperback edition 2014

A catalogue record for this publication is available from the British Library

ISBN 978-1-107-42687-0 Paperback

To

MY HONOURED TEACHER

A. E. HOUSMAN

PREFACE

IT is a remarkable fact that while the importance of the *Annales* of Ennius is universally recognised by students of classical literature, the fragments have not hitherto been edited with English notes. Even at this late date, therefore, the present is in a sense a pioneer work, and as such may have the good fortune to go some way towards supplying a real need. Critically, my aim throughout has been to distinguish what is actually known to be genuine from all that is attributed to Ennius by conjecture only. Hence I have admitted to the body of the text nothing of which the authorship is not specifically vouched for by our authorities; lines quoted "anonymously," which appear to be authentic are placed in an appendix following the book to which they would naturally belong, while more doubtful cases are reserved for the general appendix A (*Fragmenta Dubia*). Asterisks distinguish those lines which are placed doubtfully in the books in which they stand. Within the books, I have endeavoured to arrange the lines in the order which seems, wherever it is possible to trace the development of the theme, to offer that which is most natural and harmonious. It is here that the sharpest divisions of opinion are bound to arise, but I have carefully indicated in the commentary all points in which the generally accepted arrangement and interpretation differ from my own proposals. Excursus I (on the narrative of the Punic Wars) is a case in point. The same problem is intensified in those books, such as the first, of which we possess a large number of fragments. Here an interesting suggestion, which has a high degree of *prima facie* probability, is that Macrobius in his series of quotations

(*Sat.* VI. 1. 11–15) follows the actual order of the text of Ennius. But the traditional interpretation of *Nec pol homo*, etc. (quoted in VI. 1. 15) and *Accipe daque fidem*, etc. (quoted in VI. 1. 13), from which I have seen no reason to depart, compels us to reverse Macrobius' order, while my own explanation of *Quom superum*, etc. (quoted in VI. 1. 14) makes it the earliest of the three (*cf.* notes *ad loc.*[1]). In matters so controversial, individual interpretations of detached fragments and scattered lines cannot commend themselves to all critics, but I have sought, without fanciful reconstructions, to present a consistent picture of the whole poem as a work of art.

Reference has been made throughout to the following editions:

J. Vahlen, First edition, Leipzig 1854 (V i); Second edition, Leipzig 1903 (V ii).

L. Müller, as given in the *Corpus Poetarum Latinorum* (of Postgate), representing the 1888 revision of his text of 1884 (M).

L. Valmaggi, Torino 1900 (Val.).

G. Pascoli, in *Epos*, Livorno 1911 (P).

To other books references are made as they arise in the course of the commentary; but I must specially acknowledge my debt to the great work of Vahlen, to the stimulating *Ennius und Vergilius* of Professor E. Norden, and to the *Early Latin Verse* (as well as to a multitude of other publications by the same author) of the *doyen* of such studies in Great Britain, Professor W. M. Lindsay.

My thanks are due to the following also for much help

---

[1] The fragments in question are those numbered by me 12, 19, 32, 37, 41. Following Macrobius we should accept 12, 19, 41, 32, 37 as the correct order.

of various kinds: the late Monsignor Duchesne of the French
School at Rome; the late Professor James Seth of Edinburgh;
Emeritus Professor E. V. Arnold, Bangor; Dr T. Ashby,
The British School at Rome; Professor R. S. Conway,
Manchester; "Mm. La Direction," Bibliothèque Nationale,
Paris; Dr P. Giles, Master of Emmanuel College, Cambridge;
Professor H. Stuart Jones, Oxford; Mrs Arthur Strong,
British School at Rome; Professor W. J. Watson, Edinburgh.
I have further to thank my brother, the Rev. F. A. Steuart,
M.A., B.D., who supplied the substance of my note on
Book VII, Fr. 3 (on Sarra as a name for Tyre), and my father,
John A. Steuart, to whose constant interest, no less than to
his wide literary experience, I owe so much.

For grants of money in aid of this work I am indebted
to the Mistress and Council of Girton College, Cambridge,
and the Court of the University of Edinburgh, acting as
trustees of the Earl of Moray Endowment Fund.

Finally, I must record my obligation to the readers of the
Cambridge Press for their unfailing skill and care.

E. M. S.

August 1925.

CONTENTS

ANNALS OF QUINTUS ENNIUS

BOOK I

FR. 1*

Musae quae pedibus magnum pulsatis Olympum.

Varro, *L.L.* VII. 20; cf. *id. R.R.* I. 1. 4; Serv. ad *Aen.* XI. 660.

> Varro, *L.L.* VII. 20: 'Musae' e.q.s.: caelum dicunt Graeci Olympum, montem in Macedonia omnes. *Id. R.R.* I. 1.4: et quoniam, ut aiunt, dei facientes adiuuant, prius inuocabo eos, nec, ut Homerus et Ennius, 'Musas' e.q.s. Serv. ad *Aen.* XI. 660: Ennius ad Musas 'quae pedibus pulsatis Olympum.'

FR. 2*

Lunai portum, est operae, cognoscite, ciues,
†Nam latos populos res atque poemata nostra
Cluebant†.

Pers. VI. 9ff.; Probus, 231 K.

> Pers. VI. 9ff.: 'Lunai portum, est operae, cognoscite ciues.' | Cor iubet hoc Enni postquam destertuit esse | Maeonides, quintus pauone ex Pythagoreo. Probus, 231 K.: neutro genere in casibus supra dictis sine ambiguitate breuis est [syllaba]....Ennius in primo 'Nam latos' e.q.s.

'Cluebunt' Dousa. 'Latos | Per populos terrasque poemata nostra cluebunt | Clara' Ilbergius. 'Nostra Latinos per populos terrasque poemata clara cluebunt' M et P. VI Ilbergium sequitur, VII Probi lectionem refert.

FR. 3*

Visus Homerus adesse poeta.

Cic. *Acad. Pr.* II. 16. 51 et 27. 88; cf. *id. de Repub.* VI. 10. 10.

> Cic. *Acad. Pr.* II. 16. 51: num censes Ennium, cum in hortis cum Seruio Galba ambulauisset, dixisse 'uisus sum mihi cum Galba ambulare'? At cum somniauit narrauit 'Visus' e.q.s. *ib.* 27. 88: dormientium, et uinolentorum, et furiosorum uisa imbecilliora esse dicebas quam uigilantium, siccorum, sanorum. Quo modo? quia cum experrectus esset Ennius, non se uidisse Homerum, sed uisum esse. *Id. de Repub.* VI. 10.10: fit enim fere ut cogitationes sermonesque nostri pariant aliquid in somno tale quale de Homero scribit Ennius de quo uidelicet saepissime uigilans solebat cogitare et loqui.

'In somnis mihi' add. Columna conl. *Aen.* II. 270.

Fr. 4*

O pietas animi!

Cic. *Acad. Pr.* II. 27. 88; Donat. ad Ter. *Eun.* 560.

> Cic. *Acad. Pr.* II. 27. 88: nisi uero Ennium non putamus ita totum illud audiuisse 'O' e.q.s., si modo id somniauit ut si uigilans audiret. Donat. ad Ter. *Eun.* 560: 'O festus dies hominis' pro 'homo festi diei.' Sic dicitur etiam scelus homo. Ennius 'O' e.q.s.

Fr. 5*

Memini me fiere pauum.

Charis. 98 K.; Donat. ad Ter. *Andr.* 429; *id.* ad eiusdem *Phorm.* 74, et *Adelph.* 106.

> Charis. 98 K.: pauus...Ennius 'Meminit me fieri pauum.' Donat. ad Ter. *Andr.* 429: 'Memini uidere' pro 'uidisse.' Ennius 'Meminit me fieri pauum.' *Id.* ad *Phorm.* 74: Et sic dixit 'Memini relinqui'...ut 'me minime fieri pauum' (uel 'paruum' uel 'prauum') Ennius; ad *Adelph.* 106: 'Fieret' producta prima syllaba. Ennius 'Memini me quum (uel) quam fieri pauum (uel pauidum).'

Fiere] 'fieri' codd., corr. Ilbergius conl. Macrobii *Exc. Bob. G.L.K.* v. p. 645. 'Quom memini fieri me pauom' Merula. 'Commemini' Scaliger.

Fr. 6*

Quom ueter occubuit Priamus sub Marte Pelasgo.

Prisc. III. 97 H.

> Prisc. III. 97 H.: ...'ueterrimus' quasi a 'ueter' positiuo quod Capri quoque approbat auctoritas et usus antiquissimorum. Ennius 'Quom ueter' e.q.s.

Cum Fr. 14 coniunx. M.

Fr. 7*

Assaraco natus Capys optumus, isque pium ex se Anchisam generat.

Serv. (D.) ad *Geo.* III. 35.

> Serv. (D.) ad *Geo.* III. 35: Assaracus auus Anchisae: Ennius 'Assaraco' e.q.s.

Anchisam] 'Anchisen' Serv. (D.), corr. Val.

FR. 8*

Doctusque Anchisa, Venus quem pulcherruma dium
Fari donauit, diuinum pectus habere.

Probus ad *Ecl*. VI. 31; Schol. Ver. ad *Aen*. II. 687.

Probus ad *Ecl*. VI. 31: cur ibi Anchisen facit disputantem quod hic
Silenum Deum? Nisi quod poeta Ennius Anchisen augurii ac per hoc
diuini quiddam habuisse praesumit sic 'Doctusque Anchisesque Venus
quem pulchra dearum | Fari donauit diuinum pectus habere.' Schol.
Ver. ad *Aen*. II. 687: peritum multarum disciplinarum Anchisen fuisse—
[po]ssunt Naeu[ius]—qui ita de eo ait 'Doctus Anchisa Venus quem
pulcherrima diu | Fata docet diuinum ut pectus haberet.'

Doctusque Anchisa] scripsit Fleckeisenus. 'Doctus parens A.' M.
pulcherruma dium] scripsit Fleckeisenus.
v. 2: 'Fata docet fari' edd. Bernaysium secuti. Ad Probi lectionem redit
VII.

FR. 9

Transnauit cita per teneras caliginis auras.

Serv. (D.) ad *Geo*. IV. 59.

Serv. (D.) ad *Geo*. IV. 59: 'nare' pro 'uolare' ut apud Ennium in primo
'Transnauit' e.q.s.

FR. 10

Constitit inde loci propter sos dia dearum.

Fest. p. 386. 34 L.; Paul. p. 387. 4 L.

Fest. p. 386. 34 L.: 'sos' pro 'eos' antiqui dicebant, ut Ennius lib. I.
'Constitit' e.q.s. Paul. p. 387. 4 L.: 'sos' pro 'eos' antiqui dicebant,
ut Ennius 'Constitit' e.q.s.

dia dearum] 'de adiarum' Fest., corr. Aug.

FR. 11

face uero

Quod tecum precibus pater orat.

Fest. p. 218. 11 L.

Fest. p. 218. 11 L.: 'orare' antiquos dixisse pro 'agere' testimonio...
Ennius quoque cum dixit in lib. I Annalium 'face uero' e.q.s.

face uero] 'facere uero' W, corr. Columna. 'tu face uero' Aug. 'tu uero
face' VI. 'tum uero face' VII, unum tantum uersum significans.

Fr. 12

Est locus, Hesperiam quem mortales perhibebant.

Macr. vi. 1. 11.

    Macr. vi. 1. 11: est locus Hesperiam Grai cognomine dicunt. Ennius in primo 'Est locus' e.q.s.

Fr. 13*

Quam prisci casci populi tenuere Latini.

Varro, *L.L.* vii. 28; Cic. *Tusc.* i. 12. 27.

    Varro, *L.L.* vii. 28: 'cascum' 'uetus' esse significat Ennius quod ait 'Quam prisci' e.q.s. Cic. *Tusc.* i. 12. 27: itaque unum illud erat insitum priscis illis quos 'cascos' appellat Ennius esse in morte sensum e.q.s.

tenuere] 'genuere' Varr., corr. Columna.

Fr. 14*

Quos homines quondam Laurentis terra recepit.

Prisc. vii. 337 H.

    Prisc. vii. 337 H.: 'Laurentis' etiam pro 'Laurens' dicebant. Ennius in Annalibus 'Quos homines' e.q.s.

Fr. 15*

Saturno

Quem Caelus genuit.

Non. p. 289. 10 L.; Charis. 72 K.

    Non. p. 289. 10 L.: 'Caelum' neutro. Masculino...Ennius...'Saturno' e.q.s. Charis. 72 K.: 'Caelum' hoc, cum sit neutrum, etiam masculine ueteres dixerunt, et Ennius 'Quem Caelus genuit.'

Fr. 16*

Saturnia terra.

Varro, *L.L.* v. 42.

    Varro, *L.L.* v. 42: hunc antea montem (*sc.* Capitolium) Saturnium appellatum prodiderunt et ab eo late 'Saturniam terram' ut etiam Ennius appellat.

'Late' add. edd. uerbo e Varrone allato, seclus. Vii.

Fr. 17*

Excita quom tremulis anus attulit artubus lumen,
Talia tum memorat lacrumans, exterrita somno:—
Eurydica prognata, pater quam noster amauit,
Vires uitaque corpus meum nunc deserit omne.
Nam me uisus homo pulcher, per amoena sàlicta   5
Et ripas raptare, locosque nouos; ita sola
Postilla, germana soror, errare uidebar,
Tardaque uestigare et quaerere te, neque posse
Corde capessere; semita nulla pedem stabilibat.
Exin compellare pater me uoce uidetur   10
His uerbis:—O gnata, tibi sunt ante ferendae
Aerumnae, post ex fluuio fortuna resistet:—
Haec ecfatus pater, germana, repente recessit,
Nec sese dedit in conspectum corde cupitus;
Quamquam multa manus ad caeli caerula templa   15
Tendebam lacrumans, et blanda uoce uocabam.
Vix aegro cum corde meo me somnus reliquit.

Cic. *de Diu.* I. 20. 40.

Cic. *de Diu.* I. 20. 40: nunc te ad fabulas reuoco uel nostrorum uel
Graecorum poetarum. Narrat enim et apud Ennium Vestalis illa
'Excita' e.q.s.
11. ferendae] 'gerendae' (uel 'gerenda') codd., corr. Dauisius conl. fr. 20.
'ferendae' VI. 'gerendae' VII.
vv. 12–13 inuerso ordine in codd. opt. leguntur; transp. Dauisius.

Fr. 18

Te nunc sancta precor Venus, te, genetrix patris nostri,
Vt me de caelo uisas, cognata, parumper.

Non. p. 603. 6 L.

Non. p. 603. 6 L.: 'parumper,' ut saepe, interim et paruo tempore.
'Parumper,' cito et uelociter…Ennius Annali lib. I. 'Te †sane neta†
precor' e.q.s.
nunc sancta] Columna. 'sale nata' V. 'dea sancta' Ilbergius. 'uenerata'
Baehrensius. 'rogitata' Hauptius. 'sane alta' P.
te, g.] 'et' codd. 'te' VI cum edd. 'et' VII.

FR. 19

Teque, pater Tiberine, tuo cum flumine sancto.

Macr. VI. 1. 12.

> Macr. VI. 1. 12: 'Tuque, o Thybri, tuo, genitor cum flumine sancto.'
> Ennius in primo 'Teque pater' e.q.s.

FR. 20*

Ilia, dia nepos, quas aerumnas tetulisti.

Charis. 90 K.; Non. p. 317. 9 L.; Fest. p. 364. 4 L.

> Charis. 90 K.: neptis grammatici nolunt dici...et aduocari Ennium
> quod dixerit ita 'Ilia' e.q.s. Non. p. 317. 9 L.: nepos dici et femina
> potest Ennio auctore, quae nunc neptis dicitur 'Ilia' e.q.s. Fest.
> p. 364. 4 L.: antiquae id consuetudinis fuit, ut cum ait Ennius
> quoque...'Ilia dia nepos.'

tetulisti] 'ne tulisti' Non.

FR. 21*

cetera, quos peperisti

Ne cures.

Serv. (D.) ad *Aen.* IX. 653.

> Serv. (D.) ad *Aen.* IX. 653: 'cetera' id est in ceterum: est autem
> Ennianum 'cetera quos' e.q.s.

FR. 22*

Olli respondit rex Albai Longai.

Atil. Fortun. 284 K.; Donat. 396 K.; Pompeius (comm. in Donat.) 297 K.

> Atil. Fortun. 284 K.: (hexameter) minimus habet XII (syllabas), ut est
> Ennianum 'Olli' e.q.s. Donat. 396 K.: diaeresis est discissio syllabae
> unius in duas facta, ut 'Olli' e.q.s. Pompeius, 297 K.: diaeresis est
> 'Albai Longai' pro eo quod est 'Albae Longae.'

FR. 23

Haec ecfatus; ibique latrones dicta facessunt.

Non. p. 477. 2 L.

> Non. p. 477. 2 L.: 'facessere' est 'facere.' Ennius Annalibus lib. I.
> 'Haec ecfatus' e.q.s.

ecfatus] 'et fatus' codd. corr. Scaliger.

FR. 24*

At Ilia reddita nuptum.

Serv. (D.) ad *Aen.* III. 333.

Serv. (D.) ad *Aen.* III. 333: reddita more ueteri pro data accipiendum est: 're' ergo abundat. Ennius Annalibus 'ad illa reddita nuptum.'

At Ilia] Commelinus. 'ut illa' Daniel.

FR. 25

Destituunt campos riuosque remanant.

Fest. p. 354. 36 L.; Paul. p. 355. 11 L.

Fest. p. 354. 36 L.: 'remanant,' repetunt. Ennius lib. I 'Desunt riuos camposque remant.' Paul. p. 355. 11 L.: 'Remant' repetant. Ennius 'Riuos camposque remant.'

Destituunt] Scaliger. 'campos riuoque' Baehrensius. 'campos ripisque' M. 'undae' add. M. 'cliuis decedunt, riuos camposque' VI. Ad Festi lectionem redit VII.

FR. 26*

Postquam consistit fluuius qui est omnibus princeps
†Qui sub ciuilia†.

Fronto (*de Orat.*), p. 160 Nab.; Cic. *Orat.* XLVIII. 161.

Fronto, p. 160 Nab.: Tiber amnis et dominus et fluentium circa regnator undarum Ennius 'Postquam' e.q.s.

consistit] 'consis...se' Fronto corr. Beckerius, non probante VII. Volgo dicitur apud Frontonem inueniri 'qui omnium'; at testante B. Kueblero, apud VII, legitur 'omnib.' non 'omnium.' Testante eodem, ab Ennii uersu tredecim fere litterarum spatio secreta sunt quae sequuntur 'qui sub ciuilia'; quae igitur secl. VII. Cic. *Orat.* XLVIII. 161: Ita enim loquebamur 'qui est omnibu princeps' non 'omnibus princeps.'
Qui sub caeruleo] Ilbergius, VI, Val. P. 'qui sub caeruleus' Beckerus. 'qui sunt sub caelo' M.

FR. 27*

Lupus femina feta repente.

Serv. (D.) ad *Aen.* II. 355.

Serv. (D.) ad *Aen.* II. 355: sane apud ueteres 'lupus' promiscuum erat ut Ennius 'Lupus' e.q.s.

feta] 'facta' cod. C. Seruii.

FR. 28*

Fici dulciferae lactantes ubere toto.

Charis. 128 K.

> Charis. 128 K.; 'Fici.' Ennius 'Fici' e.q.s.

FR. 29

Indotuetur ibi lupus femina, conspicit omnis;
Hinc campum celeri passu permensa parumper
Conicit in siluam sese.…

Non. p. 603. 8 L.

> Non. p. 603. 8 L.: 'parumper' ut saepe interim et paruo tempore.
> 'Parumper' cito et uelociter. Vergilius lib. VI. 'pulsusque' e.q.s. Ennius
> Annali lib. I. 'te sane' e.q.s. (uide supra Fr. 18): idem in eodem
> 'Indotuetur' e.q.s.
> Hinc campum] 'in campo,' codd., corr. Columna. 'campos' Ilbergius.
> 'campum' VII.

FR. 30*

pars ludicre saxa
Iactant, inter se licitantur.

Non. p. 195. 1 L.

> Non. p. 195. 1 L.: 'Licitari' congredi, pugnare. Ennius 'pars' e.q.s.

FR. 31*

Occiduntur ubi potitur ratus Romulus praedam.

Fest. p. 340. 24 L.

> Fest. p. 340. 24 L.: 'ratus sum' significat 'putaui,' sed alioqui pro
> 'firmo,' 'certo' ponitur 'ratus' et 'ratum.' Ennius 'Occiduntur' e.q.s.

FR. 32

Quom superum lumen nox intempesta teneret.

Macr. VI. 1. 14.

> Macr. VI. 1. 14: 'et lunam in nimbo nox intempesta tenebat.' Ennius
> in primo 'Cum superum' e.q.s.

Fr. 33

Curantes magna cum cura tum cupientes
Regni dant operam simul auspicio augurioque:
...in monte...........................
Remus auspicio se deuouet, atque secundam
Solus auem seruat. At Romulus pulcher in alto   5
Quaerit Auentino, seruat genus altiuolantum.
Certabant urbem Romam Remoramne uocarent.
Omnibus cura uiris uter esset induperator.
Exspectant ueluti, consul quom mittere signum
Volt, omnes auidi spectant ad carceris oras,   10
Quam mox emittat pictis e faucibus currus;
Sic exspectabat populus, atque ora tenebat
Rebus, utri magni uictoria sit data regni.
Interea sol albus recessit in infera noctis.
Exin candida se radiis dedit icta foras lux,   15
.Et simul ex alto, longe pulcherrima praepes,
Laeua uolauit auis; simul aureus exoritur sol.
Cedunt de caelo ter quattuor corpora sancta
Auium, praepetibus sese pulchrisque locis dant.
Conspicit inde sibi data Romulus esse propritim,   20
Auspicio regni stabilita scamna solumque.

Cic. *de Diu*. I. 48. 107; Gell. VI. 6.

Cic. *de Diu*. I. 48. 107: itaque Romulus augur, ut apud Ennium est,
cum fratre item augure 'Curantes' e.q.s. Gell. VI. 6: locos porro
praepetes et augures appellant: et Ennius in Annalium primo dixit
'praepetibus sese pulchrisque locis dant.'

3. in monte] codd. omnes. 'Hinc Remus' uolgo.
12. tenebat] 'timebat' VII, cf. *Relat. Acad. Boruss.* 1894, pp. 1143 *sqq.*
('Stadtgründungsaugurium bei Ennius').
20. propritim] 'priora' cod. (B). 'propriam' cett., corr. M.

Fr. 34

Iuppiter, ut muro fretus magis quamde manus ui!

Fest. p. 312. 34 L.

Fest. p. 312. 34 L.: 'quamde' pro 'quam' usos esse antiquos, cum
multi ueteres testimonio sunt †tamen huius† ('tum Ennius' Ursinus)

in primo 'Iuppiter ut muro fretus quamde manus †impe†' (spat. 3–4 litt. relict.).

manus ui] Scaliger. 'manu stat' Lambinus. 'manu sa' olim M.

FR. 35

Ast hic quem nunc tu tam toruiter increpuisti.

Non. p. 830. 14 L.

Non. p. 830. 14 L.: 'toruiter' Pomponius 'Auctorato' 'Occidit' e.q.s.
Ennius lib. I. 'Ast hic' e.q.s.

hic] 'ic' codd., corr. Scaliger.
toruiter] 'torbiter' codd.

FR. 36

At tu, non ut sum summam seruare decet rem.

Fest. p. 384. 26 L.

Fest. p. 384. 26 L.: 'sum' pro 'eum' usus est Ennius lib. I. 'At tu' e.q.s.
At tu, non ut] Festus. 'at te non ut' Columna. 'astu non ui' VI et edd.
ad Festi lectionem redit VII.

FR. 37

Nec pol homo quisquam faciet impune animatus
Hoc, nec tu; nam mi calido dabis sanguine poenas.

Macr. VI. I. 15.

Macr. VI. I. 15: 'tu tamen interea calido mihi sanguine poenas
Persolues.' Ennius in primo 'Nec pol' e.q.s.

nec tu] 'nisi' codd., corr. Baehrensius.

FR. 38

Virgines; nam sibi quisque domi Romanus habet sas.

Fest. p. 432. 23 L.

Fest. p. 432. 23 L.: 'sas' Verrius putat significare eas, teste Ennio,
qui dicat in lib. I. 'Virgines' e.q.s., cum 'suas' magis uideatur significare.

FR. 39

Nam ui depugnare sues stolidi soliti sunt.

Fest. p. 416. 36 L.

Fest. p. 416. 36 L.: 'stolidus,' stultus. Ennius lib. I. 'Nam ui' e.q.s.
soliti] 'solidi' cod., corr. Scaliger.

FR. 40

Aeternum seritote diem concorditer ambo.

Charis. 196 K.

Charis. 196 K.: 'concorditer' Ennius Annalium libro I. ('Aeternum' e.q.s.).

FR. 41

Accipe daque fidem, foedusque feri bene firmum.

Macr. VI. 1. 13.

Macr. VI. 1. 13: 'Accipe daque fidem, sunt nobis fortia bello | Pectora.' Ennius in primo: 'Accipe' e.q.s.

FR. 42

Quod mihi reique, fide, regno, uobisque, Quirites,
Se fortunatim, feliciter ac bene uortat.

Non. p. 160. 8 L.

Non. p. 160. 8 L.: 'fortunatim' prospere. Ennius Annali lib. I. 'Quod mihi' e.q.s.

Quod mihi reique, fide] 'ea mihi reliquiae' codd., corr. M (quod VI). 'reique fidei' Rothius; cf. Lindsayius in *Cl. Rev.* x. 425 n. 'quod mihi meaeque fide et' VI. 'resque ea mi, fidei' Baehrensius. V (post primam editionem sed ante secundam) 'ea uti res (uel 'ea res ut') mique meaeque fide et': ipsam Nonii lectionem refert VII.

FR. 43

Nerienem Mauortis et Herem.

Gell. XIII. 23. 18.

Gell. XIII. 23. 18: Ennius autem in primo Annali in hoc uersu 'Nerienem' e.q.s., si quod minime solet, numerum seruauit, primam syllabam intendit, tertiam corripuit.

Herem] 'herclem' codd., corr. Meursius.

FR. 44*

Cenacula maxima caeli.

Tertull. *adu. Valent.* VII.; Schol. Ver. ad *Aen.* x. 1.

Tertull. *adu. Valent.* VII.: primus omnium Ennius, poeta Romanus, 'Cenacula maxima caeli' simpliciter pronuntiauit de elati situs nomine, uel quia Iouem illic epulantem legerat apud Homerum. Schol. Ver. ad *Aen.* x. 1: Ennius non tantum 'domum,' sed etiam 'cenacula caeli.'

FR. 45

Qui caelum uersat stellis fulgentibus aptum.

Macr. VI. I. 9.

> Macr. VI. I. 9: 'axem humero torquet stellis ardentibus aptum.'
> Ennius in primo 'Qui caelum' e.q.s.

FR. 46*

Respondit Iuno Saturnia, sancta dearum.

Serv. ad *Aen*. IV. 576; Donat. 394 K.; Expl. in Donat. 563 K.; Pompeius, 291 K.

> Serv. ad *Aen*. IV. 576: 'sancte dearum' dixit secundum Ennium
> 'Respondit' e.q.s. Donat. 394 K.: fiunt soloecismi...per comparationes
> 'Respondit' e.q.s. Expl. in Donat. 563 K.: fiunt soloecismi...per com-
> parationem sic 'Respondit' e.q.s. Pompeius, 291 K.: soloecismus est
> ...per comparationem 'Respondit' e.q.s.

FR. 47

⟨Teque⟩, Quirine pater, ueneror, Horamque Quirini.

Non. p. 172. 12 L.

> Non. p. 172. 12 L.: Hora, Iuuentutis dea. Ennius Annali lib. I.
> 'Quirine pater' e.q.s.

Teque] add. Columna.

FR. 48*

Romulus in caelo cum dis genitalibus aeuum
Degit.

Serv. ad *Aen*. VI. 763; Cic. *Tusc*. I. 12. 28.

> Serv. ad *Aen*. VI. 763: quem tibi longaeuo, id est deo: aeuum enim
> proprie aeternitas est quae non nisi in deos uenit. Ennius 'Romulus'
> e.q.s. Cic. *Tusc*. I. 12. 28: ex hoc et nostrorum opinione Romulus in
> caelo cum dis agit aeuum, ut famae adsentiens dixit Ennius.

APPENDIX TO BOOK I

FR. 49*

Somno leni placidoque reuinctus.

Fronto, p. 74 N.

Fronto, p. 74 N.: si quando te somno leui, ut poeta ait, placidoque
reuinctus uideo in somnis, nunquam est quin amplectar et exosculer...
hoc unum ex Annalibus sumptum amoris mei argumentum poeticum
et sane somniculosum.

FR. 50*

Vnus erit quem tu tolles in caerula caeli
Templa.

Varro, *L.L.* VII. 6; Ov. *Met.* XIV. 812; *id. Fasti*, II. 487.

Varro, *L.L.* VII. 6: incipiam (*sc.* de uerbis quae a poetis sunt posita)
hinc 'Vnus erit' e.q.s. Ov. *Met.* XIV. 812: Tu mihi concilio quondam
praesente deorum | (Nam memoro, memorique animo pia uerba
notaui) | Vnus erit quem tu tolles in caerula caeli, | Dixisti. *Id. Fasti*, II.
487: unus erit quem tu tolles in caerula caeli | Tu mihi dixisti: sint
rata dicta Iouis.

Addenda sunt testimonia:

1. Grammatici cuiusdam anonymi *Breuis Expositio Vergilii Georgicorum*,
ad II. 384: Romulus cum aedificaret templum Iouis (Feretrii) pelles
unctas strauit et sic ludos edidit ut et caestibus dimicarent et cursu con-
tenderent, quam rem Ennius in Annalibus testatur.

2. Varro, *L.L.* v. 55: ager Romanus primum diuisus in partes tres, a
quo tribus appellata, Titiensium, Ramnium, Lucerum. Nominatae, ut
ait Ennius, Titienses ab Tatio, Ramnenses a Romulo, Luceres, ut Iunio,
ab Lucomone.

BOOK II

FR. 1

†Pectora diu tenet desiderium post optimi regis obitum†
                                        simul inter
Sese sic memorant:—O Romule, Romule die
Qualem te patriae custodem di genuerunt!
O pater, o genitor, o sanguen dis oriundum!
Tu produxisti nos intra luminis oras.

Cic. *de Rep.* 1. 41. 64; Prisc. VI. 250 H.; Lact. 1. 15. 30.

> Cic. *de Rep.*1.41.64: iusto quidem rege cum est populus orbatus,pectora
> diu tenet desiderium, sicut ait Ennius, post optimi regis obitum simul
> inter...oriundum. Non eros nec dominos appellabant eos,quibus iuste
> paruerunt, denique ne reges quidem, sed patriae custodes sed patres
> et deos. Nec sine causa: quid enim adiungunt 'Tu' e.q.s. Prisc. VI.
> 250 H.: ...ueteres 'hoc sanguen' dixerunt...Ennius...in II. Annali
> 'O genitor o sanguen dis oriundum.' Lact. I. 15. 30: nam Romulum
> desiderio suis fuisse declarat Ennius, apud quem populus amissum
> regem dolens haec loquitur 'O Romule, Romule' e.q.s.

†diu†] Cod. Cic. man. 1. 'dia' man. 2. 'dura' Steinackerius. 'fida'
Krarupius. 'pia' Havetius.

FR. 2

Et simul effugit, speres ita funditus nostras.

Fest. p. 446. 13 L.

> Fest. p. 446. 13 L.: 'speres' antiqui pluraliter dicebant, ut Ennius
> lib. II. 'Et simul' e.q.s.

FR. 3*

Et qui se sperat Romae regnare Quadratae?

Fest. p. 312. 2 L.

> Fest. p. 312. 2 L.: Quadrata Roma in Palatio ante templum Apollinis
> dicitur, ubi reposita sunt quae solent boni ominis gratia in urbe con-
> denda adhiberi quia saxo munitus est initio in speciem quadratam.
> Eius loci Ennius meminit cum ait 'Et quis est erat Romae regnare
> quadratae.'

Et qui se sperat] Salmasius. 'et qui sextus erat' Hertzius, probante VII.

Fr. 4*

Olli respondit suauis sonus Egeriai.

Varro, *L.L.* vii. 42.

> Varro, *L.L.* vii. 42: apud Ennium 'Olli respondit' e.q.s. 'olli' ualet dictum 'illi' ab olla et ollo.

Egeriai] 'egria' codd., corr. Victorinus.

Fr. 5*

Mensas constituit, idemque ancilia...
Libaque, fictores, Argeos, et tutulatos.

Varro, *L.L.* vii. 43–4; Fest. p. 486. 1 L.; Paul. p. 485. 14 L.

> Varro, *L.L.* vii. 43–4: apud Ennium 'Mensas... ancilia' dicta ab ambicisu, quod ea arma ab utraque parte ut Thracum incisa. 'Libaque... tutulatos.' Liba quod libandi causa fiunt. Fictores dicti a fingendis libis. Argei ab Argis. Fest. p. 486. 1 L.: 'Tutulum uocari aiunt flaminicarum capitis ornamentum quod fiat uitta purpurea innexa crinibus, et exstructum in altitudinem. Quidam pilleum lanatum forma metali figuratum quo flamines ac pontifices utantur, eodem nomine uocari. Ennius 'Libaque' e.q.s. Paul. p.485. 14 L.: Tutulum dicebant flaminicarum capitis ornamentum uitta purpurea innexa crinibus et in altitudinem exstructum. Ennius 'fictores' e.q.s.

Libaque] 'Salibaque' (uel 'quae') codd., corr. Victorinus.
tutulatos] om. Festus.

Fr. 6

Si quid me fuerit humanitus, ut teneatis.

Fest. p. 152. 17 L.

> Fest. p. 152. 17 L.: 'me' pro 'mihi' dicebant antiqui, ut Ennius cum ait lib. ii. 'Si quid' e.q.s.

Fr. 7*

Mettoi Fubettoi.

Quint. i. 5. 12.

> Quint. i. 5. 12: duos in uno nomine faciebat barbarismos Tinca Placentinus...'preculam' pro 'pergula' dicens...at in eadem uitii geminatione 'Mettoi Fubettoi' dicens Ennius poetico iure defenditur.

'Metti eo et fuuetio eo' uel 'ettieo fufectio e' uel 'ettieo fufectio eo' uel 'mettieo suffectieo eo' codd. 'Mettoi Fubettoi' VI; quod iam improbat VII, G. Hermannum secutus, qui 'Metioeo Fufetioeo' scripsit.

FR. 8

Quamde tuas omnes legiones ac populares.

Fest. p. 314. 2 L.

Fest. p. 312. 32 L.: 'Quamde' pro 'quam' usos esse antiquos cum multi
ueteres testimonio sunt †tamen huius† in primo 'Iuppiter' e.q.s. (uide
1. 34)...secundo 'Quamde tuas' e.q.s.

Quamde tuas] 'quandit uas' Fest., corr. Ursinus.

FR. 9

Qui ferro minitere, atque in te ningulus.

Fest. p. 184. 17 L.

Fest.p.184. 17 L.: 'ningulus' nullus, ut Ennius lib. 11. 'Qui ferro' e.q.s.

FR. 10

Hic occasus datust, at Horatius inclutus saltu.

Fest. p. 190. 2 L.

Fest. p. 188. 27 L.: 'occasus' interitus, uel solis cum decidit a superis
infra terras: quo uocabulo Ennius pro 'occasione' est usus in lib. 11.;
'Hic occasus' e.q.s.

Horatius] 'Oratius' Fest.

FR. 11

Ingens cura mis cum concordibus aequiperare.

Prisc. XIII. vol. 11. p. 3 H.

Prisc. XIII. vol. 11. p. 3 H.: Ennius in 11. 'Ingens cura mis cum cordibus
(uel 'concordibus') aequiperare,' 'mis' dixit pro 'mei.'

'Cura mihi concordibus' Scaliger. 'curast mis concordibus' Ribbeckius.

FR. 12

Adnuit sese mecum decernere ferro.

Prisc. x. 504 H.

Prisc. x. 504 H.: illud quoque sciendum quod in 'ui' diuisas termi-
nantia praeteritum perfectum cum soleant corripere paenultimam, tamen
uetustissimi inueniuntur etiam produxisse eandem paenultimam...
Ennius in 11. 'Adnuit' e.q.s.

Fr. 13

At sese sum quae dederat in luminis oras.

Fest. p. 384. 27 L.

Fest. p. 384. 27 L.: 'sum' pro 'eum' usus est Ennius lib. I. 'At tu non' e.q.s. (uide I. 36) et lib. II. 'At sese sum' e.q.s.

Fr. 14

Ferro se caedi quam dictis his toleraret.

Fest. p. 490. 8 L.

Fest. p. 490. 8 L.: 'tolerare' patienter ferre. Accius in Neoptolemo 'Aut quisquam' e.q.s. Ennius lib. II. 'ferro se' e.q.s.

caedi] 'caede' Fest., corr. Ursinus.

Fr. 15

Haec inter se totum ✱ ✱ ✱ ✱ ⟨tuditan⟩tes.

Fest. p. 480. 31 L.

Fest. p. 480. 31 L.: '⟨t⟩uditantes,' tundentes, ⟨negotium id est ag⟩entes, significare ait Cincius ⟨de uerbis priscis. E⟩nnius lib. II. 'Haec inter' e.q.s.

'se tota ui' Scaliger. 'sese tuditant ui contendentes' Ilbergius. 'tota tum ui' M. 'egere diem tuditantes' VII.

Fr. 16*

tractatus per aequora campi.

Macr. de Verb. (G.L.K. IV. 561 K.).

Macr. de Verb. (G.L.K. IV. 561 K.): 'tractare' saepe trahere: Ennius 'tractatus' e.q.s.

Fr. 17*

Volturus in siluis miserum mandebat homonem
Heu, quam crudeli condebat membra sepulchro!

Prisc. VI. 206 H.; Serv. ad Aen. VI. 595; Charis. 147 K.; Schol. Bamb. ad Stat. Theb. III. 508.

Prisc. VI. 206 H.: uetustissimi tamen etiam 'homo, homonis' de-clinauerunt. Ennius 'Vulturus in siluis' e.q.s. (nam et 'uultur,' et 'uulturus,' et 'uulturius' dicitur). Serv. ad Aen. VI. 595: sane in usu est 'uultur' licet Cicero 'uulturius' dixerit, quod quidem potest esse

et deriuatiuum: Ennius 'uulturus in campo miserum mandebat homonem.' Charis. 147 K.: 'Volturus,' Ennius 'Vulturus in spineto
supinum mandebat hominem.'
'Vulturus' Prisc. codd. 3, Charis., Serv. codd. 3. 'uulturis' cett., nisi
quod Servii F 'uultur,' et S 'uulturius.'
in siluis] Prisc. et Serv. codd. 3. 'in campo' Serv. codd. 3. 'in campos'
Serv. R. 'in spineto' Charis.
miserum] 'supinum' Charis. et Serv. codd. 3.

FR. 18*

At tuba terribili sonitu taratantara dixit.

Prisc. VIII. 450 H.; Serv. ad *Aen.* IX. 501.

Prisc. VIII. 450 H.: ...in nominationibus, id est ὀνοματοποιίαις, siue
nominum seu uerborum nouis conformationibus non omnes declinationis motus sunt quaerendi...'taratantara,' Ennius 'At tuba' e.q.s.
Serv. ad *Aen.* IX. 501: 'At tuba terribilem sonitum.' Hemistichium
Ennii: nam sequentia iste mutauit. Ille enim ad exprimendum tubae
sonum ait 'taratantara dixit.'

FR. 19*

Isque dies postquam Ancus Marcius regna recepit.

Serv. (D.) ad *Aen.* III. 333.

Serv. (D.) ad *Aen.* III. 333: 'reddita' more ueteri pro 'data' accipiendum
est: 're' ergo abundat. Ennius Annalibus 'ad illa reddita' (uide I. 24)
et alibi 'Isque dies post aut Marcus quam regna recepit' pro 'accepit.'
postquam Ancus Marcius] Ilbergius.

FR. 20

Ostia munita est. Idem loca nauibus celsis
Munda facit, nautisque mari quaesentibus uitam.

Fest. p. 126. 2 L. et p. 312. 9 L.

Fest. p. 126. 2 L.: ⟨'mundus' quoque appellatur lautus et purus.⟩
Ennius 'idem loca nauibus celsis munda facit nautisque mari ⟨quae-
sentibus uitam⟩.' *Id.* p. 312. 9 L.: 'quaeso,' ut significat idem quod
rogo, ita 'quaesere' ponitur ab antiquis pro 'quaerere,' ut est apud
Ennium lib. II. 'Ostia' e.q.s.
celsis] Fest. primo loco; 'pulchris' secundo loco.

FR. 21*

Isdem campus habet textrinum nauibus longis.

Serv. (D.) ad *Aen.* XI. 326; Cic. *Or.* XLVII. 157.

> Serv. (D.) ad *Aen.* XI. 326: quidam 'texamus' proprie dictum tradunt
> quia loca in quibus naues fiunt Graece ναυπήγια, Latine textrina dici:
> Ennius Idem campus habet' e.q.s. Cic. *Or.* XLVII. 157: 'isdem campus
> habet' inquit Ennius et 'in templis isdem.' At 'eisdem' erat uerius,
> nec tamen probauit ut opimius: male sonabat 'iisdem.'

Isdem] 'idem' Serv. corr. e Cic. edd.

FR. 22

* * * ⟨pont⟩i caerula prata.

Fest. p. 362. 22 L.

> Fest. p. 362. 22 L.: 'Rigido' * * * * * * * * Ennius iocatus uidetur
> * * * * * * * * * * * * li est enim a manis no * * * * * * * * * * re usus
> est. Et lib. II. * * * * * * * * * * * * * * 'i caerula prata.'

'⟨pont⟩i' suppl. Scaliger. '⟨Neptun⟩i' alii. '⟨cael⟩i' Lindsayius.

BOOK III

FR. 1

Olim de caelo laeuum dedit inclutus signum.

Non. p. 72. 25 L.

> Non. p. 72. 25 L.: 'laeuum' significari ueteres putant quasi a leuando.
> Vergilium quoque sub hac ostentatione posuisse uoluerunt Georgi-
> corum lib. IV. 'si quem Numina' e.q.s. Ennius Annali lib. III. 'Olim
> de caelo' e.q.s.

inclutus] 'inlitlytus' (L.) Nonii. 'inclytus' cett.

FR. 2

Et densis aquila pinnis obnixa uolabat
Vento quem perhibent Graium genus aera lingua.

Prob. ad *Ecl.* VI. 31.

> Prob. ad *Ecl.* VI. 31: pro aere uenti hic extrinsecus accipiuntur. Ad
> quod argumentum collegimus Ennii exemplum de Annalium tertio
> 'Et densis' e.q.s.

FR. 3*

ab laeua rite probatum.

Schol. Bern. ad *Geo.* IV. 7.

Schol. Bern. ad *Geo.* IV. 7: 'laeua' prospera...ut Ennius ait 'ab laeua'
e.q.s.

FR. 4*

Postquam lumina sis oculis etiam bonus Ancus reliquit.

Fest. p. 388. 6 L.; Paul. p. 387. 14 L.

Fest. p. 388. 6 L.: interdum pro 'suos' ponebant (sc. 'sos'), ut cum
per datiuum casum idem Ennius effert 'Postquam lumina' e.q.s. Paul.
p. 387. 14 L.: 'sos' interdum pro 'suos' ponebant: per datiuum casum
idem Ennius effert 'Postquam lumina sis oculis.'

FR. 5

Tarquinio dedit imperium simul et sola regni.

Fest. p. 386. 21 L.

Fest. p. 386. 21 L.: 'solum' terram. Ennius lib. III. 'Tarquinio' e.q.s.

FR. 6*

Tarquinii corpus bona femina lauit et unxit.

Serv. ad *Aen.* VI. 219; Donat. in Ter. *Hec.* 135.

Serv. ad *Aen.* VI. 219: uersus Ennii, qui ait 'Tarquinii corpus' e.q.s.
Donat. in Ter. *Hec.* 135: (uxor dicitur) quod lotos maritos ipsae
unguebant cuius rei testis Ennius 'Exin Tarquinium' e.q.s.

FR. 7

Prodinunt famuli; tum candida lumina lucent.

Fest. p. 254. 24 L.; Paul. p. 255. 8 L.

Fest. p. 254. 24 L.: 'prodinunt' prodeunt, ut Ennius Annali lib. III.
'Prodinunt famuli' e.q.s. Paul. p. 255. 8 L.: 'prodinunt' prodeunt.
Ennius 'Prodinunt' e.q.s.

FR. 8

Circum sos quae sunt magnae gentes opulentae.

Fest. p. 386. 35 L.

Fest. p. 386. 35 L.: 'sos' pro 'eos' antiqui dicebant, ut Ennius lib. I
'Constitit inde' e.q.s. (uide I. 10), et lib. III. 'Circum sos' e.q.s.

Fr. 9

Hac noctu filo pendebit Etruria tota.

Macr. i. 4. 18.

    Macr. i. 4. 18: reliqua autem uerba, quae Auieno nostro noua uisa
sunt, ueterum nobis sunt testimoniis adserenda. Ennius enim—nisi
cui uidetur inter nostrae aetatis politiores munditias respuendus—
'noctu concubia' dixit his uersibus 'qua Galli' e.q.s. (uide iv. 4). Quo
in loco animaduertendum est non solum quod 'noctu concubia' sed
quod etiam 'qua noctu' dixerit. Et hoc posuit in Annalium septimo,
in quorum tertio clarius idem dixit 'Hac noctu' e.q.s.

Fr. 10

Postquam defessi sunt stare et spargere sese
Hastis ansatis, concurrunt undique telis.

Macr. vi. 1. 16.

    Macr. vi. 1. 16: 'concurrunt undique telis | Indomiti agricolae.'
Ennius in tertio 'Postquam' e.q.s.

stare et spargere] 'stant et' codd., corr. V.

Fr. 11

Caelum prospexit stellis fulgentibus aptum.

Macr. vi. 1. 9.

    Macr. vi. 1. 9: 'axem humero torquet stellis ardentibus aptum.' Ennius
in primo 'Qui caelum' e.q.s. (uide i. 45), et in tertio 'Caelum' e.q.s.

Fr. 12

Inde sibi memorat unum super esse laborem.

Gell. i. 22. 16.

    Gell. i. 22. 16: sed inuenimus in tertio Enni Annalium in hoc uersu
'Inde sibi' e.q.s. id est 'reliquum esse' et restare: quod quidem diuise
pronuntiandum est, ut non una pars orationis esse uideatur sed duae.

BOOK IV

FR. 1

Romani scalis summa nituntur opum ui.

Macr. vi. 1. 17; Serv. ad *Aen.* xii. 552.

> Macr. vi. 1. 17: 'summa nituntur opum ui.' Ennius in quarto 'Romani scalis' e.q.s. Serv. ad *Aen.* xii. 552: 'summa nituntur opum ui': hemistichium est Ennianum.

FR. 2*

Vulsculus perdidit Anxur.

Paul. e Fest. p. 20. 23 L.

> Paul. e Fest. p. 20. 23 L.: 'Anxur' uocabatur quae nunc Tarracina dicitur Vulscae gentis, sicut ait Ennius, 'Vulsculus' e.q.s.

FR. 3*

Nonis Iunis soli luna obstitit et nox.

Cic. *de Rep.* 1. 16. 25.

> Cic. *de Rep.* 1. 16. 25: erat enim tum haec noua et ignota ratio, solem lunae oppositum solere deficere, quod Thaletem Milesium primum uidisse dicunt. Id autem postea ne nostrum quidem Ennium fugit; qui ut scribit, anno trecentesimo quinquagesimo fere post Romam conditam 'Nonis' e.q.s.

FR. 4*.

Qua Galli furtim noctu summa arcis adorti
Moenia concubia uigilesque repente cruentant.

Macr. 1. 4. 18.

> Macr. 1. 4. 18: ...Ennius...'noctu concubia' dixit his uersibus 'Qua Galli' e.q.s.: uide iii. 9, quod ad fragmentum totus locus exscriptus est.

FR. 5*

Hos pestis necuit, pars occidit illa duellis.

Prisc. ix. 470 H.

> Prisc. ix. 470 H.: sed proprie 'necatus' ferro, 'nectus' uero alia ui peremptus dicitur. Ennius 'Hos pestis' e.q.s.

BOOK V

FR. 1

Inicit inritatus, tenet occasus, iuuat res.

Fest. p. 190. 3 L.

Fest. p. 188. 27 L.: 'occasus'...Ennius pro 'occasione' usus est...
in lib. v. 'Inicit' e.q.s.: cf. II. 10 et VIII. 25.

FR. 2

Cogebant hostes lacrumantes ut misererent.

Prisc. VIII. 428 H.

Prisc. VIII. 428 H.: ...'misero'...quod uetustissimi usi sunt...
Ennius in v Annalium 'Cogebant' e.q.s.

FR. 3*

Bellum aequum manibus nox intempesta diremit.

Acro ad Hor. *Epp*. II. 2. 97.

Acro ad Hor. *Epp*. II. 2. 97: ut Romani quondam pugnauerunt cum
hostibus Samnitibus usque ad noctem: unde et Ennius inquit 'Bellum'
e.q.s.

FR. 4

Ansatas mittunt de turribus...

Non. p. 893. 13 L.

Non. p. 893. 13 L.: 'Ansatae' iaculamenta cum ansis. Ennius lib. v.
'Ansatas' e.q.s.

'Hastas' add. Columna.

FR. 5

Quod per amoenam urbem leni fluit agmine flumen.

Macr. VI. 4. 4.

Macr. VI. 4. 4: 'agmen' pro 'actu' et 'ductu' quodam ponere non
inelegans est ut 'leni fluit agmine Thybus.' Immo et antiquum est;
Ennius enim in quinto ait 'Quod per' e.q.s.

FR. 6

Nomine Burrus, uti memorant, a stirpe supremo.

Fest. p. 364. 3 L.; Non. p. 336. 32 L.

Fest. p. 364. 3 L.: recto fronte...Cato...Antiquae id consuetudinis
fuit ut cum ait Ennius quoque 'a stirpe supremo.' Non. p. 336. 32 L.:
stirpem generis feminini...masculino Ennius Annalium lib. v. 'Nomine' e.q.s.

BOOK VI

FR. 1

Quis potis ingentis oras euoluere belli?

Quint. VI. 3. 86; Macr. VI. 1. 18; Diom. 385 K.; Serv. (D.) ad *Aen.* IX. 526.

Quint. VI. 3. 86: dissimulauit Cicero, cum Sex. Annalis testis reum
laesisset, et instaret identidem accusator ei: dic, M. Tulli, numquid
potes de Sexto Annali? Versus enim dicere coepit de libro Ennii
Annali sexto 'Quis potis' e.q.s. Macr. VI. 1. 18: 'et mecum ingentes
oras euoluite belli': Ennius in sexto 'Quis potis' e.q.s. Diom. 385 K.:
item 'potis est' pro 'potest,' ut apud eundem Ennium 'Quis potis' e.q.s.
Serv. (D.) ad *Aen.* IX. 526: hoc est, narrate non tantum initia, sed etiam
extrema bellorum: nam orae sunt extremitates. Est autem Ennianum
'Qui potis' e.q.s.

oras] 'causas' Quint.

FR. 2

Nauus repertus homo, Graio patre, Graius homo, rex.

Fest. p. 168. 5 L.

Fest. p. 168. 5 L.: 'Nauus,' celer ac strenuus, a nauium uelocitate
uidetur dictus. Ennius lib. VI. 'Nauus' e.q.s.

FR. 3*

Aio te, Aeacida, Romanos uincere posse.

Cic. *de Diu.* II. 56. 116; Aurel. Vict. *de Vir. Illus.* 35; Amm. Marc. 23. 5;
Minuc. Fel. *Oct.* 26; August. *de Ciu. Dei*, III. 17; Quint. VII. 9. 7; Charis.
271 K.; Diom. 450 K.; Prisc. XVIII. 234 H.; Isid. I. 33; Donat. 369 K.;
Prob. 221 K.; Vel. Long. 55 K.

Cic. *de Diu.* II. 56. 116: num minus ille potuit de Croeso quam de
Pyrrho fingere Ennius? Quis enim est qui credat Apollinis ex oraculo
Pyrrho esse responsum 'Aio' e.q.s.? Aurel. Vict. *de Vir. Illus.* 35:
Pyrrhus rex Epirotarum...cum imperium orbis agitaret, et Romanos
potentes uideret, Apollinem de bello consuluit. Ille ambigue respondit

'Aio' e.q.s. Amm. Marc. 23. 5: nam et oracula dubia legimus...
sortemque his posteriorem ueram quidem sed non minus ambiguam
'Aio' e.q.s. Minuc. Fel. *Oct.* 26: de Pyrrho Ennius Apollinis Pythii
responsa confinxit, cum iam Apollo uersus facere desisset; cuius tunc
cautum illud et ambiguum defecit oraculum, cum et politiores homines
et minus creduli esse coeperunt. Aug. *de Ciu. Dei*, III. 17: cui sane
de rerum futuro euentu consulenti satis urbane Apollo sic ambiguum
oraculum edidit, ut e duobus quidquid accidisset, ipse diuinus habe-
retur. Ait enim 'dico te, Pyrrhe, uincere posse Romanos.' Charis.
271 K.: amphibolia est dictio sententiae dubiae significationis...ut
'Aio' e.q.s. Diom. 450 K.: amphibolia est uitio compositionis in
ambiguo posita sententia 'Aio' e.q.s. Nec aliter eodem uersu (non-
nominato Ennio) utuntur Quintilianus et Isidorus. Prisc. XVIII. 234 H.:
et aptius quidem est priori casui prius sociari uerbum. Sed auctores
frequentissime ὑπερβατοῖς id est transitionibus utuntur ut 'Aio' e.q.s.
Donat. 369 K.: syllabarum aliae sunt breues, aliae longae, aliae com-
munes...longae...positione cum correpta uocalis...desinit...in 'i'
litteram solam inter duas uocales loco consonantis positam (quam nonnulli geminant) ut 'Aio' e.q.s. Prob. 221 K.: illa ergo ratione 'i'
littera duplicem sonum designat, una quamuis figura sit, si undique
fuerit cincta uocalibus ut...'Aio' e.q.s. Vel. Long. 55 K.: sed quotiens, ut supra diximus, duabus uocalibus interiecta haec littera (*sc.* 'i')
est, duarum consonantium obtinet uicem. Sic non erit acephalus
uersus 'Aio' e.q.s.

FR. 4*

Mulserat huc nauem conpulsam fluctibus pontus.

Prisc. IX. 486 H.

Prisc. IX. 486 H.: 'mulgeo' quoque 'mulsi' facit...Ennius in VII Annalium 'Mulserat' e.q.s.

FR. 5*

Et melior nauis quam quae stlataria portat.

Schol. Vallae ad Juv. *Sat.* VII. 134.

Schol. Vallae ad Juv. *Sat.* VII. 134: 'stlataria.' Probus exponit 'illece-
brosa,' Ennius: 'Et melior' e.q.s.

FR. 6

Intus in occulto mussabant.

Fest. p. 384. 20 L.

Fest. p. 384. 20 L.: ⟨summ⟩ussi dicebantur ⟨murmuratores⟩...Ennius
in sexto...'⟨i⟩ntus in occulto mussa⟨bant⟩.'

intus] 'ntus' cod. Suppl. O. Muellerius.

FR. 7

Balantum pecudes quatit; omnes arma requirunt.

Macr. VI. 1. 54.

> Macr. VI. 1. 54: 'puluerulentus eques furit: omnes arma requirunt.'
> Ennius in sexto 'Balantum' e.q.s.

FR. 8*

taetrosque elephantos.

Isid. *Or.* x. 270.

> Isid. *Or.* x. 270: 'tetrum' enim ueteres pro 'fero' ut Ennius....

FR. 9

Incedunt arbusta per alta, securibus caedunt,
Percellunt magnas quercus, exciditur ilex,
Fraxinus frangitur, atque abies consternitur alta,
Pinus proceras peruortunt; omne sonabat
Arbustum fremitu siluai frondosai.

Macr. VI. 2. 27.

> Macr. VI. 2. 27: 'itur in antiquam siluam...ingentes montibus ornos.
> Ennius in sexto 'Incedunt' e.q.s.

FR. 10*

Nec mi aurum posco, nec mi pretium dederitis;
Nec cauponantes bellum, sed belligerantes
Ferro non auro uitam cernamus utrique:
Vosne uelit an me regnare era, quidue ferat Fors,
Virtute experiamur. Et hoc simul accipe dictum;   5
Quorum uirtuti belli fortuna pepercit,
Eorundem libertati me parcere certum est.
Dono, ducite, doque uolentibus cum magnis dis.

Cic. *de Off.* I. 12. 38; Serv. ad *Aen.* XII. 709 et X. 532.

> Cic. *de Off.* I. 12. 38: Pyrrhi quidem de captiuis reddendis illa praeclara
> sententia est. 'Nec mi' e.q.s. regalis sane et digna Aeacidarum genere
> sententia. Serv. ad *Aen.* XII. 709: 'inter se coisse uiros et cernere ferro':
> uera et antiqua haec est lectio. Nam Ennium secutus est qui ait: 'olli

cernabant magnis de rebus agentes,' et idem 'ferro...utrique.' *Id.*
ad *Aen.* x. 532: 'parce' autem est secundum antiquos 'serua,' ut
apud Lucilium et Ennium inuenitur.

7. libertati me] 'me libertati' codd. Cic., corr. Lachmannus.

FR. 11*

Quo uobis mentes rectae quae stare solebant
Antehac, dementes sese flexere uiai?

Cic. *de Sen.* VI. 16.

> Cic. *de Sen.* VI. 16: (Appius Claudius) cum sententia senatus inclinaret
> ad pacem cum Pyrrho foedusque faciendum, non dubitauit dicere illa,
> quae uersibus persecutus est Ennius 'Quo uobis' e.q.s.

uiai] 'uia' codd., corr. Lambinus ad Hor. *Carm.* III. 5. 45.

FR. 12

Sed quid ego hic animo lamentor?

Donat. ad Ter. *Phorm.* 821.

> Donat. ad Ter. *Phorm.* 821: 'parare animo': uenuste additum animo.
> Ennius in sexto 'Sed quid ego' e.q.s.

FR. 13*

Orator sine pace redit regique refert rem.

Varro, *L.L.* VII. 41.

> Varro, *L.L.* VII. 41: apud Ennium 'Orator' e.q.s. Orator dictus ab
> oratione.

FR. 14

Ast animo superant, atque aspera prima...
..........fera belli spernunt...

Schol. Ver. ad *Aen.* v. 473.

> Schol. Ver. ad *Aen.* v. 473: Ennius in VI. 'Aut animos superant atque
> asp...rima...fera belli spernunt.'

Ast] 'aut' cod., corr. V.
animo] 'animos' cod., corr. Keilius.
aspera prima] Keilius. 'asperrima' Maius.
'Mortiferi belli' M. 'munera' Keilius. 'uolnera' VI.
...'era' VII, quod ipso in codice nihil ante 'era' apparere credit.

FR. 15*

stolidum genus Aeacidarum
Bellipotentes sunt magis quam sapientipotentes.

Cic. *de Diu.* II. 56.

> Cic. *de Diu.* II. 56: quamquam semper fuit ut apud Ennium est 'stolidum' e.q.s.

FR. 16

...Diui hoc audite parumper
Vt pro Romano populo prognariter armis
Certando prudens animam de corpore mitto.

Non. p. 218. 19 L.

> Non. p. 218. 19 L.: 'prognariter' strenue, fortiter et constanter.... Ennius Annalium lib. VI. 'Diui' e.q.s.

Diui] 'diu' codd., corr. Junius.

FR. 17

Tum cum corde suo diuum pater atque hominum rex
Effatur.

Macr. VI. 1. 10.

> Macr. VI. 1. 10: 'conciliumque uocat diuum pater atque hominum rex.' Ennius in sexto 'Tum cum corde' e.q.s.

FR. 18

Vertitur interea caelum cum ingentibus signis.

Macr. VI. 1. 8.

> Macr. VI. 1. 8: 'uertitur interea caelum et ruit oceano nox.' Ennius in libro sexto 'Vertitur' e.q.s.

FR. 19

Vt primum tenebris abiectis indalbabat.

Achill. Stat. ad Catull. LXIII. 40.

> Achill. Stat. ad Catull. LXIII. 40: 'lustrauit aethera album.' Ennius de sole (uide I. 33). Et in sexto 'Vt primum' e.q.s.

FR. 20

lumen scitus agaso.

Fest. p. 444. 6.

> Fest. p. 444. 6: ⟨scitae alias quae sunt⟩ bona facie, a⟨li⟩as bonis ⟨artibus mulieres a⟩ poetis usurpantur....Ennius in lib. VI. 'lumen' e.q.s.

FR. 21

Explorant Numidae; totam quatit ungula terram.

Macr. VI. I. 22.

> Macr. VI. I. 22: 'quadrupedante putrem sonitu quatit ungula campum.' Ennius in sexto 'Explorant' e.q.s.

BOOK VII

FR. I

Haece locutus uocat quocum bene saepe libenter
Mensam sermonesque suos rerumque suarum
Comiter inpartit, magnam cum lassus diei
Partem triuisset de summis rebus regendis,
Consilio indu foro lato sanctoque senatu;   5
Quoi res audacter magnas paruasque iocumque
Eloqueretur se cura, malaque et bona dictu
Euomeret, si qui uellet, tutoque locaret;
Quocum multa uolup ⟨ac⟩ gaudia clamque palamque,
Ingenium quoi nulla malum sententia suadet   10
Vt faceret facinus leuis aut malus; doctus, fidelis,
Suauis homo, facundus, suo contentus, beatus,
Scitus, secunda loquens in tempore, commodus, uerbum
Paucum, multa tenens antiqua, sepulta uetustas
Quae facit, et mores ueteresque nouosque, tenens res   15
Multorum ueterum, leges diuumque hominumque,
Prudenter qui dicta loquiue tacereue posset.
Hunc inter pugnas Seruilius sic conpellat.

Gell. XII. 4. 4.

> Gell. XII. 4. 4: descriptum definitumque est a Quinto Ennio in Annali septimo graphice admodum sciteque sub historia Gemini Seruilii, uiri

nobilis quo ingenio, qua comitate...amicum esse conueniat hominis
genere et fortuna superioris. 'Haece' e.q.s. L. Aelium Stilonem dicere
solitum ferunt, Q. Ennium de semet ipso haec scripsisse picturamque
istam morum et ingenii ipsius Q. Ennii factam esse.

1. Haece locutus] 'haec eloqu(cu)tus' (uel 'locutus') codd., corr. Stephanus.
3. Comiter] 'comitū' Z. 'cōmunit' T. 'comiĭt' Y.
magnam c. l. d. p. triuisset] Baehrensius. 'fuisse' B. 'fuisset' cett.
'fuuisset' Lipsius. 'magna cum lapsa dies iam Parte fuisset' Turnebius.
5. lato] 'late' Y. 'Latio' Bergkius.
7. se cura, malaque] Hosius. 'et cuncta malaque et bona' (Q, Z, B, Y).
'et cuncta malusque et bona' (X, O, Π). '7 (= et) cuncta mala bonaque'
(T). '& cunctam aliisq. & bona' (N). 'et haud cunctans' Bergkius.
'el. nec cunctans' Marxius. 'el. et unose' V. olim. 'et iniunctans'
Huschkius. 'et cuncta malaque et bona' VII. 'et cuncta simul malaque
et bona' Hugius.
9. multa uolup ac gaudia] Hugius. 'uolup gaudia' (X, O, Π, N) et 2
fere litt. spat. relic. post 'uolup' (B). 'uoluptate gaudia' (T, Y). 'gaudia'
secl. VII, coni. 'multa uolup sibi fecit.'
11. aut] 'haut' (Q, B). 'haud' cett.
15. tenens res] 'tenentem' codd. VII. 'tenens res' VI.
17. Prudenter] 'prudentem' codd. VII. 'prudenter' VI.
posset] 'possit' X.
18. Seruilius sic conpellat] 'conpellat S. sic' codd., corr. Dousa.

FR. 2

Nec quisquam sophiam sapientia quae perhibetur
In somnis uidit prius quam sam discere coepit.

Fest. p. 432. 27 L.; Paul. p. 433. 4 L.

Fest. p. 432. 27 L.: 'sas' Verrius putat significare 'eas,' teste Ennio,
qui dicat in lib. I. (uide I. 38) 'Virgines' e.q.s., cum 'suas' magis
uideatur significare. Sicuti eiusdem lib. VII., fatendum est 'eam'
significari, cum ait: 'Nec quisquam philosophiam' (quae doctrina
Latina lingua nomen habet) 'sapientia quae' e.q.s. Paul. p. 433. 4 L.:
'sam' eam. Idem Ennius 'Ne quisquam philosophiam in somnis' e.q.s.
sophiam] Scaliger.
perhibetur] Scaliger. 'peribetur' Fest. 'sapientia q. p.' om. Paul.

FR. 3*

Poenos Sarra oriundos.

BOOK VII 31

Prob. ad *Geo.* II. 506.

Prob. ad *Geo.* II. 506: Tyron Sarram appellatam Homerus docet,
quem etiam Ennius sequitur auctorem cum dicit 'Poenos' e.q.s.

FR. 4*

Poeni suos soliti dis sacrificare puellos.

Fest. p. 290. 36 L.; Non. p. 233. 7 L.

Fest. p. 290. 36 L.: 'puelli' per deminutionem a 'pueris' dicti sunt.
Itaque et Ennius ait 'Poeni solitis uos sacrificare puellos.' Non. p. 232.
7 L.: 'puellos' pueros. Varro...Lucilius...Lucretius...Ennius 'suos
diuis sacrificare puellos.'

Poeni suos soliti dis] V.

FR. 5*

scripsere alii rem
Versibus quos olim Fauni uatesque canebant
Quom neque Musarum scopulos..........
Quisquam, nec dicti studiosus erat........
Ante hunc.............................
Nos ausi reserare.....................

Cic. *Brut.* XIX. 76 et XVIII. 71; *id. Or.* XLVII. 157 et LI. 171; *id. de Diu.*
I. 50. 114; Varro, *L.L.* VII. 36; Quint. IX. 4. 115.

Cic. *Brut.* XIX. 76: tamen illius, quem in Vatibus et Faunis adnumerat
Ennius, Bellum Punicum quasi Myronis opus delectat. Sit Ennius
sane ut est certe perfectior: qui si illum ut simulat contemneret non
omnia bella persequens primum illud Punicum, acerrimum bellum,
reliquisset. Sed ipse dicit cur id faciat: 'scripsere' inquit 'alii rem
uersibus.' Et luculente quidem scripserunt, etiam si minus quam tu
polite: nec uero tibi aliter uideri debet, qui a Naeuio uel sumpsisti
multa si fateris, uel si negas surripuisti. *Id. ib.* XVIII. 71: quid? nostri
ueteres uersus ubi sunt? 'quos olim...scopulos nec dicti studiosus
quisquam erat ante hunc' ait ipse de se nec mentitur in gloriando.
Id. Or. XLVII. 157: nec uero reprehenderim 'scripsere alii rem': 'scripserunt' esse uerius sentio. *Id. ib.* LI. 171: ergo Ennio licuit uetera
contemnenti dicere 'uersibus...canebant,' mihi de antiquis eodem
modo non licebit? Praesertim cum dicturus non sim 'ante hunc'
ut ille, nec quae sequuntur 'nos ausi reserare.' *Id. de Diu.* I. 50. 114:
eodem enim modo multa a uaticinantibus saepe praedicta sunt neque
solum uerbis sed etiam 'uersibus—canebant.' Varro, *L.L.* VII. 36:
'uersibus...canebant.' Fauni dei Latinorum, ita ut Faunus et Fauna
sit: hos uersibus quos uocant Saturnios in siluestribus locis traditum

est solitos fari futura, a quo fando Faunos dictos. Antiquos poetas
uates appellabant a uersibus uiendis. Quint. IX. 4. 115: ante enim
carmen ortum est quam obseruatio carminis. Ideoque illud 'Fauni
uatesque canebant.'

Fauni] 'Fauni et' Varro. 'Faunei' V.

Volgo legitur 'quom neque Musarum scopulos quisquam superarat';
quod uerbum (superarat) primum in ed. Victoriana (an. 1536) inuenitur.

FR. 6

⟨Heu⟩ quianam dictis nostris sententia flexast.

Fest. p. 306. 31 L.

> Fest. p. 306. 31 L.: 'quianam' pro 'quare' et 'cur' positum est apud
> antiquos ut.... Ennium in lib. VII. 'quianam dictis' e.q.s.

Heu] add. Scaliger.

FR. 7

Dum censent terrere minis hortantur ibi sos.

Fest. p. 388. 1 L.

> Fest. p. 386. 32 L.: 'sos' pro 'eos' antiqui dicebant, ut Ennius...
> lib. VII. 'Dum censent' e.q.s.

ibi] 'be' Festus. 'ibei' O. Muellerius.

FR. 8

Non semper uestra euertit: nunc Iuppiter hac stat.

Macr. VI. 1. 19.

> Macr. VI. 1. 19: 'nequa meis dictis esto mora: Iuppiter hac stat.'
> Ennius in septimo 'Non semper' e.q.s.

FR. 9

Fortibus est fortuna uiris data.

Macr. VI. 1. 62.

> Macr. VI. 1. 62: 'audentes fortuna iuuat.' Ennius in septimo 'Fortibus'
> e.q.s.

FR. 10

Poste recumbite, uestraque pectora pellite tonsis.

Fest. p. 488. 34 L.

> Fest. p. 488. 34 L.: 'tonsam' Ennius significat remum quod quasi
> tondeatur ferro, cum ait lib. VII. 'poste' e.q.s.: item 'pone petunt' e.q.s.

FR. 11*

Pone petunt, exim referunt ad pectora tonsas.

Fest. p. 488. 35 L.; Paul. p. 489. 13 L.

Fest. p. 488. 35 L. (cf. Fr. 10); Paul. p. 489. 13 L.: 'tonsa' remus, quod quasi tondeatur ferro. Ennius 'Pone' e.q.s.

FR. 12

Alter nare cupit, alter pugnare paratust.

Fest. p. 166. 33 L.

Fest. p. 166. 33 L.: 'nare' a 'naue' ductum Cornificius ait, quod aqua feratur natans ut nauis. Ennius lib. VII. 'Alter' e.q.s.

paratust] paratus.t. (*i.e.* Titus) Fest.

FR. 13

Denique ui magna quadrupes eques atque elephanti
Proiciunt sese.

Gell. XVIII. 5; Non. p. 152. 13 L.; Macr. VI. 9. 10; Serv. (D.) ad *Geo.* III. 116.

Gell. XVIII. 5: quem (*sc.* Enniastam quendam qui Ennii annales legebat) cum iam inter ingentes clamores legentem inuenissemus (legebat autem librum ex annalibus Ennii septimum, hos eum primum uersus perperam pronuntiantem audiuimus 'denique...ecus'...neque multis postea uersibus additis, celebrantibus eum laudantibusque discessit. Tum Iulianus egrediens e theatro: quid uobis, inquit, de hoc anagnosta et de quadrupede equo uidetur? Sic enim profecto legit: 'denique... ecus'...ecquid putatis si magistrum praelectoremque habuisset alicuius aeris 'quadrupes equus' dicturum fuisse ac non 'quadrupes eques'? Quod ab Ennio ita scriptum relictumque esse nemo unus litterarum ueterum diligens dubitauit....Sed enim contentus, inquit, ego his non fui: et ut non turbidae fidei nec ambiguae sed ut purae liquentisque esset, equusne an eques Ennius scriptum reliquisset, librum summae atque reuerendae uetustatis, quem fere constabat Lampadionis manu emendatum, studio pretioque multo unius uersus inspiciendi gratia conduxi: et 'eques' non 'equus' scriptum in eo uersu inueni. Non. p. 152. 13 L.: 'equitem' pro 'equo.'...Ennius Annali lib. VII. 'An non quadrupedes equites.' Macr. VI. 9. 9: omnes enim antiqui scriptores ut hominem equo insidentem, ita et equum, cum portaret hominem, 'equitem' uocauerunt, et 'equitare' non hominem tantum sed equum quoque dixerunt. Ennius libro Annalium septimo ait 'Denique...sese.' Numquid dubium est quin 'equitem' in hoc

loco ipsum equum dixerit cum addidisset illi epitheton 'quadrupes'?
Serv. (D.) ad *Geo.* III. 116: hic 'equitem' sine dubio 'equum' dicit,
maxime cum inferat 'insultare solo.' Ennius Annalium septimo 'Denique' e.q.s.

Fr. 14*

Illyrii restant sicis sibynisque fodentes.

Paul. p. 453. 11 L.

Paul. p. 453. 11 L.: 'sybinam' appellant Illyrii telum uenabuli simile.
Ennius 'Illyrii' e.q.s.

sibynis] E. 'sibinis' M, L. 'sibunis' Merula.

Fr. 15

Deducunt habiles gladios filo gracilento.

Non. p. 166. 12 L.

Non. p. 166. 12 L.: 'gracilitudo' [et 'gracilens' pro 'gracilis' et 'graci-
lentum' pro 'gracili' et 'gracilium'] pro 'gracilitas'....Ennius lib. VII.
'Deducunt' e.q.s.

Fr. 16

Legio redit ut rumore secundo.

Non. p. 615. 8 L.

Non. p. 614.23 L.: 'rumor' 'fauor' 'auxiliatio.'...Ennius Annali lib. VII.
'legio †redditu† rumore' ⟨et⟩ 'ruinas mox auferre domos populi
rumore secundo.'

redit ut] Baehrensius. 'redditu' Nonius.
secundo] add. M.

Fr. 17

                                          ruina
Mox auferre domos populi rumore secundo.

Non. p. 615. 10 L.

Cf. Fr. 16: 16 et 17 coniunx. VII, legendo 'murumque ruinas Mox' e.q.s.
ruina] 'ruinas' codd., corr. M.

Fr. 18

Sulphureas posuit spiramina Naris ad undas.

Prisc. VI. 223 H.

Prisc. VI. 223 H.: sed Nar seruauit 'a' productam etiam in obliquis:
Ennius in VII. Annalium 'Sulphureas' e.q.s.

FR. 19

Russescunt frundes.

Charis. 130 K.

> Charis. 130 K.: frus, 'haec frus,' quia sic ab Ennio est declinatum Annalium libro VII. 'Russescunt frundes' non frondes.

FR. 20

longique cupressi
Stant rectis foliis et amaro corpore buxum.

Serv. (D.) ad *Geo.* II. 449.

> Serv. (D.) ad *Geo.* II. 449: buxum lignum non arborem dixit, quamuis Ennii exemplo et arborem potuerat dicere neutro genere: ille enim sic in septimo 'longique cupressi Stant sectis foliis et amaro corpore buxum.'

rectis] Vrsinus.
amaro] Vrsinus.

APPENDIX TO BOOK VII

FR. 21

Appius indixit Karthaginiensibus bellum.

Cic. *de Inu.* I. 19. 27.

> Cic. *de Inu.* I. 19. 27: historia est gesta res ab aetatis nostrae memoria remota; quod genus 'Appius' e.q.s.

FR. 22

Quem nemo ferro potuit superare nec auro.

Cic. *de Rep.* III. 3. 6.

> Cic. *de Rep.* III. 3. 6: ex qua uita (*sc.* 'ciuili') sic summi uiri ornantur, ut uel M' Curius 'Quem nemo' e.q.s.

BOOK VIII

Fr. 1*

Postquam Discordia taetra
Belli ferratos postes portasque refregit,
Corpore Tartarino prognata paluda uirago
Quoi par imber et ignis spiritus et grauis terra.

Hor. *Sat.* i. 4. 60 f.; Porph. et Acron. ad loc.; Serv. ad *Aen.* vii. 622; Fest. p. 494. 7 L.; Prob. ad *Ecl.* vi. 31; Varro, *L.L.* vii. 37.

Hor. *Sat.* i. 4. 60 f.: non ut si soluas 'postquam Discordia taetra | Belli ferratos postes portasque refregit' | Inuenias etiam disiecti membra poetae. Porph. ad loc.: est sensus: si dissoluas uersus uel meos uel Lucilii, non inuenies eadem membra quae sunt in Ennianis uersibus, qui magno scilicet spiritu et uerbis altioribus compositi sunt, uelut hi sunt 'postquam...refregit.' Acron. ad loc.: 'postquam...refregit':... haec Ennii uerba sunt. Serv. ad *Aen.* vii. 622: acyrologiam fecit commutando Ennii uersum, nam ille ait 'belli...refregit.' Fest. p. 494. 7 L.: 'Tartarino' cum dixit Ennius 'horrendo et terribili' Verrius uult accipi, a Tartaro qui locus [est] apud inferos. Prob. ad *Ecl.* vi. 31: 'spiritus intus alit': aerem dictum praesumamus. Hic est etiam qui nobis uiuendi spiritum commeatum largitur. Hoc illud et Ennius appellauit in Annalibus 'Corpore' e.q.s. Varro, *L.L.* vii. 37: 'Corpore... uirago': 'Tartarino' dictum a Tartaro...'paluda' a paludamentis.

vv. 3–4 cum 1–2 inuerso ordine coniunx. Nord.

Fr. 2

†proeliis promulgatis†
Pellitur e medio sapientia ui geritur res,
Spernitur orator bonus, horridus miles amatur;
Haud doctis dictis certantes, sed maledictis
Miscent inter sese inimicitiam agitantes,   5
Non ex iure manum consertum, sed magis ferro
Rem repetunt, regnumque petunt, uadunt solida ui.

Gell. xx. 10. 1; Cic. *pro Mur.* xiv. 30; *id. ad Fam.* vii. 13. 2; Lact. v. 1.

Gell. xx. 10. 1: 'ex iure manum consertum'—ex Ennio ergo, inquam, est, magister, quod quaero; Ennius enim uerbis hisce usus est...tum ego hos uersus ex octauo Annali absentes dixi: nam forte eos tamquam insigniter praeter alios factos memineram 'Pellitur' e.q.s. Cic. *pro*

Mur. XIV. 30: etenim, ut ait ingeniosus poeta et auctor ualde bonus,
'proeliis promulgatis Pellitur e medio' non solum ista uestra uerbosa
simulatio prudentiae, sed etiam ipsa illa domina rerum sapientia: ui
geritur res, spernitur orator non solum odiosus in dicendo ac loquax,
uerum etiam bonus: horridus miles amatur. Vestrum uero studium
totum iacet. Non ex iure manum consertum, sed ferro, inquit, rem
repetunt. *Id. ad Fam.* VII. 13. 2: tantum metuo, ne artificium tuum
tibi parum prosit. Nam, ut audio, istic 'Non ex iure...repetunt.'
Lact. V. 1: disceptatione sublata 'pellitur...res' ut ait Ennius.

1. †proeliis promulgatis†] om. Gellius.
2. Pellitur] Lact. 'tollitur' Cic. *pro Mur.* 'pelliture' Gell. Z.
ui geritur res, Spernitur] 'uigeri turres' Gell. Z. 'uidetur respui spernitur'
et 'uidetur re spernitur' et 'uidetur r. p. spernitur' codd. Cic. *pro Mur.*
3. amatur] 'amit˜' Gell. Z.
4. sed] 'nec' codd. ('n̄' Z; uacat O): corr. Columna, non probante VII.
5. agitantes] 'minitantes' M metri causa.
6. manum] Π, K, Gell., cum Med. Cic. *Ep.* et codd. nonnullis *Pro Mur.*
'manu' cett.
magis ferro] Med. Cic. *Ep.* 'magis errore' Gell. 'magis' om. *Pro Mur.*
Rem repetunt] Cic. utrobique. 'rei repetunt' uel 'petunt' Gell.
7. solida ui] 'solitaui' X, Π, Gell. 'solita uicum' Q. 'solita iucum' Z.

FR. 3*

At non sic duplex fuit hostis
Aeacida Burrus.

Ekkehartius ad Oros. IV. 14. 3.

Ekkehartius ad Oros. IV. 14. 3: de quo (*sc.* Hannibale) Ennius, 'At non
sic dubius fuit hostis Eacida Pyrrhus.'
duplex] Baehrensius; quod improbat VII

FR. 4*

Qualis consiliis, quantumque potesset in armis.

Ekkehartius ad Oros. IV. 6. 21.

Ekkehartius ad Oros. IV. 6. 21: Ennius 'Qualis consiliis' e.q.s.
qualis] 'quantum' M.
in] 'is' M.

Fr. 5

praecoca pugna est.

Non. p. 219. 10 L.

Non. p. 219. 10 L.: 'praecox' et 'praecoca,' quod est inmatura. Ennius
Annali Lib. VIII. 'praecox pugna est.'

praecoca] 'praecox' Non., corr. M, non probante VII.

Fr. 6

Certare abnueo; metuo legionibus labem.

Diom. 382 K.

Diom. 382 K.: apud ueteres 'abnueo' dictum adnotamus, ut Ennius
octauo Annalium 'Certare' e.q.s.

Fr. 7

Multa dies in bello conficit unus,
Et rursus multae fortunae forte recumbunt.
Haudquaquam quemquam semper fortuna secuta est.

Macr. VI. 2. 16.

Macr. VI. 2. 16: 'Multa dies...locauit': Ennius in octauo 'Multa'
e.q.s.

Fr. 8

Iamque fere puluis ad caelum uasta uidetur.

Non. p. 320. 19 L.

Non. p. 320. 19 L.: 'puluis' generis masculini, ut saepe. Feminini
Ennius lib. VIII. Annalium 'Iamque fere' e.q.s.

Fr. 9

Consequitur, summo sonitu quatit ungula terram.

Macr. VI. 1. 22.

Macr. VI. 1. 22: 'quadrupedante putrem' e.q.s. Ennius in sexto
'Explorant' e.q.s. (uide VI. 21); idem in octauo 'Consequitur' e.q.s.

FR. 10

Amplius exaugere obstipo lumine solis.

Fest. p. 210. 13 L.

  Fest. p. 210. 13 L.: 'obstipum,' obliquum. Ennius...in lib. VIII.
  'Amplius' e.q.s.
exaugere] 'exaugure' X: ed. princ.
obstipo lumine] 'obstipolumue' W, ed. princ. 'obstipoliumue' X.

FR. 11

Hastati spargunt hastas, fit ferreus imber.

Macr. VI. 1. 52.

  Macr. VI. 1. 52: 'ac ferreus ingruit imber': Ennius in octauo 'Hastati'
  e.q.s.

FR. 12

Densantur campis horrentia tela uirorum.

Prisc. IX. 480 H.

  Prisc. IX. 480 H.: 'Denso': Ennius in VIII. Annalium 'Densantur' e.q.s.

FR. 13

His pernas succidit iniqua superbia Poeni.

Fest. p. 396. 26 L.; Paul. p. 397. 8 L.

  Fest. p. 396. 26 L.: '⟨sup⟩pernati' dicu⟨ntur, quibus femi⟩na sunt
  succisa...⟨Ennius⟩ 'Is pernas succ.........Poeni.' Paul. p. 397. 8 L.:
  'suppernati' dicuntur quibus femina sunt succisa in modum suillarum
  pernarum. Ennius 'His pernas succidit iniqua superbia Poeni.'

FR. 14*

Quintus pater quartum fit consul.

Non. p. 701. 3 L.; Gell. X. 1. 6.

  Non. p. 700. 21 L.: 'quartum' et 'quarto' prudentes differre dixerunt.
  Varro Disciplinarum V. 'aliud est quarto praetorem fieri ac quartum:
  quarto locum significat et tres ante factos: quartum tempus significat
  et ter ante factum.' Ennius recte 'Quintus pater' e.q.s. Gell. X. 1. 6:
  uerba M. Varronis ex libro Disciplinarum quinto haec sunt 'aliud est...
  ter ante factum.' Igitur Ennius recte quod scripsit 'Quintus pater'
  e.q.s.

FR. 15*

De muris rem gerit Opscus.

Fest. p. 218. 13 L.

> Fest. p. 218. 13 L.: 'Oscos' quos dicimus, ait Verrius, 'Opscos' antea dictos teste Ennio cum dicat 'De muris' e.q.s.

Opscus] 'opsus' ex 'obscus' X.

FR. 16*

Ob Romam noctu legiones ducere coepit.

Paul. p. 187. 11 L.; Fest. p. 188. 1 L.; *Id.* p. 206. 25 L.

> Paul. p. 187. 11 L.: 'Ob' praepositio alias ponitur pro 'circum'... alias in uicem praepositionis, quae est 'propter,'...alias pro 'ad,' ut Ennius 'Ob Romam' e.q.s. Fest. p. 186. 1 L.: ⟨'Ob' praepositio alias⟩ ponitur...⟨pro 'ad' ut Ennius⟩ 'Ob Romam noc'.... *Id.* p. 206. 25 L.: 'Oboritur' agnascitur: nam praepositionem 'ob' pro 'ad' solitam poni testis hic uersus 'tantum gaudium' e.q.s.; et Ennius 'Ob Romam' e.q.s.

FR. 17*

Summus ibi capitur meddix, occiditur alter.

Paul. p. 110. 20 L.

> Paul. p. 110. 20 L.: 'meddix' apud Oscos nomen magistratus est. Ennius 'Summus' e.q.s.

FR. 18*

Optima caelicolum, Saturnia, magna dearum.

Prisc. XVII. 192 H.

> Prisc. XVII. 192 H.: solent auctores uariare figuras...per species, ut Ennius 'Optima' e.q.s.

FR. 19

Tibia Musarum pangit melos.

Schol. Bern. ad *Geo.* IV. 71.

> Schol. Bern. ad *Geo.* IV. 71: inde Ennius in VIII. ait 'Tibia' e.q.s.

Musarum] 'musaeum' M.

FR. 20*

Romanis Iuno coepit placata fauere.

Serv. ad *Aen.* i. 281.

> Serv. ad *Aen.* i. 281: 'consilia in melius,' quia bello Punico secundo, ut ait Ennius, 'placata Iuno coepit fauere Romanis.'

FR. 21

Poenos Didone oriundos.

Prisc. vi. 210 H.

> Prisc. vi. 210 H.: et sciendum quod quinque inueniuntur in 'o' terminantia quae...addita 'nis' faciunt genitiuum, ut Dido, Didonis.... Ennius in viii. 'Poenos' e.q.s.

Poenos] 'penos' codd. nisi quod unus 'phoenos.'

FR. 22*

tunicata iuuentus.

Gell. vii. 12; Non. p. 861. 3 L.

> Gell. vii. 12: Q. quoque Ennius Carthaginiensium tunicatam iuuentutem non uidetur sine probro dixisse. Non. p. 861. 3 L.: Ennius probro Carthaginiensium tunicatam iuuentutem uoluit dicere.

FR. 23

tonsam ante tenentes,
Parerent, obseruarent, portisculus signum
Quom dare coepisset.

Non. p. 222. 1 L.

> Non. p. 221. 17 L.: 'portisculus' proprie est hortator remigum, id est, qui eam perticam tenet, quae portisculus dicitur, qua et cursum et exhortamenta moderatur....Ennius lib. viii. Annalium 'tonsam' e.q.s.

tonsam ante] 'tusante' codd., corr. Scaliger. 'tonsas' Columna. 'tonsamque' Carrio. 'tonsam arte' Merula. 'tusam' Lindsayius.

FR. 24

Nunc hostes uino domiti somnoque sepulti.

Macr. vi. 1. 20.

> Macr. vi. 1. 20: 'inuadunt urbem somno uinoque sepultum': Ennius in octauo 'Nunc hostes' e.q.s.

FR. 25

Ast occasus ubi tempusue audere repressit.

Fest. p. 190. 4 L.

> Fest. p. 188. 27 L.: 'occasus'...Ennius pro 'occasione' est usus...
> in lib. VIII. 'Ast occasus' e.q.s.

APPENDIX TO BOOK VIII

FR. 26*

Hostis qui feriet, mihi erit Karthaginiensis
Quisquis erit; quoiatis siet....

Cic. pro Balb. XXII. 51.

> Cic. pro Balb. XXII. 51: neque ille summus poeta noster Hannibalis
> illam magis cohortationem quam communem imperatoriam uoluit esse
> 'Hostis' e.q.s.

BOOK IX

FR. 1

Additur orator Cornelius, suauiloquenti
Ore, Cethegus Marcus, Tuditano conlega
Marci filius............................
...Is dictus ollis popularibus olim,
Qui tum uiuebant homines atque aetatem agitabant,
Flos delibatus populi, Suadaeque medulla.

Cic. Brut. xv. 58; id. de Sen. XIV.; Gell. XII. 2. 3; Quint. II. 15. 4; id. XI.
3. 31; Serv. ad Aen. VIII. 500.

> Cic. Brut. xv. 58: quem uero exstet et de quo sit memoriae proditum
> eloquentem fuisse et ita esse habitum, primus est M. Cornelius
> Cethegus, cuius eloquentiae est auctor...Q. Ennius....Est igitur sic
> apud illum in nono, ut opinor, Annali 'Additur...Marci filius.' Et
> oratorem appellat et suauiloquentiam tribuit...sed est ea laus elo-
> quentiae certe maxima: 'Is dictus...populi.' Probe uero. Vt enim
> hominis decus ingenium sic ingeni ipsius lumen est eloquentia, qua
> uirum excellentem praeclare tum illi homines florem populi esse
> dixerunt 'Suadaeque medulla.' Id. de Sen. XIV.: M. uero Cethegum

quem recte Suadae medullam dixit Ennius. Gell. XII. 2. 3: in libro enim uicesimo secundo epistularum moralium quas ad Lucilium composuit (A. Seneca) deridiculos uersus Q. Ennium de Cethego, antiquo uiro fecisse hos dicit 'Is dictus' e.q.s.: ac deinde scribit de iisdem uersibus uerba haec: 'admiror eloquentissimos uiros et deditos Ennio pro optimis ridicula laudasse. Cicero certe inter bonos eius uersus et hos refert.' Quint. II. 15. 4: (Isocrates) finem artis temere comprehendit dicens esse rhetoricen persuadendi opificem, id est πειθοῦς δημιουργόν; neque enim mihi permiserim eadem uti declinatione qua Ennius M. Cethegum 'Suadae medulla' uocat. Id. XI. 3. 31: nam sonis homines ut aera tinnitu dignoscimus. Ita fiet illud quod Ennius probat cum dicit suauiloquenti ore Cethegum fuisse. Serv. ad Aen. VIII. 500: 'flos ueterum' Ennianum.

FR. 2

praeda exercitus undat.

Breuis Expositio Georgicorum ad II. 437.

Breuis Expositio Georgicorum ad II. 437: 'undantem,' abundantem. Ennius in lib. VIIII. Annalium: 'praeda' e.q.s.

FR. 3

Rastros dentiferos capsit causa poliendi
Agri.

Non. p. 92. 22 L.

Non. p. 92. 22 L.: politiones, agrorum cultus diligentes, ut polita omnia dicimus exculta et ad nitorem deducta. Ennius...Annali lib. IX. 'Rastros' e.q.s.

dentiferos] 'dentefabres' codd., corr. Hugius. 'dentifabros' On.

FR. 4

Libertatemque ut perpetuassit,
Quaeque axim.

Non. p. 220. 10 L.

Non. p. 220. 10 L.: 'perpetuassit' ⟨sit⟩ perpetua, aeterna. Ennius Annali lib. IX. 'libertatemque' e.q.s.

perpetuassit] 'perpetias sint' (L). 'perpetuuas sint' (BA). 'perpetuassint' volg., corr. Lindsayius. 'perpetuita sint quam maxime' VII.

Quaeque axim] M. 'que maxime' codd. 'que' secl. Merula.

Fr. 5

Sed quid ego haec memoro? Dictum factumque facit frux.

Prisc. VI. 278 H.

> Prisc. VI. 278 H.: 'frux'...Ennius...in VIIII. pro 'frugi homo' frux
> ponit, quod est adiectiuum: 'Sed quid' e.q.s.

Fr. 6

mortalem summum fortuna repente
Reddidit e summo regno ut famul oltimus esset.

Non. p. 157. 11 L.

> Non. p. 157. 11 L.: 'famul' famulus. Ennius in lib. IX. 'mortalem'
> e.q.s.

summum] 'summa' L.

'Reddidit summo regno famul ut optimus' codd., corr. V. 'ultimus'
Faber. 'infimus' V, cum Lipsio. 'm. s. miserum f. r. Reddidit exutus
r. u. f. infimus e.' M. 'M. s. f. r. recidit summotus r. f. u. uelut infimus e.'
Baehrensius.

Fr. 7

uiri ualidis cum uiribus luctant.

Non. p. 757. 5 L.

> Non. p. 757. 5 L.: 'luctant' pro 'luctantur' Ennius lib. IX. 'uiri' e.q.s.

uiri] 'uaria' codd. (CA, DA). 'uiri a' cett. corr. ed. princ. 'fortuna uaria'
V. 'Illyria' Havetius.

cum] add. Dousa ap. Merulam.

Fr. 8

puluis fulua uolat.

Non. p. 320. 21 L.

> Non. p. 320. 21 L.: 'puluis'...feminini (generis)....Ennius lib. IX.
> 'puluis' e.q.s.

Fr. 9*

Poeni stipendia pendunt.

Varro, *L.L.* V. 182.

> Varro, *L.L.* V. 182: militis stipendia ideo, quod eam stipem pendebant:
> ab eo etiam Ennius scribit 'Poeni' e.q.s.

FR. 10

Debil homo.

Non. p. 136. 3 L.

   Non. p. 136. 3 L.: 'debil' debilis. Ennius lib. IX. 'Debil homo.'
Debil] 'debilo' codd., corr. Lipsius.

FR. 11

lychnorum lumina bis sex.

Macr. VI. 4. 17.

   Macr. VI. 4. 17: inseruit operi suo et Graeca uerba, sed non primus hoc
ausus; auctorum enim ueterum audaciam secutus est: 'Dependent...
aureis,' sicut Ennius in nono 'lychnorum' e.q.s. 'Florebant flammis'
add. VII.

FR. 12

Cyclopis uenter uelut olim turserat alte,
Carnibus humanis distentus.

Prisc. IX. 486 H.

   Prisc. IX. 486 H.: Ennius...in VIIII. 'Cyclopis' e.q.s.
alte] 'alti' codd., corr. Dousa ap. Merulam.

BOOK X

FR. 1*

Insece, Musa, manu Romanorum induperator
Quod quisque in bello gessit cum rege Philippo.

Gell. XVII. 9. 2.

   Gell. XVII. 9. 2: 'insequendo' enim scribi, inquit, debet, non 'insecendo,' quoniam insequens significat: dictum est 'inseque' quasi 'perge
dicere' et 'insequere,' itaque ab Ennio scriptum in his uersibus 'inseque' e.q.s....Velio Longo, non homini indocto, fidem esse habendam,
qui in commentario, quod fecit de usu antiquae locutionis, scripserit
non 'inseque' sed 'insece'...ego arbitror et a M. Catone 'insecendo'
et a Q. Ennio 'insece' scriptum sine 'u' littera.

FR. 2

Leucatam campsant.

Prisc. x. 541 H.

Prisc. x. 541 H.: 'cambio' 'ἀμείβω' ponit Charisius et eius praeteritum 'campsi' quod ἀπὸ τοῦ κάμπτω ἔκαμψα. Graeco esse uidetur, unde et 'campso,' 'campsas' solebant uetustissimi dicere. Ennius in x. 'Leucatam campsant.'

Leucatam] 'Leucaten' uel 'leocaten' uel 'leucatem' codd., corr. V.

FR. 3*

Egregie cordatus homo, catus Aelius Sextus.

Cic. Tusc. I. 9. 18; id. de Rep. I. 18. 30; id. de Orat. I. 45. 198; Varro, L.L. vii. 46.

Cic. Tusc. I. 9. 18: aliis cor ipsum animus uidetur, ex quo excordes, uecordes, concordesque dicuntur; et Nasica ille prudens bis Consul Corculum et 'egregie' e.q.s. Id. de Rep. I. 18. 30: in ipsius paterno genere fuit noster ille amicus, dignus huic ad imitandum 'egregie' e.q.s. qui egregie cordatus et catus fuit et ab Ennio dictus est. Id. de Orat. I. 45. 198: ut ille qui propter hanc iuris ciuilis scientiam sic appellatus a summo poeta est 'egregie' e.q.s. Varro, L.L. vii. 46: 'cata' acuta: hoc enim uerbo dicunt Sabini: quare 'catus Aelius Sextus,' non, ut aiunt, 'sapiens' sed 'acutus.'

FR. 4

Insignita fere tum milia militum octo
Duxit, delectos, bellum tolerare potentes.

Prisc. I. 30 H.

Prisc. I. 30 H.: finalis dictionis subtrahitur 'm' in metro plerumque si a uocali incipit sequens dictio...uetustissimi tamen non semper eam subtrahebant: Ennius in x. Annalium 'Insignita' e.q.s.

FR. 5

Hinc nox processit, stellis fulgentibus apta.

Macr. vi. 1. 9.

Macr. vi. 1. 9: 'uertitur interea caelum et ruit Oceano nox.' Ennius... in decimo 'Hinc nox' e.q.s.

FR. 6

horitatur...induperator.

Diom. p. 382 K.

Diom. p. 382 K.: item 'hortatur' quod uolgo dicimus ueteres nonnulli 'horitur' dixerunt, ut Ennius sexto decimo Annalium 'prandere' e.q.s. (uide XVI. 17), idem in X. 'horitatur induperator' quasi specie iteratiua.

horitatur] 'horitur' codd., corr. Hugius.

FR. 7

Aspectabat uirtutem legionis suai
Exspectans si mussaret, quae denique pausa
Pugnandi fieret aut duri ⟨finis⟩ laboris.

Serv. (D.) ad *Geo.* IV. 188.

Serv. (D). ad *Geo.* IV. 188: 'mussant' autem 'murmurant.' Ennius in X. sic ait 'Aspectabat uirtutem legionis siue spectans si mussaret dubitaret-que denique causam pugnandi fieret aut duri laboris.'

suai] Bergkius.
Exspectans] Bergkius. 'suspectans' Dousa.
dubitaret] secl. edd.
pausa] Bergkius, non probante VII.
finis] add. Bergkius. 'pausa' Dousa.

FR. 8

ueluti quando uinclis uenatica uelox
Apta solet, si forte ⟨feras⟩ ex nare sagaci
Sensit, uoce sua nictit ululatque ibi acute.

Fest. p. 184. 5 L.; Paul. p. 185. 2 L.

Fest. p. 184. 5 L.: nictit canis in odorandis ferarum uestigiis leuiter ganniens ut Ennius in lib. X. 'ueluti' e.q.s. Paul. p. 185. 2 L.: nictit canis in odorandis ferarum uestigiis leuiter ganniens. Ennius 'nare sagaci' e.q.s.

ueluti] 'ueluti si' Fest., corr. Turnebius.
uinclis] 'uinculis' Fest., corr. Turnebius.
uenatica uelox Apta] 'ueneno xapta' Fest., corr. Turnebius.
feras] add. O. Muellerius.
nictit] 'nictu' Fest., corr. epit.
acute] 'acuta et' Fest., corr. Scaliger.

FR. 9

Aegro corde †comis† passis late palmis pater.

Non. p. 589. 18 L.

> Non. p. 589. 18 L.: passum, extensum, patens: unde et 'passus'
> dicimus; quod gressibus mutuis pedes patescunt. Ennius Annalium
> lib. x. 'Aegro' e.q.s.

FR. 10

pinsunt terram genibus.

Diom. p. 373 K.

> Diom. p. 373 K.: apud ueteres...'pinso,' quod est 'tundo' et 'pinsit'
> secundum tertium ordinem, ut Ennius decimo Annalium 'pinsunt'
> e.q.s.

FR. 11

Regni uersatam iam summouere columnam.

Don. ad Ter. *Phorm.* 287.

> Don. ad Ter. *Phorm.* 287: 'columen uero familiae': columen culmen
> an columen columna?...Horatius contra pro columine columnam
> (*Carm.* I. 35. 14) Ennius x. 'Regni' e.q.s.

uersatam iam summouere columnam] 'uersatum summam uero columnam' codd., corr. Scaliger.

FR. 12

Fiere.

Macr. de Verbo, *G.L.K.* IV. p. 645.

> Macr. de Verbo, *G.L.K.* IV. p. 645: a 'fio' fiere esse deberet, sed licet
> usus aliter obtinuerit ('fieri' enim nunc dicitur). Ennius tamen in x.
> Annalium 'fiere' dixit non 'fieri.'

APPENDIX TO BOOK X

FR. 13

Graecia Sulpicio sorti data Gallia Cottae.

Isid. I. 35. 3.

> Isid. I. 35. 3: zeugma...ut...'Graecia' e.q.s.

Fr. 14

O Tite, si quid ego adiuero, curamue leuasso
Quae nunc te coquit et uersat in pectore fixa,
Ecquid erit praemi?

Cic. *de Sen.* I. 1.

> Cic. *de Sen.* I. 1: 'O Tite...praemi?': Licet enim mihi uersibus eisdem
> affari te, Attice, quibus affatur Flamininum 'ille uir' e.q.s. (uide fr. 15),
> quamquam certo scio non, ut Flamininum, 'sollicitari' e.q.s. (uide
> fr. 16).

adiuero] 'adiuuero' uel 'adiuto' codd. Cic.

Fr. 15

Ille uir haud magna cum re sed plenus fidei.

Cic. *de Sen.* I. 1.

> Vide ad Fr. 14, ubi totus locus exscriptus est.

Fr. 16

Sollicitari te, Tite, sic noctesque diesque.

Ib.

BOOK XI

Fr. 1*

Quippe solent reges omnes in rebus secundis?

Fest. p. 306. 23 L.

> Fest. p. 306. 23 L.: 'Quippe' significare 'quidni' testimonio est En-
> nius lib. XL. 'Quippe' e.q.s.

Fr. 2

Contendunt Graecos, Graios memorare solent sos
................ngua longos per...

Fest. p. 362. 11 L.; *id.* p. 388. 2 L.

> Fest. p. 362. 11 L.: ✱✱✱✱✱✱s appellat Enni ✱✱✱✱✱✱cos, Grai⟨os⟩
> memo ✱✱✱✱✱✱ngua longos per. *Id.* p. 386. 2 L.: 'sos' pro 'eos'
> antiqui dicebant ut Ennius...lib. XI. 'Contendunt Graecos, Graios
> memorare solent sos.'

Fest. 2 loco 'graios grecos,' corr. V.

FR. 3

Quae neque Dardaniis campis potuere perire
Nec cum capta capi nec cum combusta cremari.

Macr. VI. 1. 60.

> Macr. VI. 1. 60: 'num capti...Troia uiros?' Ennius in undecimo cum
> de Pergamis loqueretur 'Quae' e.q.s.

FR. 4

Pendent peniculamenta unum ad quemque pediclum.

Non. p. 218. 10 L.

> Non. p. 218. 10 L.: 'peniculamentum' a ueteribus pars uestis dicitur.
> Ennius lib. XI. Annalis 'Pendent' e.q.s.
>
> pediclum] 'pedum' codd., corr. Baehrensius.   'ad quodque pedule'
> Scaliger. 'peditum' Lindsayius.

FR. 5

malo cruce, fatur, uti des

Iuppiter!

Non. p. 287. 3 L.

> Non. p. 287. 3 L.: 'crux' generis feminini saepe. Masculini Ennius
> Annalium lib. XI. 'malo' e.q.s.

FR. 6

Et simul erubuit ceu lacte et purpura mixta.

Non. p. 775. 8 L.

> Non. p. 775. 8 L.: 'lacte' nominatiuo casu, ab eo quod est 'lac.'
> Ennius lib. XI. 'Et simul' e.q.s.

FR. 7

Missaque per pectus, dum transit, striderat hasta.

Prisc. VIII. 419 H.

> Prisc. VIII. 419 H.: a 'strido' quoque alii 'stridui' alii 'stridi' pro-
> tulerunt. Ennius in Annalium XI. 'Missaque' e.q.s.

FR. 8

Tum clupei resonunt, et ferri stridit acumen

Prisc. VIII. 445 H. et IX. 473 H.

> Prisc. VIII. 445 H.: 'sono,' 'sonas' et 'sonis' Ennius in XI. Annalium
> 'Tum clipei' e.q.s. *Id.* IX. 473 H.: alia uero in 'ui' diuisas praeteritum
> desinentia 'ui' in 'itum' conuertunt in supino paenultima correpta
> 'domui,' 'domitum'... haec tamen ipsa et secundum tertiam uetustis-
> simi protulisse inueniuntur coniugationem ut Ennius in XI. Annali
> 'Tunc clipei' e.q.s.

FR. 9*

Hispane, non Romane memoretis loqui me.

Charis. 200 K.

> Charis. 200 K.: 'Hispane' Ennius Annalium libro 'Hispane' e.q.s.

FR. 10

Alte delata petrisque ingentibus tecta.

Fest. p. 226. 15 L.

> Fest. p. 226. 15 L.: petrarum genera sunt duo, quorum alterum
> naturale saxum prominens in mare cuius Ennius meminit lib. XI. 'alte'
> e.q.s.

petrisque] 'ceterisque (caet.)' cod. et ed. princ., corr. Augustinus.

FR. 11
utrique.

Fest. p. 346. 1 L.

> Fest. p. 346. 1 L.: in loco tam uasto nihil restat quod referri possit.
> Quantum ad libri numerum, testante Lindsayio, potest uel XI. esse,
> uel XII., uel XIII., uel XIIII.

BOOK XII

FR. 1

Vnus homo nobis cunctando restituit rem.
Noenum rumores ponebat ante salutem;
Ergo postque magisque uiri nunc gloria claret.

Macr. VI. 1. 23; Cic. *de Sen.* IV. 10; *id. de Off.* I. 24. 84; *id. ad Att.* II. 19;
Serv. ad *Aen.* VI. 845; Liv. XXX. 26. 9; Sen. *de Ben.* IV. 27; Suet. *Tib.*
XXXI.; Ov. *Fast.* II. 241; Samm. Seren. *de Med.* 1101.

> Macr. VI. 1. 23: 'Vnus qui nobis cunctando restituit rem.' Ennius in
> duodecimo 'Vnus...rem.' Cic. *de Sen.* IV. 10: de quo (Fabio) praeclare
> familiaris noster Ennius 'Vnus' e.q.s.   *Id. de Off.* I. 24. 84: quanto
> Q. Maximus melius de quo Ennius 'Vnus' e.q.s.   *Id. ad Att.* II. 19:
> Bibulus in caelo est, nec quare scio, sed ita laudatur quasi 'unus...
> rem.' Serv. ad *Aen.* VI. 845: Fabius Maximus:...ille est de quo ait
> Ennius 'Vnus...rem.' Sciens enim Vergilius quasi pro exemplo hunc
> uersum posuit. Liv. XXX. 26. 9: eodem anno Q. Fabius Maximus
> moritur...nihil certius est quam unum hominem nobis cunctando
> rem restituisse sicut Ennius ait. Suet. *Tib.* XXXI.: omnes confitentur
> uersum illum in te posse dici 'Vnus h.n.uigilando r.r.' Ov. *Fast.* II. 241:
> scilicet ut posses olim tu, Maxime, nasci Cui res cunctando restituenda
> foret. Samm. Seren. *de Med.* 1101: hinc quondam Fabio uerum
> cognomen adhaesit Qui solus patriae cunctando restituit rem.

Noenum] 'non enim' codd., corr. Lachmannus, non probante VII.

FR. 2

Omnes mortales, uictores, cordibus imis
Laetantes, uino curatos, somnus repente
In campo passim mollissimus perculit acris.

Prisc. V. 153 H.; *id.* VI. 230 H.

> Prisc. V. 153 H.: 'acer' et 'alacer' et 'saluber' et 'celeber' quamuis
> 'acris' et 'alacris' plerumque faciant et 'salubris' et 'celebris' feminina,
> in utraque tamen terminatione communis etiam generis inueniuntur
> prolata....Ennius...in XII. 'Omnes' e.q.s.   *Id.* VI. 230 H.: 'c' quoque
> antecedente...'er' in 'ris' conuertunt in genitiuo si sint communia uel
> in 'is' facientia feminina...et sciendum quod in utraque terminatione
> utriusque generis inueniuntur haec....Ennius in XII. 'Omnes' e.q.s.

mis] 'huius' codd. (R, H, G). 'uiuis' dett., corr. Fruterius.

BOOK XIII

FR. 1

Hannibal audaci cum pectore de me hortatur
Ne bellum faciam, quem credidit esse meum cor
Suasorem summum et studiosum robore belli?

Gell. VII. 2. 3; Non. p. 287. 11 L.

> Gell. VII. 2. 3: scripsit autem Caesellius, Q. Ennium in XIII. libro An-
> nalium 'cor' dixisse masculino genere. Verba Caesellii subiecta sunt:
> 'masculino genere cor, ut multa alia, enuntiauit Ennius, nam in XIII.
> Annali "quem cor" dixit.' Ascripsit deinde uersus Ennii duo. [Han-
> nibal...meum cor.] Antiochus est qui hoc dicit, Asiae rex....Hoc
> Caesellius quidem, sed aliud longe Ennius. Nam tres uersus sunt,
> non duo, ad hanc Ennii sententiam pertinentes, ex quibus tertium
> uersum Caesellius non respexit. Non. p. 287. 11 L.: cor generis est
> neutri, ut dubium non est. Masculini Ennius lib. XIII. 'Hannibal'
> e.q.s.

audaci cum] Gell. 'laudacium' Non.

FR. 2*

Matronae moeros complent spectare fauentes.

Serv. (D.) ad *Geo.* I. 18.

> Serv. (D.) ad *Geo.* I. 18: 'fauere' ueteres etiam 'uelle' dixerunt. Ennius
> 'Matronae' e.q.s.

FR. 3

satin uates uerant aetate in agenda?

Gell. XVIII. 2. 16.

> Gell. XVIII. 2. 16: quaesitum hoc est, uerbum 'uerant,' quod significat
> 'uera dicunt,' quisnam ueterum poetarum dixerit....Nemo enim tum
> commeminerat dictum esse a Q. Ennio id uerbum in tertio decimo
> Annalium in isto uersu 'satin' e.q.s.

BOOK XIV

Fr. 1

Verrunt extemplo placidum mare marmore flauo,
Caeruleum spumat sale conferta rate pulsum
Per mare....

Gell. II. 26. 21; Prisc. v. 171 H.

> Gell. II. 26. 21: sed cum omnia libens audiui quae peritissime dixisti,
> tum maxime quod uarietatem flaui coloris enarrasti fecistique ut in-
> tellegerem uerba illa ex Annali quarto decimo Ennii amoenissima, quae
> minime intellegebam: 'Verrunt' e.q.s. Non enim uidebatur 'caeruleum
> mare' cum 'marmore flauo' conuenire. Sed cum sit, ita ut dixisti,
> flauus color uiridi et albo mixtus, pulcherrime prorsus spumas uirentis
> maris 'flauum marmor' appellauit. Prisc. v. 171 H.: etiam 'hoc sale'
> Ennius protulit in XIIII. Annalium 'Caeruleum' e.q.s.

sale] 'mare' Gell., corr. e Prisc. edd.

Fr. 2

Quom procul aspiciunt hostes accedere uentis
Nauibus ueliuolis.

Macr. VI. 5. 10.

> Macr. VI. 5. 10: 'despiciens mare ueliuolum':...Ennius in quarto
> decimo 'Cum procul' e.q.s.

Fr. 3

Labitur uncta carina, uolat super impetus undas.

Macr. VI. 1. 51.

> Macr. VI. 1. 51: 'Labitur uncta uadis abies.' Ennius in quarto decimo
> 'Labitur' e.q.s.

Fr. 4

litora lata sonunt.

Prisc. IX. 473 H.

> Prisc. IX. 473 H.: ...haec tamen ipsa et secundum tertiam uetustissimi
> protulisse inueniuntur coniugationem, ut Ennius...in XIV. 'litora'
> e.q.s. (cf. XI. 8).

Fr. 5

Nunc est illa dies quom gloria maxima sese
Nobis ostendat, si uiuimus siue morimur.

Prisc. x. 501 H.

> Prisc. x. 501 H.: deponentia in 'rior' desinentia, 'orior' et 'morior'
> tam secundum tertiam quam secundum quartam coniugationem de-
> clinauerunt auctores....Ennius in xiiii. Annalium 'Nunc est' e.q.s.

Fr. 6

Horrescit telis exercitus asper utrimque.

Macr. vi. 4. 6.

> Macr. vi. 4. 6: 'tum ferreus hastis | Horret ager.' 'Horret' mire se habet.
> Sed et Ennius in quarto decimo 'Horrescit' e.q.s....sed et ante omnes
> Homerus ἔφριξεν δὲ μάχη φθισίμβροτος ἐγχείῃσι.

Fr. 7
Rumpia

Gell. x. 25. 4.

> Gell. x. 25. 4: item 'rumpia,' genus teli Thraecae nationis, positumque
> hoc uocabulum in Quinti Ennii Annalium xiiii.

Fr. 8

Infit, O ciues, quae me fortuna fero sic
Contudit indignum bello, confecit acerbo

Prisc. x. 518 H.

> Prisc. x. 518 H.: uetustissimi tamen tam producebant quam corripie-
> bant supradicti uerbi (id est 'tutudi') paenultimam. Ennius in xiiii.
> 'Infit' e.q.s.

indignum] 'indigno' codd., corr. I. Maehlyius.

Fr. 9

Omnes occisi obcensique in nocte serena.

Fest. p. 218. 22 L.

> Fest. p. 218. 22 L.: 'ob' praepositione antiquos usos esse pro 'ad'
> testis est Ennius cum ait lib. xiv. 'Omnes' e.q.s.

56   ANNALS OF QUINTUS ENNIUS

BOOK XV

Fr. 1

Malos diffindunt, fiunt tabulata falaeque.

Non. p. 163. 14 L.

> Non. p. 163. 14 L.: 'falae' turres sunt ligneae. Ennius lib. xv. 'Malos'
> e.q.s.

Fr. 2

Obcumbunt multi letum ferroque lapique
Aut intra muros aut extra praecipe casu.

Prisc. vi. 250 H.; *id.* vi. 281 H.

> Prisc. vi. 250 H.: uetustissimi tamen etiam 'huius lapis' protulerunt.
> Ennius in xv. Annali 'Obcumbunt' e.q.s. *Id.* vi. 281 H.: ...uetustis-
> simi etiam 'praecipis' genetiuum, qui a nominatiuo 'praeceps' est,
> secundum analogiam nominatiui protulerunt....Ennius in xv. Annali
> 'Obcumbunt' e.q.s.

Fr. 3

Arcus subspiciunt, mortalibus quae perhibentur.

Prisc. vi. 259 H.

> Prisc. vi. 259 H.: 'arcus'...inuenitur tamen apud ueteres etiam femi-
> nini generis, secundum quod bene quartae est declinationis. Ennius
> in xv. Annali 'Arcus ubi aspiciunt' e.q.s.
> subspiciunt] V.

Fr. 4*

Sicut fortis equus, spatio qui saepe supremo
Vicit Olympia, nunc senio confectus quiescit.

Cic. *de Sen.* v. 14.

> Cic. *de Sen.* v. 14: sua enim uitia insipientes, et suam culpam in senec-
> tutem conferunt, quod non faciebat is, cuius modo mentionem feci,
> Ennius 'Sicut' e.q.s. equi fortis et uictoris senectuti comparat suam.

ADDENDUM

Addendum est testimonium: "Sunt alii loci plurimorum uersuum quos Maro in
opus suum cum paucorum immutatione uerborum a ueteribus transtulit......de Pan-
daro et Bitia aperientibus portas locus acceptus est ex libro quinto decimo Ennii, qui
induxit Histros duos in obsidione erupisse porta et stragem de obsidente hoste fecisse."
Macr. vi. 2. 33.

BOOK XVI

Fr. 1

Quippe uetusta uirum non est satis bella moueri?

Fest. p. 306. 24 L.

Fest. p. 306. 24 L.: 'quippe' significare 'quidni' testimonio est Ennius
...lib. xvi. 'Quippe uetusta' e.q.s. Item alii complures.

Fr. 2

Post aetate pigret subferre laborem.

Non. p. 324. 3 L.

Non. p. 324. 3 L.: 'pigret' Ennius lib. xvi. 'Post aetate' e.q.s.

Fr. 3

Postremo longinqua dies quod fregerit aetas.

Gell. ix. r4. 5.

Gell. ix. 14. 5: Q. Ennius in sexto decimo Annali 'dies' scripsit pro
'diei,' in hoc uersu 'Postremo' e.q.s.

Postremo] 'postrema' codd., corr. Bergkius. 'postremae' Columna.

quod fregerit] 'quod fecerit' uel 'confecerit' uel 'confecerat' codd., corr.
Val.

Fr. 4

Reges per regnum statuasque sepulchraque quaerunt,
Aedificant nomen, summa nituntur opum ui.

Macr. vi. 1. 17.

Macr. vi. 1. 17: 'summa nituntur opum ui': Ennius...in sexto decimo
'Reges' e.q.s.

Fr. 5

Quos ubi rex Epulo spexit de cautibus celsis.

Fest. p. 446. 5 L.; Varro, L.L. vi. 82.

Fest. p. 446. 5 L.: 'spici' quoque sine praepositione dixerunt antiqui,
Plautus 'Flagitium est' e.q.s. Et 'spexit' Ennius lib. xvi. 'Quos ubi'
e.q.s. Varro, L.L. vi. 82: 'spectare' dictum ab antiquo, quo etiam
Ennius usus: '⟨q⟩uos Epulo postquam spexit.'

cautibus] 'contibus' Fest., corr. Vi, quod iam improbat Vii, Bergkium
secutus, qui 'cotibus' scripsit.

Fr. 6

Montibus obstipis obstantibus, unde oritur nox.

Fest. p. 210. 12 L.

> Fest. p. 210. 12 L.: 'obstipum,' obliquum. Ennius lib. xvi. 'Montibus'
> e.q.s.

obstipum] 'obstitum' codd.

Fr. 7

Si luci, si nox, si mox, si iam data sit frux.

Prisc. vi. 278 H.

> Prisc. vi. 278 H.: 'frux' etiam 'frugis' facit genetiuum quia ἀπὸ τοῦ
> φρύγω Graeco uerbo nascitur. Ennius in xvi. Annali 'Si luci' e.q.s.

Fr. 8

Nox quando mediis signis praecincta uolabit.

Fest. p. 310. 32 L.

> Fest. p. 310. 32 L.: ⟨quando cum graui uoce pro⟩nuntiatur significat
> ⟨quoniam; acuta est temporis aduerbium⟩ (suppl. Lindsayius) ut...
> Ennius lib. xvi. 'Nox' e.q.s.

Fr. 9

                                                    interea fax
Occidit, oceanumque rubra tractim obruit aethra.

Macr. vi. 4. 19.

> Macr. vi. 4. 19: 'nec lucidus aethra Siderea polus,' Ennius prior
> dixerat in sexto decimo 'interea fax' e.q.s.

Fr. 10

Hic insidiantes uigilant, partim requiescunt
Protecti gladiis, sub scutis ore fauentes.

Serv. (D.) ad *Geo.* iv. 230; *id.* ad *Geo.* i. 18.

> Serv. (D.) ad *Geo.* iv. 230: 'ore faue': cum religione ac silentio accede
> ...in xvi. Ennius 'Hic' e.q.s. *Id.* ad *Geo.* i. 18: nonnunquam 'fauere'
> et pro 'tacere' ponitur, ut idem Ennius 'ore fauentes.'

Protecti] 'tecti' Serv. (D.), corr. Columna. 'contecti' Merula. 'tecti cum'
Baehrensius.

Fr. 11

Nauorum imperium seruare est induperantum.

Fest. p. 168. 7 L.

Fest. p. 168. 7 L.: 'nauus' celer ac strenuus a nauium uelocitate uidetur dictus Ennius...lib. xvi. 'Nauorum' e.q.s.

induperantum] 'insuperantum' Fest., corr. Scaliger.

Fr. 12

Quo res sapsa loco sese ostentatque iubetque.

Fest. p. 432. 32 L.; Paul. p. 433. 6 L.

Fest. p. 432. 32 L.: idem (*sc.* Ennius), cum ait 'sapsam' pro 'ipsa nec alia,' ponit in lib. xvi. 'Quo res' e.q.s. Paul. p. 433. 6 L.: 'sapsa' ipsa. Idem Ennius 'Quo res' e.q.s.

Fr. 13

Spero, si speres quicquam prodesse potis sunt.

Fest. p. 446. 13 L.

Fest. p. 446. 13 L.: 'speres' antiqui pluraliter dicebant, ut Ennius... lib. xvi. 'Spero' e.q.s.

Fr. 14

Non in sperando cupide rem prodere summam.

Fest. p. 254. 32 L.; Paul. p. 255. 14 L.

Fest. p. 254. 32 L.: 'prodit' memoriae porro dat, et fallit; item ex interiore loco procedit; item perdit ut Ennius lib. xvi. 'Non' e.q.s. Quae eadem refert Paulus.

Fr. 15*

Vndique conueniunt uelut imber tela tribuno,
Configunt parmam, tinnit hastilibus umbo
Aerato sonitu galeae; sed nec pote quisquam
Vndique nitendo corpus discerpere ferro;
Semper abundantes hastas frangitque quatitque,   5
Totum sudor habet corpus, multumque laborat,
Nec respirandi fit copia; praepete ferro
Histri tela manu iacientes sollicitabant.

Macr. vi. 3. 3.

Macr. VI. 3. 2: Homerus de Aiacis forti pugna ait Αἴας δ' οὐκέτ' ἔμιμνε κ.τ.λ. (Π. 102): hunc locum Ennius in duodecimo ad pugnam C. Aelii tribuni his uersibus transfert 'Vndique' e.q.s.: hinc Vergilius eundem locum de incluso Turno gratia elegantiore composuit 'ergo nec clipeo' e.q.s.

FR. 16

Concidit, et sonitum simul insuper arma dedere.

Macr. VI. 1. 24.

Macr. VI. 1. 24: 'corruit in uolnus: sonitum super arma dedere': Ennius in sexto decimo 'Concidit' e.q.s.

FR. 17

prandere iubet horiturque.

Diom. 382 K.

Diom. 382 K.: item 'hortatur' quod uolgo dicimus ueteres nonnulli 'horitur' dixerunt, ut Ennius sexto decimo Annalium 'prandere' e.q.s.

FR. 18*

rex deinde citatus

Conuellit sese.

Serv. (D.) ad *Aen.* XI. 19.

Serv. (D.) ad *Aen.* XI. 19: ...alii 'uelle mouere' accipiunt. Ennius 'rex' e.q.s.

FR. 19*

Clamor ad caelum uoluendus per aethera uagit.

Varro, *L.L.* VII. 104.

Varro, *L.L.* VII. 104: En⟨n⟩ii...ab ⟨ha⟩edo 'Clamor' e.q.s.

FR. 20

Qui clamos oppugnantis uagore uolanti.

Fest. p. 514. 2 L.

Fest. p. 514. 2 L.: 'uagorem' pro uagitu Ennius lib. XVI. 'Qui' e.q.s.

Fr. 21

Ingenio forti dextrum latus pertudit hasta.

Prisc. x. 518 H.

   Prisc. x. 518 H.: ...Ennius...in xvi. 'Ingenio' e.q.s. Vide ad xiv. 8,
ubi totus locus exscriptus est.

Fr. 22

tamen induuolans secum abstulit hasta
Insigne.

Macr. vi. 1. 53.

   Macr. vi. 1. 53: 'apicem tamen incita summum Hasta tulit.' Ennius
in sexto decimo 'tamen' e.q.s.

Fr. 23

Tunc timido manat ex omni corpore sudor.

Macr. vi. 1. 50.

   Macr. vi. 1. 50: 'tum gelidus toto manabat corpore sudor.' Ennius
in sexto decimo 'Tunc timido' e.q.s.

Fr. 24

Primus senex bradys in regimen bellique peritus.

Fest. p. 348. 17 L.

   Fest. p. 348. 17 L.: 'regimen' pro 'regimento' usurpant poetae. Ennius
lib. xvi. 'Primus' e.q.s.
bradys] 'bradyn' Fest., corr. Merula.

Fr. 25

Aestatem autumnus sequitur, post acer hiems it.

Prisc. v. p. 179 K.; Serv. ad *Aen*. vi. 685.

   Prisc. v. p. 179 K.: Ennius in xvi. 'Aestatem' e.q.s. Vide ad xii. 2, ubi
totus locus exscriptus est. Serv. ad *Aen*. vi. 685: sciendum antiquos
et 'alacris' et 'alacer' et 'acris' et 'acer' tam de masculino quam de
feminino genere dixisse....Ennius...'Aestatem' e.q.s.

FR. 26

hebem.

Charis. 132 K.

Charis. 132 K.: 'hebem'...Ennius XVI., ubi Fl. Caper 'non ut ad-
iunctiuo sed appellatiuo est locutus.'

BOOK XVII

FR. 1

Noenus decet mussare bonos qui facta labore
Nixi militiae peperere.

Serv. (D.) ad *Geo.* IV. 188; Paul. p. 131. 11 L.

Serv. (D.) ad *Geo.* IV. 188: 'mussant'...quae uox ponitur et in tacendi
significatione, ut apud Ennium 'non possunt mussare boni qui factam
labore enixi militiam peperere.' Paul. p. 131. 11 L.: uulgo uero pro
tacere dicitur (mussare) ut idem Ennius 'non decet mussare bonos.'
Noenus] V.
facta] Dousa.
Nixi militiae] Dousa.

FR. 2

It eques, et plausu caua concutit ungula terram.

Macr. VI. 1. 22.

Macr. VI. 1. 22: 'quadrupedante' e.q.s. Ennius...in septimo decimo
'It eques' e.q.s.

FR. 3

Tollitur in caelum clamor exortus utrimque.

Macr. VI. 1. 21.

Macr. VI. 1. 21: 'Tollitur in caelum clamor, cunctique Latini': Ennius
in septimo decimo 'Tollitur' e.q.s.

FR. 4

Concurrunt ueluti uenti quom spiritus Austri
Imbricitor Aquiloque suo cum flamine contra
Indu mari magno fluctus extollere certant.

Macr. VI. 2. 28.

Macr. VI. 2. 28: 'diuersi...Eurus equis': Ennius in septimo decimo
'Concurrunt' e.q.s.

indu] 'inde' (P), corr. H. Stephanus.

FR. 5

dux ipse uias.

Prisc. VI. 199 H.

Prisc. VI. 199 H.: eiusdem (id est primae) declinationis feminarum
genetiuum etiam in 'as' more Graeco solebant antiquissimi terminare...
Ennius in XVII. Annali 'dux ipse uias' pro 'uiae.'

FR. 6

Tum caua sub monte late specus intus patebat.

Fest. p. 462. 19 L.; Non. p. 329. 18 L.; Prisc. VI. 260 H.; Sen. (D.) ad
Aen. VII. 568.

Fest. p. 462. 19 L.: 'specus' feminino genere pronuntiabant antiqui,
ut 'metus' et 'nepos'...ut Ennius 'Tum' e.q.s. Non. p. 329. 18 L.:
'specus' genere masculino...feminino Ennius Annalium lib. XVII.
'Concaua' e.q.s. Prisc. VI. 260 H.: (specus) feminino tamen hoc nomen
quoque inuenitur....Ennius in XVII. Annalium 'Tum caua' e.q.s.
Serv. (D.) ad *Aen.* VII. 568: 'hic specus horrendum': hoc nomen apud
maiores trium generum fuit. Ennius feminino posuit 'sub' e.q.s.

Tum caua] 'tum causa' Fest. 'concaua' Non., corr. e Prisc. edd.
monte] Prisc., Fest. 'montis' Non.
late] 'latet' Non.

FR. 7

Neque corpora firma

Longiscunt quicquam.

Non. p. 195. 9 L.

Non. p. 195. 9 L.: 'Longiscere' longum fieri uel frangi. Ennius lib.
XVII. 'Neque corpora' e.q.s.

BOOK XVIII

FR. 1*

Sol aestate diem faciens longiscere longe.

Non. p. 195. 12 L.

> Non. p. 195. 12 L.: 'longiscere,' longum fieri uel frangi. Ennius lib.
> XVII. 'neque corpora' e.q.s.: idem 'cum sola est eadem facient lon-
> giscere longe.'
> Sol aestate diem] Baehrensius. 'cum soles eadem' VII.
> faciens] Bergkius.

FR. 2

Degrumare forum.

Non. p. 87. 18 L.

> Non. p. 87. 18 L.: 'grumae' sunt loca media in quae directae quattuor
> congregantur et conueniunt uiae. Est autem 'gruma' mensura quaedam
> qua fixa uiae ad lineam deriguntur, ut est agrimensorum et talium....
> Ennius lib. XVIII. gruma derigere dixit 'Degrumari ferrum.'
> Degrumare forum] V.

FR. 3

aere fulua.

Gell. XIII. 20. 14.

> Gell. XIII. 20. 14: contra uero idem Ennius in Annali duodeuicesimo
> 'aere fulua' dixit non 'fuluo,' non ob id solum quod Homerus ἠέρα
> βαθεῖαν dicit, sed quod hic sonus, opinor, uocabilior est uisus et
> amoenior.

INCERTAE SEDIS FRAGMENTA

FR. 1*

Atque manu magna Romanos impulit amnis.

Schol. Ver. ad Aen. v. 241.

> Schol. Ver. ad Aen. v. 241: Ennius 'Atque manu' e.q.s.

FR. 2

Atque atque accedit muros Romana iuuentus.

Gell. x. 29. 2; Non. p. 850. 18 L.

Gell. x. 29. 2: ('atque' particula) gemina si fiat auget intenditque rem de qua agitur, ut animaduertimus in Q. Ennii Annalibus, nisi memoria in hoc uersu labor 'Atque' e.q.s. Non. p. 850. 18 L.: 'atque' particula si diligentius intellegitur, multam habet significantiam: ut uel illud est Enni 'Atque' e.q.s.

Atque atque] Gell. 'atque' Non.
accedit] Gell. 'accendit' Non.

FR. 3*

Audire est operae pretium procedere recte
Qui rem Romanam Latiumque augescere uoltis.

Acro ad Hor. *Sat.* 1. 2. 37; Varro ap. Non. p. 767. 15 L.

Acro ad Hor. *Sat.* 1. 2. 37: urbane abutitur Ennianis uersibus: ille enim ait 'Audire' e.q.s. Varro ap. Non. p. 767. 15 L.: e mea φιλοφθονίᾳ natis, quos Menippea haeresis nutricata est tutores do 'Qui rem' e.q.s.

FR. 4*

Auersabuntur semper uos, uostraque uulta.

Non. p. 341. 21 L.

Non. p. 341. 21 L.: 'uultus' masculino genere appellatur...neutro.... Ennius 'Auersabuntur' e.q.s.

Auersabuntur] 'aduersabantur' codd., corr. Quicheratus.

FR. 5*

Aut permarceret paries percussa trifaci.

Paul. p. 504. 15 L.

Paul. p. 504. 15 L.: 'trifax' telum, longitudinis trium cubitorum quod catapulta mittitur. Ennius 'Aut' e.q.s.

permarceret] 'permaceret' (M, L, Par.). 'permaneret' T.

FR. 6

Brundisium pulchro praecinctum praepete portu.

Gell. VII. 6. 2.

> Gell. VII. 6. 2: cur autem non Q. quoque Ennium reprehendit (Iulius Hyginus), qui in Annalibus non 'pennas Daedali' sed longe diuersius 'Brundisium,' inquit, 'pulchro' e.q.s.

Brundisium, inquit] 'Braundisium (uel Brundusium) quid' Gell., corr. V.
portu] 'portus et' codd., corr. 'portu sed' M et Scioppius.

FR. 7*

Bruttace bilingui.

Porph. in Hor. *Sat.* I. 10. 30; Paul. p. 31. 25 L.

> Porph. in Hor. *Sat.* I. 10. 30: 'bilinguis' dicitur quoniam utraque lingua usi sunt (Canusini), sicut per omnem illum tractum Italiae... ideo ergo Bruttios †brichacae† bilingui. Paul. p. 31. 25 L.: bilingues Bruttaces Ennius dixit, quod Brutti et Osce et Graece loqui soliti sunt.

Bruttace] corr. e Porph. edd.

FR. 8*

Capitibus nutantis pinos rectosque cupressos.

Gell. XIII. 20. 13; Non. p. 287. 14 L.

> Gell. XIII. 20. 13: Ennius item 'rectos cupressos' dixit contra receptum uocabuli genus hoc uersu 'Capitibus' e.q.s. Non. p. 287. 14 L.: 'cupressus' generis feminini ut dubium non est. Masculini Ennius 'Capitibus' e.q.s.

nutantis] Gell. 'nutantibus' Non.

FR. 9*

Cum legionibus quom proficiscitur induperator.

Cassiod. 207 K.

> Cassiod. 207 K.: 'Cum' praepositio per 'c' scribenda est, 'quum' aduerbium temporis, quod significat 'quando,' per 'q'...discretionis causa, ut apud Ennium 'Cum' e.q.s.

FR. 10*

Cum magno strepitu Volcanum uentus uegebat.

Fest. p. 138. 20 L.

Fest. p. 138. 20 L.: metonymia est tropos, cum...a superiore re
inferior (significatur), ut Ennius 'Cum magno' e.q.s.

uegebat] 'uegerat' F, corr. Scaliger.

FR. 11*

Decretum est stare et fossari corpora telis.

Varro, *L.L.* VII. 100.

Varro, *L.L.* VII. 100: apud Ennium 'Decretum est stare corpora telis.'
Hoc uerbum Ennii dictum a fodiendo a quo 'fossa.'

et fossari] suppl. Bergkius. 'est fossari' (om. 'stare') Columna.

FR. 12*

dictis Romanis incutit iram.

Serv. (D.) ad *Aen.* I. 69.

Serv. (D.) ad *Aen.* I. 69: 'incute'...si...'fac' (significat) septimus
casus est (uentis) et erit sensus 'fac uim Troianis per uentos': Ennius
'dictis' e.q.s.

incutit] 'inculit' codd., corr. Commelinus.

FR. 13*

Diuumque hominumque pater, rex.

Varro, *L.L.* v. 65.

Varro, *L.L.* v. 65: Ennius...eundem (Iouem) appellans dicit 'Diuumque' e.q.s.

FR. 14*

Dum quidem unus homo Romanus toga superescit.

Fest. p. 394. 7 L.

Fest. p. 394. 7 L.: 'superescit' significat 'supererit.' Ennius 'Dum
quidem' e.q.s.

FR. 15*

Dum clauum rectum teneam, nauemque gubernem.

Isid. XIX. 2; Quint. II. 17. 24.

> Isid. XIX. 2: 'clauus est quo regitur gubernaculum': de quo Ennius
> 'Dum clauum' e.q.s. Quint. II. 17. 24: nam et gubernator uult salua
> naue in portum peruenire. Si tamen tempestate fuerit abreptus, non
> ideo minus erit gubernator, dicetque notum illud 'Dum clauum' e.q.s.

FR. 16*

Effudit uoces proprio cum pectore sancto.

Serv. ad *Geo.* II. 424.

> Serv. ad *Geo.* II. 424: 'cum' abundat.... Ennius 'Effudit' e.q.s. id est,
> 'proprio pectore' nam 'cum' uacat.

FR. 17*

Ei mihi qualis erat.

Serv. ad *Aen.* II. 274.

> Serv. ad *Aen.* II. 274: 'Ei mihi' Ennii uersus.

FR. 18*

Et tum sicut equus, qui de praesepibus fartus
Vincla suis magnis animis abrupit, et inde
Fert sese campi per caerula laetaque prata
Celso pectore, saepe iubam quassat simul altam,
Spiritus ex anima calida spumas agit albas.

Macr. VI. 3. 7.

> Macr. VI. 3. 7: Homerica descriptio est equi fugientis in haec uerba
> 'ὡς δ' ὅτε τις στατὸς ἵππος' κ.τ.λ. (N, 131, ff.). Ennius hinc traxit 'Et
> tum sicut' e.q.s.

FR. 19

Et detondit agros laetos atque oppida cepit.

Prisc. IX. 482 H.

> Prisc. IX. 482 H.: 'detondeo' detondi. Vetustissimi tamen etiam 'deto-
> tondi' protulerunt. Ennius in Annalibus 'Et detondit' e.q.s.

detondit] 'detotondit' codd., corr. Bamb. 'deque totondit' Merula.

FR. 20

Euax aquast aspersa Latinis.

Charis. 240 K.

    Charis. 240 K.: 'Euax'...Ennius in Annalium libro 'aquast' e.q.s.
euax] om. Charis.

FR. 21

Exin per terras postquam celerissimus rumor.

Prisc. VII. 334 H.

    Prisc. VII. 334 H.: 'celerissimus' pro 'celerrimus' superlatiuum pro-
tulerunt....Ennius in Annalibus 'Exin' e.q.s.
Exin] 'exit' Merula.

FR. 22*

Flamma loci, postquam concussa est turbine saeuo.

Schol. Bemb. ad Ter. *Heaut.* 245.

    Schol. Bemb. ad Ter. *Heaut.* 245: 'loci': parhelcon. Nam 'loci' omni
significationi addi solet. Ennius 'Flamma' e.q.s.
concussa est] 'concussa pre' corr. Baehrensius. 'concussast' Umphen-
bachius. 'conclusast' Faernius.

FR. 23*

furentibus uentis.

Serv. ad *Aen.* I. 51.

    Serv. ad *Aen.* I. 51: 'Austris': figura est celebrata apud Vergilium et
est species pro genere. Legerat apud Ennium 'furentibus uentis,' sed
quasi asperum fugit et posuit 'Austris' pro 'uentis.'

FR. 24*

Fortis Romani sunt, quamquam caelus profundus.

Non. p. 289. 16 L.; Charis. 72 K.

    Non. p. 289. 16 L.: 'caelum' neutro. Masculino...Ennius 'fortis
Romani' e.q.s. Charis. 72 K.: 'caelum hoc,' cum sit neutrum, etiam
masculine ueteres dixerunt: et Ennius...'quamquam' e.q.s.
sunt] add. Merula.

FR. 25*

Fortunasque suas coepere latrones
Inter se memorare.

Non. p. 196. 1 L.

Non. p. 196. 1 L.: 'latrocinari,' militare mercede.... Ennius 'Fortunasque' e.q.s.

FR. 26*

funduntque elatis nauibus lucem.

Serv. ad *Aen.* XII. 115; Mar. Vict. 28 K.

Serv. ad *Aen.* XII. 115: Ennianus uersus est ordine commutato; ille
enim ait 'funduntque' e.q.s. Mar. Vict. 28 K.: uidetur plurimis esse
quintus communium syllabarum modus, qui apud Lucilium et ueteres
multos est frequentatus, ut correpta uocalis desinat in 's,' et excipiatur
ab alia consonanti...ut...'efflantque naribus lucem.'

FR. 27

Interea fugit albus iubar Hyperionis cursum.

Prisc. v. 170 H.

Prisc. v. 170 H.: 'iubar' quoque tam masculinum quam neutrum pro-
ferebant. Ennius in Annalibus 'Interea' e.q.s.

FR. 28*

Inde Parum.................ulabant.

Fest. p. 362. 24 L.

Fest. p. 362. 24 L.: ✻ ✻ ✻ Ennius iocatus uidetur ✻ ✻ ✻ et alibi 'Inde
Parum ✻ ✻ ✻ ulabant.' Parum insulam refert.

FR. 29*

It nigrum campis agmen.

Serv. ad *Aen.* IV. 404.

Serv. ad *Aen.* IV. 404: 'It nigrum' hemistichium Ennii de elephantis
dictum, quod ante Accius est usus de Indis.

FR. 30*

Impetus haud longe mediis regionibus restat.

Fest. p. 356. 33 L.; Paul. p. 357. 7 L.

> Fest. p. 356. 33 L.: 'restat' pro 'distat' ait....Ennium ponere cum is dicat 'Impetus' e.q.s. Paul. p. 357. 7 L.: 'restat' Ennius posuit pro 'distat.'

haud] 'aut' Fest., corr. Turnebius.

FR. 31*

Iam cata signa fere sonitum dare uoce parabant.

Varro, *L.L.* VII. 46.

> Varro, *L.L.* VII. 46: apud Ennium 'Iam cata signa ferae' e.q.s.: 'cata' acuta: hoc enim uerbo dicunt Sabini.

fere] Laetus.

FR. 32*

Inde patefecit radiis rota candida caelum.

Isid. *Or.* XVIII. 36; Serv. ad *Aen.* VI. 748.

> Isid. *Or.* XVIII. 36: ideo autem rotis quadrigas currere dicunt siue quia mundus iste circuli sui celeritate transcurrit, siue propter solem quia uolubili ambitu rotat, sicut ait Ennius 'Inde patefecit' e.q.s. Serv. ad *Aen.* VI. 748: 'rotam uoluere per annos'...Est autem sermo Ennii.

FR. 33*

Inde loci lituus sonitus effudit acutos.

Paul. p. 103. 28 L.

> Paul. p. 103. 28 L.: lituus appellatus, quod litis sit testis. Est enim genus bucinae incuruae quo qui cecinerit dicitur liticen. Ennius 'Inde loci' e.q.s.

FR. 34*

Irarum effunde quadrigas.

Serv. ad *Aen.* XII. 499.

> Serv. ad *Aen.* XII. 499: et hic moderate locutus est, nam Ennius ait 'Irarum' e.q.s.

Fr. 35*

Ingenti uadit cursu qua redditus termo est.

Fest. p. 498. 3 L.

> Fest. p. 498. 3 L.: 'termonem' Ennius Graeca consuetudine dixit, quem nos nunc 'terminum,' hoc modo 'Ingenti' e.q.s.

Fr. 36*

Incedit ueles uolgo sicilibus latis.

Paul. p. 453. 20 L.

> Paul. p. 453. 20 L.: 'siciles' hastarum spicula lata. Ennius 'Incedit' e.q.s.

Fr. 37*

It equitatus uti celerissimus.

Charis. 83 K.

> Charis. 83 K.: 'celer,' 'celerior,' 'celerrimus' facit...nam quod Ennius ait 'It' e.q.s. barbarismus est.

Fr. 38*

Iuppiter hic risit, tempestatesque serenae
Riserunt omnes risu Iouis omnipotentis.

Serv. (D.) ad *Aen.* I. 254.

> Serv. (D.) ad *Aen.* I. 254: ...laetum ostendit Iouem et talem qualis esse solet cum facit serenum: poetarum enim est elementorum habitum dare numinibus....Ennius 'Iuppiter' e.q.s.

Fr. 39*

Heia machaeras!

Serv. ad *Aen.* IX. 37.

> Serv. ad *Aen.* IX. 37: hic distinguendum, ut 'heia' militum sit properantium clamor. Et est Ennianum, qui ait 'Heia machaeras.'

Fr. 40*

Hortatore bono, prius quam iam finibus termo.

Fest. p. 498. 4 L.

> Fest. p. 498. 4 L.: 'termonem' Ennius Graeca consuetudine dixit.... 'Hortatore' e.q.s.

iam] 'qui' VII.

FR. 41*

Hic pede pes premitur hic armis arma teruntur.

Auct. *Bell. Hisp.* xxxi.

Auct. *Bell. Hisp.* xxxi.: 'Hic' ut ait Ennius, 'pes pede premitur, armis teruntur arma.'

FR. 42*

hic tum nostri cessere parumper.

Auct. *Bell. Hisp.* xxiii.

Auct. *Bell. Hisp.* xxiii.: 'hic tum,' ut ait Ennius, 'nostri' e.q.s.
hic tum] om. V.

FR. 43*

Liuius inde redit magno mactatus triumpho.

Serv. (D.) ad *Aen.* ix. 641.

Serv. (D.) ad *Aen.* ix. 641: 'mactus' autem apud ueteres etiam 'mactatus' dicebatur, ut Ennius 'Liuius' e.q.s.

FR. 44*

Labitur uncta carina per aequora cana celocis.

Isid. *Orig.* xix. 1.

Isid. *Orig.* xix. 1: 'celoces' quas Graeci κέλητας uocant id est ueloces biremes uel triremes agiles et ad ministerium aptae. Ennius 'Labitur' e.q.s.

FR. 45*

leuesque sequuntur in hastis.

Serv. (D.) ad *Aen.* v. 37.

Serv. (D.) ad *Aen.* v. 37: 'in iaculis': in hastis Ennius 'leuesque' e.q.s.

FR. 46*

Moribus antiquis res stat Romana uirisque.

Aug. *de Ciu. Dei*, ii. 21.

Aug. *de Ciu. Dei*, ii. 21: Tullius...in principio quinti libri commemorato prius Ennii poetae uersu quo dixerat 'Moribus' e.q.s. quem quidem ille uersum, inquit, uel breuitate uel ueritate tamquam ex oraculo mihi quodam esse effatus uidetur.

Fr. 47*

Multa foro ponit et agoeae longa replentur.

Isid. *Orig.* XIX. 2. 4.

> Isid. *Orig.* XIX. 2. 4: 'agea' uiae sunt uel loca in naui per quae ad remiges hortator accedit: de qua Ennius 'Multa' e.q.s.

ponit et agoeae] 'ponet et agea' uel 'p. e. agiauia' Isid., corr. Val.

Fr. 48*

Nam me grauis impetus Orci
Percutit in latus.

Serv. (D.) ad *Aen.* I. 81.

> Serv. (D.) ad *Aen.* I. 81: alii 'in latus' pro 'latus' accipiunt. Ennius 'Nam me' e.q.s.

Fr. 49*

Nauibus explebant sese terrasque replebant.

Serv. ad *Aen.* VI. 545.

> Serv. ad *Aen.* VI. 545: ut diximus supra 'explebo' est 'minuam' nam ait Ennius 'Nauibus' e.q.s.

Fr. 50*

Non si, lingua loqui saperet, quibus, ora decem sint,
Innumerum, ferro cor sit pectusque reuinctum.

Schol. Bern. ad *Geo.* II. 43; cod. Par. 7960.

> Schol. Bern. ad *Geo.* II. 43: Homericus sensus: sic etiam Ennius 'ora decem.' Cod. Par. 7960: ...'mǒn si lingua loqui saperet at ora decem sint in metrum ferro cor sit pecusque reuinctum.'

non si] Mommsenus. 'monstra si sibi' Baehrensius.

quibus] VII. Cf. idem V. in *Rh. Mus.* XVII. 143.

Innumerum] VII.

pectusque] Mommsenus.

Fr. 51*

Nec metus ulla tenet, freti uirtute quiescunt.

Non. p. 315. 23 L.

> Non. p. 315. 23 L.: metus masculino. Feminino....Ennius 'Nec metus ulla' e.q.s.

Nec] 'ni' codd., corr. Mercerius non probante VII.

freti] 'rite' codd., corr. Mercerius. 'uirtutem rite' VII.

FR. 52*

Nobis unde forent fructus uitaeque propagmen.

Non. p. 90. 9 L.; *id.* p. 327. 2 L.

Non. p. 90. 9 L.: 'propages' est series et adfixio continuo uel longe ducta. . . .Ennius 'Nobis' e.q.s. *Id.* p. 327. 2 L.: 'propago,' propages . . .neutri Ennius 'Nobis' e.q.s.

Nobis] 'nouis' (primo loco), 'bonis' (sec. loco) codd. Non., corr. Junius.

propagmen] 'propaginem' (pr. loco), 'propagmen' uel 'propagimen' (L.) (sec. loco) codd.

FR. 53*

Omnes mortales sese laudarier optant.

Aug. *de Trin.* XIII. 6; *id. Ep.* 231. 3.

Aug. *de Trin.* XIII. 6: illud etiam quod uetus poeta dixit Ennius 'Omnes' e.q.s. profecto et de se ipso et de iis quos expertus fuerat coniecit. *Id. Ep.* 231. 3: ego autem quod ait Ennius 'Omnes' e.q.s. partim puto approbandum, partim cauendum.

FR. 54*

Oscitat in campis caput a ceruice reuolsum
Semianimesque micant oculi lucemque requirunt.

Serv. ad *Aen.* X. 396.

Serv. ad *Aen.* X. 396: Ennii est, ut 'Oscitat' e.q.s.: quem uersum ita ut fuit transtulit ad suum carmen Varro Atacinus.

FR. 55*

Optima cum pulchris animis Romana iuuentus.

Don. ad *Phorm.* 465.

Don. ad *Phorm.* 465: 'cum istoc animo' pro 'huius animi.' Ennius 'Optima' e.q.s.

FR. 56

Proletarius publicitus scutisque feroque
Ornatur ferro, muros urbemque forumque
Excubiis curant.

Gell. XVI. 10; Non. p. 288. 19 L.

Gell. XVI. 10: legebatur in consessu forte complurium Ennii liber ex Annalibus. In eo libro uersus hi fuerunt 'Proletarius' e.q.s. Non.

p. 288. 19 L.: 'Proletarii' ciues dicebantur qui in plebe tenuissima erant et non amplius quam mille et quingentos aeris in censum de ferebant. Ennius Annali 'Proletarius' e.q.s.

Ornatur ferro] Gell. 'ornatus' (om. 'ferro') Non.

Excubiis curant] om. Non.

FR. 57*

Pandite, sultis, genas, et corde relinquite somnum.

Fest. p. 462. 9 L.; Paul. p. 463. 1 L.

Fest. p. 462. 9 L.: 'sultis,' 'si uoltis' significat, composito uocabulo, ita ut alia sunt....Ennius 'Pandite' e.q.s. Paul. p. 463. 1 L.: 'sultis,' 'si uultis.' Ennius 'Pandite' e.q.s.

FR. 58*

patrem diuumque hominumque.

Cic. de Nat. Deor. II. 2. 4.

Cic. de Nat. Deor. II. 2. 4: quod ni ita esset, qui potuisset assensu omnium dicere Ennius 'aspice...Iouem' (Thyestes). Illum uero et Iouem et dominatorem rerum et omnia nutu regentem et, ut idem Ennius 'patrem' e.q.s.

FR. 59*

Perque fabam repunt et mollia crura reponunt.

Serv. ad Geo. III. 76.

Serv. ad Geo. III. 76: Ennius de gruibus 'Perque' e.q.s.

FR. 60*

Pila retunduntur uenientibus obuia pilis.

Schol. Bern. ad Luc. Phars. I. 6.

Schol. Bern. ad Luc. Phars. I. 6: Enni uersus 'Pila' e.q.s.

FR. 61*

Quom saeuo obsidio magnus Titanus premebat.

Non. p. 320. 5 L.

Non. p. 320. 5 L.: 'obsidio' feminino....Neutro Ennius 'Cum saeuo' e.q.s.

Quom] Val.

saeuo] 'suo' codd., corr. Junius.

Titanus] 'Titanum' codd., corr. Merula.

Fr. 62*

Quom sese exsiccat somno Romana iuuentus.

Lact. ad Stat. *Theb.* vi. 27.

> Lact. ad Stat. *Theb.* vi. 27: 'et cornu...inani': sic a pictoribus simulatur ut liquidum somnum ex cornu super dormientes uideatur effundere. Sic Ennius 'Quom' e.q.s.

Fr. 63*

Quom e carcere fusi
Currus cum sonitu magno permittere certant.

Schol. Bern. ad *Geo.* I. 51. 2.

> Schol. Bern. ad *Geo.* I. 51. 2: ...Ennius 'Quom' e.q.s.
> e] 'a' cod., corr. Hagenus.

Fr. 64*

Quianam legiones caedimus ferro?

Serv. ad *Aen.* x. 6.

> Serv. ad *Aen.* x. 6: 'quianam,' 'cur,' 'quare': Ennianus sermo est 'Quianam' e.q.s.

Fr. 65*

Quom nihil horridius unquam lex ulla iuberet.

Ekkehartus, ad Oros. II. 9. 4.

> Ekkehartus, ad Oros. II. 9. 4: ...anno autem post hunc...uirgo uestalis damnata est uiuaque obruta in campo qui nunc sceleratus uocatur.... Ennius 'Quom nihil' e.q.s.

Fr. 66*

Qui uicit non est uictor nisi uictus fatetur.

Serv. (D.) ad *Aen.* xi. 306.

> Serv. (D.) ad *Aen.* xi. 306: mire ait ac si diceret etiamsi uelim eos a bellis discedere, natura non patitur. Ennius 'Qui' e.q.s.

Fr. 67*

Quem non uirtutis egentem.

Serv. ad *Aen.* xi. 27.

> Serv. ad *Aen.* xi. 27: 'Quem...egentem' Ennii uersus est.

Fr. 68*

quo tam temere itis.

Serv. (D.) ad *Aen.* IX. 327.

Serv. (D.) ad *Aen.* IX. 327: 'temere'...significat et 'subito.' Ennius
'quod tam' e.q.s.
quo] Masvicius.

Fr. 69*

qui fulmine claro
omnia per sonitum arcet.

Serv. (D.) ad *Aen.* I. 31; Prob. ad *Ecl.* VI. 31.

Serv. (D.) ad *Aen.* I. 31: 'arcebat'...significat autem et 'continet.'
Ennius 'qui fulmine' e.q.s., id est 'continet.' Prob. ad *Ecl.* VI. 31:
...plane trinam esse mundi originem, et Lucretius confitetur dicens
'omnia per sonitum arcet, terram, mare, caelum.'

Fr. 70*

Quae ualide......ueniunt; falarica missa.

Non. p. 891. 14 L.

Non. p. 891. 14 L.: 'falarica' telum maximum....Ennius 'Quae' e.q.s.

Fr. 71*

Quomque caput caderet, carmen tuba sola peregit
Et pereunte uiro raucus sonus aere cucurrit.

Lact. ad Stat. *Theb.* XI. 56.

Lact. ad Stat. *Theb.* XI. 56: 'carmen tuba...peregit.' Ennius 'Quomque' e.q.s.

Fr. 72*

ratibusque fremebant
Imber Neptuni.

Serv. (D.) ad *Aen.* XI. 299; *id.* ad *Geo.* I. 12.

Serv. (D.) ad *Aen.* XI. 299: antiqui aquae sonitus 'fremitus' dicebant:
Ennius 'ratibusque' e.q.s. *Id.* ad *Geo.* I. 12: ueteres murmura aquae
'fremitum' dicebant. Ennius...'ratibusque' e.q.s.

FR. 73*

runata recedit.

Paul. p. 317. 12 L.

Paul. p. 317. 12 L.: 'runa' genus teli significat. Ennius 'runata recedit,' id est proeliata.

FR. 74*

stant puluere campi.

Porph. ad Hor. *Od.* I. 9. I.

Porph. ad Hor. *Od.* I. 9. I : 'stet' autem 'plenum sit' significat. Ennius 'stant' e.q.s.

FR. 75*

Septingenti sunt paulo plus aut minus anni
Augusto augurio postquam incluta condita Roma est.

Varro, *R.R.* III. 12; Suet. *Oct.* VII.

Varro, *R.R.* III. 12: in hoc nunc denique est ut dici possit, non cum Ennius scripsit 'Septingenti' e.q.s. Suet. *Oct.* VII.: loca religiosa et in quibus augurato quid consecratur 'augusta' dicuntur, ab auctu uel ab auium gestu gustuue, sicut etiam Ennius docet scribens 'Augusto' e.q.s.

FR. 76*

Sed sola terrarum postquam permensa parumper.

Fest. p. 386. 21 L.; Varro, *L.L.* v. 22.

Fest. p. 386. 21 L.: 'solum,' terram. Ennius... 'Sed sola' e.q.s. Varro, *L.L.* v. 22: igitur tera terra, et ab eo poetae appellarunt summa terrae quae sola teri possunt 'sola terrae.'

FR. 77*

succincti corda machaeris.

Serv. ad *Aen.* IX. 675.

Serv. ad *Aen.* IX. 675: armati ferro aut bene instructi armis...ut Ennium sit secutus qui ait 'succincti' e.q.s.

FR. 78*

Succincti gladiis media regione cracentes.

Paul. p. 46. 16 L.

Paul. p. 46. 16 L.: 'cracentes' graciles. Ennius 'Succincti' e.q.s.

FR. 79

Sicuti si quis ferat uas uini dimidiatum.

Gell. III. 14.

Gell. III. 14: disseritque ac diuidit (Varro) subtilissime quid 'dimidium' 'dimidiato' intersit, et Q. Ennium scienter hoc in Annalibus dixisse ait 'Sicuti' e.q.s. Pars quae deest ei uaso non 'dimidiata' dicenda est sed 'dimidia.'

FR. 80*

spiras legionibus nexit.

Fest. p. 444. 28 L.

Fest. p. 444. 28 L.: 'spira' dicitur et basis columnae unius tori aut duorum....Ennius quidem hominum multitudinem ita appellat cum dicit 'spiras' e.q.s.

FR. 81*

Tanto sublatae sunt agmine tunc lapides.

Non. p. 311. 12 L.

Non. p. 311. 12 L.: 'lapides' et feminino genere dici possunt ut apud Ennium 'Tanto' e.q.s.

agmine] 'augmine' Wakefieldius.

FR. 82*

teloque trabali.

Serv. (D.) ad *Aen.* XII. 294.

Serv. (D.) ad *Aen.* XII. 294: Ennius 'teloque trabali.'

FR. 83*

tergus igitur sagus pinguis opertat.

Non. p. 331. 9 L.

Non. p. 331. 9 L.: 'sagum' generis neutri, ut plerumque. Masculini Ennius 'tergus' e.q.s.

FR. 84
terrai frugiferai.

Charis. 19 K.; Plot. Sacer. 449 K.; Mart. XI. 90.

Charis. 19 K.: dicunt quidam ueteres in prima declinatione solitos nomina genetiuo casu per 'as' proferre, item datiuo per 'i'...item adhuc morem esse poetis in datiuo casu ut 'aulai medio' Vergilius, 'terrai frugiferai' Ennius in Annalibus. Plot. Sacer. 449 K.: diaeresis est...'frugiferai.' Mart. XI. 90: attonitusque leges terrai frugiferai | Accius et quidquid Pacuuiusque uomunt.

FR. 85*
tibi uita
Seu mors in mundo est.

Charis. 201 K.

Charis. 201 K.: 'in mundo' pro 'palam' et 'in expedito' ac 'cito'... Ennius 'tibi uita' e.q.s.

FR. 86*
Tonsillas apiunt, configunt litus, aduncas.

Isid. *Orig.* XIX. 2.

Isid. *Orig.* XIX. 2: 'Tonsilla' uncinus ferreus uel ligneus ad quem in litore defixum funes nauium illigantur: de quo Ennius 'Tonsillas' e.q.s.
Tonsillas apiunt] 'tonsillas apiunt' (uel 'tonsilla sapiunt') codd. 't. rapiunt' uolgo.

FR. 87*
Vt Tiberis flumen uomit in mare salsum.

Macr. VI. 4. 3.

Macr. VI. 4. 3: 'mane salutantum totis uomit aedibus undam': pulchre 'uomit undam' et antique, nam Ennius ait 'Vt Tiberis' e.q.s.
Vt] 'et' Baehrensius.

FR. 88
uiresque ualentes
Contudit crudelis hiems.

Prisc. X. 518 H.

Prisc. X. 518 H.: uetustissimi tamen tam producebant quam corripiebant supra dicti uerbi (id est 'tutudi') paenultimam. Ennius...in Annalibus 'uiresque' e.q.s. Hic produxit paenultimam.

FR. 89*

Surum unum unus ferre tamen defendere possent.

Fest. p. 362. 26 L.; *id.* p. 382. 32 L.; Paul. p. 383. 13 L.

> Fest. p. 362. 26 L.: idem (Ennius) 'unum [u]surum surus' e.q.s.
> Suri autem sunt fustes, et hypocoristicos surculi. *Id.* p. 382. 32 L.:
> 'surum' dicebant, ex quo ⟨surculus⟩ ∗∗∗∗∗∗∗∗∗∗∗∗∗ usu est ∗∗∗
> ∗∗∗∗∗⟨Ennius. Vnus s⟩urum surus ⟨ferre tamen defende⟩re possent.
> Paul. p. 383. 13 L.: 'surum' dicebant, ex quo per deminutionem fit
> surculus. Ennius 'Vnus surus surum ferret tamen' e.q.s.

Versum paene desperatum corr. VII.

FR. 90*

uersat mucronem.

Serv. (D.) ad *Aen.* IX. 744.

> Serv. (D.) ad *Aen.* IX. 744: 'uersat' librat, iactat: et est Ennianum
> 'uersat mucronem.'

FR. 91*

Tum tonuit laeuum bene tempestate serena.

Cic. *de Diu.* II. 39. 82.

> Cic. *de Diu.* II. 39. 82: ad nostri augurii consuetudinem dixit Ennius
> 'Tum tonuit' e.q.s.

FR. 92*

uertunt crateras ahenos.

Serv. ad *Aen.* IX. 163.

> Serv. ad *Aen.* IX. 163: 'uertunt crateras aenos' potantes exhauriunt.
> Et est hemistichium Ennianum.

FR. 93*

uestro sine momine uenti.

Maius, *Auct. Class.* VIII. 33. 2.

> Maius, *Auct. Class.* VIII. 33. 2: inueni quoque 'hoc momen-nis' pro
> 'momento': unde Ennius 'uestro' e.q.s.

Fr. 94*

Vix solum complere cohum terroribus caeli.

Isid. *de Nat. Rer.* xii.

> Isid. *de Nat. Rer.* xii.: partes autem eius (*sc.* 'caeli') chous, axis, cardines, conuexa poli, sidera. Chous quod caelum continet. Vnde Ennius 'Vix' e.q.s.

solum] Isid. 'solidum' Ilbergius.

APPENDIX A

FRAGMENTA DUBIA

Fr. 1

acanthus

Schol. Bern. ad *Geo.* ii. 119.

> Schol.Bern.ad *Geo.* ii. 119: Gnifo commentatur Annalium libro decimo hanc arborem in insula Cercina regionis Africae esse opportunam tincturae, quae in floris sui colorem lanam tinguat, unde uestis Acanthia appellatur.

Fr. 2

Atque gubernator magna contorsit equos ui.

Charis. iii. 272 K.; Diom. ii. 457 K.; Quint. viii. 6. 9; Plot. Sacer. 466 K.

> Charis. iii. 272 K.: metaphorae quaedam sunt communes...quia quemadmodum in naui auriga dici potest ita in curru gubernator ut 'cumque gubernator' e.q.s. Diom. ii. 457 K.: metaphorae quaedam sunt communes...ut 'cumque' e.q.s. Quint. viii. 6. 9: (comparatio) cum in rebus animalibus aliud pro alio ponitur ut de agitatore: 'gubernator' e.q.s. Plot. Sacer. 466 K.: metaphora...fit...modis iiii; ab animali ad animale 'Atque' e.q.s.

Fr. 3

At Romanus homo, tamenetsi res bene gesta est
Corde suo trepidat.

Cic. *de Or.* iii. xlii.

> Cic. *de Or.* iii. xlii.: uidetis profecto genus hoc totum cum inflexo commutatoque uerbo res eadem enuntiatur ornatius: ...aut ex uno plures 'At' e.q.s.

FR. 4

Confrictique oleo, lentati, et ad arma parati.

Serv. (D.) ad *Aen.* III. 384.

> Serv. (D.) ad *Aen.* III. 384: et quidam 'lentandus' noue uerbum fictum
> putant, sed in Annalibus legitur 'Confrictique' e.q.s.

Confricti] 'confricati' Serv., corr. Ilbergius.
et ad arma parati] 'paratique ad arma' Serv., corr. Ilbergius.

FR. 5

Ciues Romani tunc facti sunt Campani.

Pseudo-Censorinus 612 K.

> Pseudo-Censorinus 612 K.: hexameter heroicus...totus ex spondiis
> 'Ciues' e.q.s.

FR. 6

cursus quingentos saepe ueruti.

Fest. p. 514. 22 L.

> Fest. p. 514. 22 L.: 'ueruta pila' dicuntur quod ⟨uelut uerua⟩ habent
> praefixa. Ennius lib. x. 'cursus' e.q.s.

FR. 7

Contremuit templum magnum Iouis altitonantis.

Varro, *L.L.* VII. 7.

> Varro, *L.L.* VII. 7: quocirca (*sc.* quod caelum, qua attuimur dictum
> 'templum') sic 'Contremuit' e.q.s.

FR. 8

Caelicolae, mea membra, dei, quos nostra potestas
Officiis diuisa facit.

Serv. ad *Aen.* IV. 638.

> Serv. ad *Aen.* IV. 638: sciendum Stoicos dicere unum esse deum cui
> nomina uariantur pro actibus et officiis, unde etiam duplicis sexus esse
> dicuntur...hic et Iouis oratio 'Caelicolae' e.q.s.

FR. 9

Europam Libyamque rapax ubi diuidit unda.

Cic. *Tusc.* I. 20. 45; *id. de Nat. Deor.* III. 10. 24.

Cic. *Tusc.* I. 20. 45: etenim si nunc aliquid assequi se putant qui ostium Ponti uiderunt et eas angustias per quas penetrauit ea quae est nominata Argo...aut ii qui Oceani freta illa uiderunt 'Europam' e.q.s. *Id. de Nat. Deor.* III. 10. 24: quid Chalcidico Euripo in motu identidem reciprocando putas fieri constantius, quid freto Siciliensi, quid Oceani feruore illis in locis 'Europam' e.q.s.?

FR. 10

Eripuere patres pueris plorantibus offam.

Pliny, *N.H.* XVII. 83.

Pliny, *N.H.* XVII. 83: et Ennius, antiquissimus uates obsidionis famam exprimens offam eripuisse plorantibus liberis patres commemorat.

FR. 11

Ex specula spectans.

Corp. Gloss. Lat. V. 20. 11.

Corp. Gloss. Lat. V. 20. 11: 'ex specula spectans' ex alto loco intendens.

FR. 12

Exaequant tumulis tumulos ac mortibus mortes
Accumulant.

Bell. Hisp. v.

Bell. Hisp. v.: 'hic alternis non solum morti mortem exaggerabant, sed tumulos tumulis exaequabant': uersum coniectura sua restituit Woelfflinus.

FR. 13

feruentia rapa uorare.

Sen. *Apoc.* IX.

Sen. *Apoc.* IX.: cum sit e republica esse aliquem qui cum Romulo possit 'feruentia' e.q.s.

Fr. 14

fusi sine mente
Ac sine sensu ullo iaceant.

Non. p. 488. 8 L.

> Non. p. 488. 8 L.: 'fundere' prosternere, iacere. Vergilius Aen. lib. I.
> 'quam...fundat humo' et †Aen.† lib. II. 'fusi' e.q.s.

Fr. 15

Ferme aderant ratibus repentibus aequore in alto.

Varro, *L.L.* VII. 23.

> Varro, *L.L.* VII. 23: 'Ferme aderant aequore in alto ratibus repentibus.'
> ⟨aequor⟩ mare appellatum aequatum cum commotum.

Fr. 16

Inuictus ca⟨nis, nare sagax et ui⟩ribus fretus.

Fest. p. 426. 13 L.

> Fest. p. 426. 13 L.: 'sagaces' appellantur multi ac sollertis acuminis...
> etiam canis ✳ ✳ ✳ 'inuictus ca ✳ ✳ ✳ ribus fretus.'
> Suppl. Dacerius: 'canis atque sagax et uiribus'; 'nare sagax' VII.

Fr. 17

Marsa manus, Paeligna cohors, Vestina uirum uis.

Don. 398 K.; Charis. 282 K.; Diom. 446 K.; Pomp. 303 K.

> Don. 398 K.: schesis onomaton est multitudo nominum coniunctorum
> quodam habitu copulandi ut 'Marsa' e.q.s. Charis. 282 K.: schesis
> onomaton est cum in textu plures antonomasiae ponuntur ut 'Marsa'
> e.q.s. Diom. 446 K.: schesis onomaton est cum singulis nominibus
> epitheta coniuncta sunt ut 'Marsa' e.q.s. Pomp. 303 K.: schesis
> onomaton est coaceruatio nominum...ut 'magna' e.q.s.

Fr. 18

Nos sumus Romani qui fuuimus ante Rudini.

Cic. *de Or.* III. 42.

> Cic. *de Or.* III. 42: ex pluribus intellegitur unum: 'Nos' e.q.s.

FR. 19

O genitor noster, Saturnie, maxime diuum.

Prisc. XVII. 205 H.

> Prisc. XVII. 205 H.: tertia uero possessiua, etsi naturam habeat ut per uocatiuum dici possit, ut praedictum est,...possimus enim etiam ad alienam possessionem dirigere sermonem ut 'O genitor' e.q.s.

FR. 20

Olli crateris ex auratis hauserunt.

Censor. 72 H.

> Censor. 72 H.: duodecasyllabos spondiazon 'Olli' e.q.s.

FR. 21

Quod bonus et liber populus.

Barthius, *Aduers.* XXXVIII. 15 (Lexicon Terent.).

> Barthius, *Aduers.* XXXVIII. 15: Terentius Adelphis: neque boni officium functus es, neque liberalis uiri: Ennius in eo 'Quod' e.q.s.

FR. 22

Qua murum fieri uoluit, urgemur in unum.

Non. p. 674. 18 L.

> Non. p. 674. 18 L.: 'urguere' insistere...Varro Antiquitates Rerum Humanarum 'Qua murum' e.q.s.

FR. 23

Rex ambas ultra fossam protendere coepit.

Plot. Sacer. 468 K.

> Plot. Sacer. 468 K.: synecdoche...fit modis quattuor...per id quod dicitur illud quod sequitur ut 'Rex' e.q.s.

protendere] 'retinere' codd., corr. Lachmannus.

Fr. 24

Romam ex aquilone

Raeti destringunt.

Placid. 79. 3 D.

> Placid. 79. 3 D.: 'Romam' e.q.s.: uel 'conlimitant' uel 'finibus se eius adiungunt.'

Raeti destringunt] 'retiae stringunt' codd., corr. Lachmannus. 'attingunt' Deuerlingus.

Fr. 25

spoliantur eos et corpora nuda relinquunt.

Don. 394 K.

> Don. 394 K.: fiunt soloecismi...per significationes sicut 'spoliantur' e.q.s.

Fr. 26

Tum coepit memorare simul cata dicta.

Varro, *L.L.* vii. 46.

> Varro, *L.L.* vii. 46: apud Ennium 'iam cata signa' e.q.s. 'cata' acuta: hoc enim uerbo dicunt Sabini; quare catus Aelius sextus non, ut aiunt, sapiens, sed acutus; et quod est 'Tum coepit' e.q.s. accipienda sunt 'acuta.'

Fr. 27

trabes remis rostrata per altum.

Varro, *L.L.* vii. 33.

> Varro, *L.L.* vii. 33: sic dictum a quibusdam ut 'una canes,' 'una trabes,' 'remis rostrata per altum.'

trabes] add. Columna.

Fr. 28

Vosque, Lares, tectum nostrum qui funditus curant.

Charis. 267 K.

> Charis. 267 K.: per personas (soloecismus) ut 'Vosque' e.q.s.

FR. 29

Volturnalem, Palatualem, Furinalem,
Floralemque Falacrem, et Pomonalem fecit
Hic idem.

Varro, *L.L.* VII. 45.

Varro, *L.L.* VII. 45: eundem Pompilium ait (Ennius) fecisse flamines,
qui cum omnes sint a singulis deis cognominati...sunt in quibus...
latent origines, ut in his qui sunt uersibus plerique 'Volturnalem' e.q.s.

APPENDIX B

FRAGMENTA SPURIA

FR. 1

Albani muris Albam Longam cinxerunt.

Mar. Vict. 101 K.

Mar. Vict. 101 K.: per transfigurationem quoque cum herous figuram
trimetri accipit, uelut 'Albani' e.q.s., hic enim si per dipodias percu-
tiatur, fiet trimetris.

FR. 2

Carbasus alta uolat pandam ductura carinam.

Barthius ad Stat. *Ach.* I. 558.

Barthius ad Stat. *Ach.* I. 558: carbasus nauis a 'uelo' ut Ennius 'Carbasus' e.q.s.

FR. 3

Flentes, plorantes, lacrumantes, obtestantes.

Auct. ad Herenn. IV. 12.

Auct. ad Herenn. IV. 12: 'Homoeoptoton'...ut 'Flentes' e.q.s.

FR. 4

Introducuntur legati Minturnenses.

Mar. Vict. 211 K.

Mar. Vict. 211 K.: hexameter uersus dactylicus per quot species
uariatur? Triginta et duas. Quatenus? In uersu duodecim syllabarum
species una est. Quippe hic sine ulla uarietate omnes in se spondeos
habet et uocabitur spondiazon ut 'Introducuntur' e.q.s.

Fr. 5

endo suam do.

Aus. *Technop*. 160; Charis. 278 K.; Diom. 441 K.; Prob. 263 K.; Mar.
Vict. 59 K.; Consent. 388 K.

Aus. *Technop*. 158 f.: unde Rudinus ait 'diuum domus altisonum cael.'
Et cuius de more quod astruit 'endo suam do.' Aut de fronde loquens
cur dicit 'populea frus'? Charis. 278 K.: apocope...syllaba ut 'endo
suam do' hoc est domum. Fere similia ceteri.

Fr. 6

Diuum domus altisonum cael.

Aus. *Technop*. 158. Vide ad Fr. 5.

Fr. 7

laetificum gau.

Aus. *Technop*. 144.

Aus. *Technop*. 144: Ennius ut memorat replet te laetificum gau.

Fr. 8

Musas quas memorant †nosce† nos esse ⟨Camenas⟩.

Varro, *L.L.* VII. 26.

Varro, *L.L.* VII. 26: 'Musas' e.q.s. Camenarum priscum uocabulum
ita natum ac scriptum est alibi: Carmenae ab eadem origine sunt
declinatae.

'Camenae' suppl. V.

Fr. 9

Machina multa minax minitatur maxima muris.

Diom. 447 K.

Diom. 447 K.: et aliter parhomoeon fit cum uerba similiter incipiunt
ut 'Machina' e.q.s.

Fr. 10

Maerentes, flentes, lacrumantes, commiserantes.

Diom. II. 442 P.; Charis. 282 K.

Diom. II. 442 P.: et aliter homoeopton fit cum oratio excurrit in eosdem
casus et similes fines ut Ennius 'Maerentes' e.q.s. Charis. 282 K.:
homoeopton est oratio excurrens in eosdem casus similes ut 'Maerentes'
e.q.s.

FR. 11

Miscent foede flumina candida sanguine sparso.

Diom. 499 K.

Diom. 499 K.: partipedes sunt qui in singulis pedibus singulas orationis partes adsignant ut 'miscent †fida† flumina' e.q.s.
foede] 'fida' libri plerique. 'foede' cod. man. 2.

FR. 12

Massili portabant iuuenes ad litora tanas.

Don. 401 K.

Don. 401 K.: tmesis est unius compositi aut simplicis uerbi sectio una
dictione uel pluribus interpositis ut...'saxo cere' e.q.s. et 'Massili'
e.q.s.

FR. 13

O Tite, tute, Tati, tibi tanta, tyranne, tulisti.

Auct. ad Herenn. IV. 12. 18; Prisc. XII. 591 H.; Don. 398 K.; Expl. in
Don. 565 K.; Charis. 282 K.; Pomp. 303 K.; Plot. Sacer. 454 K.

Auct. ad Herenn. IV. 12. 18: (compositio seruabitur) si uitabimus eiusdem litterae nimiam adsiduitatem, cui uitio uersus hic erit exemplo
(nam hic nihil prohibet in uitiis alienis exemplis uti) 'O Tite' e.q.s.
Prisc. XII. 591 H.: ...nominatiuo...breuem 'tĕ' syllabam pro 'met'
addere solent auctores uel 'temet'...Ennius 'O Tite' e.q.s. Don.
398 K.: parhomoeon est cum ab isdem litteris diuersa uerba sumuntur
ut 'O Tite' e.q.s. Expl. in Don. 565 K.: eiusdem Enni uersus est
'tute Tati' e.q.s. Omnes enim partes orationis 't' littera principium
sumunt. Charis. 282 K.: parhomoeon est cum uerba omnia similiter
incipiunt ut 'O Tite' e.q.s. Pomp. 303 K.: parhomoeon est quotiens
ab isdem litteris diuersa uerba sequuntur...antiqui integros uersus
ita faciebant ut 'O Tite' e.q.s. uersus est Ennianus. Plot. Sacer. 454 K.:
aprepia est absurda et indecens uerborum structura ut 'O Tite' e.q.s.

FR. 14

Phemenoe Burro! cluo purpurei Epirotae.

Porph. ad Hor. *A.P.* 403.

Porph. ad Hor. *A.P.* 403: per uersus hexametros reddidit responsa
†Phemenoet pyrro clio tamquam purphoeri poetae 'aio te Aeacida' e.q.s.
Versus restitutus est a Stowassero (*Wien. Stud.* XIII. 325 ff.).

FR. 15

perculsi pectora Poeni.

Schol. anon. ap. Columnam.

Schol. anon. ap. Columnam: hoc fragmentum mihi e Cosentia Fabius
Aquinas misit: quod a quodam suo uetustissimo Statii interprete ms.
excerpsit: cuius nomen, cum in illius libri principio et fine multae
desiderentur paginae, prorsus ignoratur. Constat tamen ex collatione
non esse Lactantium.

FR. 16

Qui inuicti fuere uiri, pater optime Olympi,
Hos ego in pugna uici, uictusque sum ab isdem.

Oros. IV. 1. 14; Paul. Diac. *Hist.* II. 16.

Oros. IV. 1. 14: sed Pyrrhus atrocitatem cladis (*sc.* Heracleensis) quam
hoc bello exceperat dis suis hominibusque testatus est, adfigens
titulum in templo Tarenti Iouis in quo haec scripsit 'Qui inuicti'
e.q.s. Eadem fere apud Paul., nisi quod uersus hac specie citat 'Qui
inuicti ante fuere uiri, pater optime Olympi, | Hos et ego' e.q.s.

FR. 17

Quem super ingens
Porta tonat caeli.

Gramm. anon. ap. Columnam p. 83.

Gramm. anon. ap. Columnam: 'in membranis anonymi cuiusdam
grammatici expresse ex Ennio.'

FR 18

saxo cere comminuit brum.

Don. 401 K.; Expl. in Don. 565 K.; Serv. ad *Aen.* 1. 412.

Don. 401 K.: tmesis...'saxo' e.q.s. Expl. in Don. 565 K.: ...Ennius
et 'saxo' e.q.s. Serv. ad *Aen.* 1. 412: figura est tmesis...in simplici
(sermone) nimis est asperum: quod tamen faciebat antiquitas ut 'saxo'
e.q.s.

FR. 19

Tum lateralis dolor certissimus nuntius mortis.

Mar. Vict. 216 K.

Mar. Vict. 216 K.: Ennius quoque ait 'uita illa dignus locoque,' quasi
'dignu locoque' dixerit. Similiter Lucilius ait 'Tum lateralis' e.q.s.

NOTES

THE PROBABLE DIVISION OF THE
SUBJECT-MATTER

BOOK I. From the Sack of Troy to the death of Romulus.

BOOK II. The reigns of Numa, Tullus and Ancus.

BOOK III. The reigns of the three last kings and the establishment of the Republic.

BOOK IV. Events down to the Gallic invasion of 390 B.C.

BOOK V. The Samnite wars to 295 B.C.; some preliminaries to the war with Pyrrhus.

BOOK VI. The war with Pyrrhus down to the appeal of Syracuse for help.

BOOK VII. A personal interlude. The conclusion of the war with Pyrrhus and the minor operations between the First and Second Punic wars. The First Punic war was not narrated.

BOOK VIII. From the outbreak of the Second Punic war to the recall of Hannibal to Africa.

BOOK IX. From the recall of Hannibal to the conclusion of the war.

BOOK X. The Macedonian wars down to the conclusion of the armistice after the battle of Cynoscephalae.

BOOK XI. ⎱ Events between the battle of Cynoscephalae and the outbreak
BOOK XII. ⎰ of the war with Antiochus. Cato and home affairs.

BOOK XIII. The war with Antiochus down to 190 B.C.

BOOK XIV. From the passage of the Hellespont to the end of the war.

BOOK XV. The Aetolian war and Fulvius Nobilior. The original *envoi*.

BOOK XVI. The Istrian war and the Tribune Aelius.

BOOK XVII. ⎱ Later events, perhaps as far as the outbreak of the Third
BOOK XVIII. ⎰ Macedonian war.

BOOK I

FR. 1. That the line is correctly placed as the first in the poem is clear from Varro (*R.R.* 1. 1. 4). It recalls the familiar Homeric formula ἔσπετε νῦν μοι, Μοῦσαι, Ὀλύμπια δώματ' ἔχουσαι; the narrative poems of both Livius and Naevius also contain similar addresses. But while Livius identified the Italian *Camena* with the Greek Μοῦσα, no such identification was possible for Ennius. His are the Greek Muses of Olympus or Helicon, and the name *Camena* is never mentioned, at least in the extant fragments. True, he refers to Egeria, who was traditionally one of the *Camenae*; but it is as the prophetic helper of Numa that he speaks of her. For him the *Camenae* presided over no poetry but that which he had himself rejected; indeed he seems to have banished the word from the literary language (in the sense of *Musa*), just as he banished *Vates* until both were restored to honour by the Augustans.

The corrupt citation in Varro (*L.L.* VII. 26) is sometimes attached to our line, but there is no evidence whatever that the line was a hexameter. Müller is probably correct in calling it a Saturnian, though we need not follow him in attributing it to Naevius (see further below on Sp. 8).

Besides the general invocation which served for the poem as a whole, special prologues were prefixed to certain important books, *e.g.* VI. (introducing the war with Pyrrhus), X. (after the conclusion of the Hannibalic war), XVI. (the narrative of contemporary events). For the phrase *pedibus pulsatis Olympum*, which refers to the Muses' dance, cf. *Theog. vv.* 1–8. Valmaggi's *Aequo pede pulsat* is most inappropriate as a parallel; he is happier with *nunc pede libero Pulsanda tellus*, but the phrase before us is too natural to require elaborate comment, and is, in fact, an excellent illustration of the truth of Cicero's general criticism of the style of Ennius—*communi more uerborum* (see *Or.* XXXVI.). *Aen.* XI. 660, for which Servius quotes our line, has the much stronger expression *flumina...pulsant*. The ancients were fond of discussing whether, in such descriptions as the present, the name *Olympus* referred to the heavens or the hill; see for example Varro, *L.L.* VII. 28, where the hill is chosen. *Olumpum* would be Ennius' own spelling of the word; Y to represent Greek *upsilon* was not introduced until the last century of the Republic (cf. Cassiod. 153. 11 K.). For convenience, however, I adopt the conventional *y, ch, ph, th*, instead of *u, c, p, t*, in Greek loan words.

FR. 2. The dream of inspiration. The *motif* is, of course, familiar in the literature of all ages and countries. It is used again by Ennius in the *Epicharmus*, but the vision of Homer in the *Annales* seems to have been specially famous. An interesting reminiscence of it is to be found in Petrarch's Latin epic *Africa* (Bk IX. *vv.* 141 ff.). Of the numerous ancient references, one of the most important is Persius, VI. 9 f., with the *scholium* ad loc.: *sic enim ait Ennius in Annalium suorum principio, ubi se dicit uidisse in somnis Homerum dicentem fuisse se quondam pauonem* (cf. Fr. 5 below) *et ex eo translatam esse animam in se.*

Lunai portum. These words must be accepted as belonging to the quotation. The archaic genitive in *ai* had become a standing joke for Martial (see XI. 90, on a person of affectedly archaic tastes), and it is most unlikely that Persius could have used such a form himself. The most obvious reason for mentioning Luna (mod. Spezia) so emphatically is that it was the scene of the dream which was to inspire poems so famous. Hence, though the line from Probus which I have placed after *Lunai portum* is usually regarded as a separate fragment, and the two are read in the reverse order, I have combined them. This arrangement enables us to retain and explain the *nam* of Probus, which none of the editors attempts to do. Whatever the correct reading of the second line may be, the connection of thought is clearly something like 'Note the name of this place; it is worth while *for* famous poems sprang thence.' I have left the MSS. reading untouched in default of a satisfactory emendation, for all those which have been proposed should, I submit, be rejected on metrical grounds. As a rule one or other of the following is accepted: (1) *Nostra Latinos | Per populos terrasque poemata clara cluebunt* (Müller), (2) *latos | Per populos os atque poemata nostra cluebunt | Clara...*, or some combination of the two such as that given by Valmaggi who reads *latos | Per populos terrasque poemata nostra cluebunt | Clara*. All these lines belong to what we may call the 'triple dactyl' type; that is, they all have dactyls in the third, fourth, and fifth feet. I suggest that this rhythm was not used by Ennius in a normal hexameter in combination with the type of caesura which they all contain (trochaic third foot break followed by unbroken fourth foot). We are heavily handicapped in our attempts to appreciate the metrical rules which Ennius formulated, but in the extant fragments of the *Annales* one 'triple dactyl' line only shows this caesura. And that line is an obvious *tour de force* aiming at a special effect— *Labitur uncta carina per aequora cana celocis*. It thus resembles the other caesuraless 'triple dactyl' lines *Poste recumbite, uestraque pectora pellite tonsis* and *Corde capessere; semita nulla pedem stabilibat*. Taken together, they seem to suggest deliberate experiment in caesura effects for this type of line; and on further investigation we find two other experimental types, both of which are very rare: 1. Unbroken third foot— strong break in fourth: *Tarquinum dedit imperium simul et sola regni*. 2. Trochaic break in both third and fourth feet: *Visus Homerus adesse poeta* (four examples altogether). Normally the 'triple dactyl' line shows: (1) The ordinary strong third foot break, with or without fourth foot break; and (2) trochaic third foot break with strong fourth foot break. Of these (1) is by far the more common, but both are perfectly satisfactory for Ennius as for Homer. We should hesitate, therefore, to accept any version of our line which introduces a rhythm so unusual. An easy correction of *cluebunt* would be *clarebunt*. The error may have arisen from *clarebant* (with *u* in the margin to correct the slip in the tense) and the confusion might be helped by a reminiscence in the scribe's mind of the Lucretian *corona...quae clara clueret*. *Clarere* is a good Ennian word; and with *clarebunt* standing at the beginning of the next line, we should have *Nam latos populos res atque poemata nostra*, which would at least clear the way towards restoring a line with a correct caesura. To read *nam late populis*, etc., would provide a tolerable meaning; and terminations are very liable to corruption. But *res atque* is not quite convincing. Indeed it must be confessed that *in primo annali* might seem more natural than *in primo* simply, and the *nam* may be merely the symbol *ann(ali)*. With this view, the sentence of Probus would become *Ennius in primo annali latos populos res atque poemata nostra cluebant*. However, I retain *nam* in the text (explaining it as stated above), for quotations from the *Annales* are often given by the number of the book only (*e.g.* by Macrobius) and the same authority is not always consistent on this point.

The famous and important passage in Lucretius (I. 116 ff.: *An pecudes...expandere dictis*) gives a clear statement that Ennius represented Homer as imparting certain philosophical information. Was that information limited to the doctrine of metempsychosis and Ennius' own mystical descent from himself? This is all that Persius tells us; and the survival and subsequent fate of the soul is the point of the discourse of *semper florens Homerus* most elaborated by Lucretius. The latter might appear to have two different and contradictory statements of Ennius in mind: (1) *Cecinit Ennius noster* (in the poem which I, Lucretius, know best and therefore mention first); (2) *Etsi praeterea* (although he did make other statements elsewhere, and imply that there was some sort of survival after death). May not Lucretius be alluding to

the *Epicharmus* as well as to the *Annales*? The compliment
with which he begins, especially the emphatic *noster*, would
be more appropriate from one didactic poet to another than
from a teacher to a writer of narrative; and, while its suita-
bility to his subject leads him to mention Ennius' theory of
the birth of individual souls, that theory itself would be out
of place in the prologue to the history of Rome. It is to be
noted that Homer is not mentioned until the first subject
has been disposed of; and the source of inspiration at the
beginning is not Olympus, the home of the Epic Muse of
Homer, but Helicon, where dwells the didactic Muse of
Hesiod. Accordingly I cannot accept as belonging to the
present context, two fragments quoted together by Varro
(*L.L.* v. 59), and generally placed close to our line. They are:
Oua parire solet genus pinnis condecoratum | *Non animam; post
inde uenit diuinitus pullis* | *Ipsa anima*... and *terraque corpus* |
Quae dedit ipsa capit neque dispendi facit hilum. Pascal, indeed,
revives the old theory that they belong to the *Epicharmus*
(*Riv. di Fil. Class.* xxv. 239 ff.); but there is no reason to
suppose that the *Epicharmus* was not altogether in Trochaic
Septenarii, the metre of all the extant fragments. Hence I
prefer to leave the lines among the *Fragmenta Incertorum
Librorum*, though they may well belong to the Satires.

Fr. 3. In Petrarch's poem, already mentioned, Ennius describes Homer as a bald, blind old man in a ragged robe, and
ends with the words *Aspice qualis erat quondam dum uixit
Homerus*. It is possible that the words *Ei mihi qualis erat!*
quoted by Servius (on *Aen.* ii. 274) belong to the same description in Ennius himself. But they are capable of very
wide reference, and, failing an exact statement from Servius,
it is impossible to assign them to any particular point in the
Annales.

Fr. 4. The beginning of Homer's speech. The Donatus

NOTES: BOOK I 99

scholia on Terence quote the fragment as a parallel to
Terence's *festus dies hominis* (*pro ' homo festi diei'*). This construction, however, savours rather of comedy than epic. There
is no difficulty in explaining our example as an ordinary
possessive genitive; 'the loving-kindness of thy heart' is a
natural phrase in Latin as in English.

Fr. 5. The form *fiere* should certainly be restored. It is
attested by Macrobius for Bk x (see *G.L.K.* v. 645), and is
the older form, driven out by the constant use of *fio* as the
passive of *facio*. We can hardly allow *fĭĕrĭ*. This so-called
'cretic shortening' is postulated by Lindsay in a number of
words (see *Early Latin Verse*, pp. 44 ff.); he accepts *commodă*
(the imperative of the verb) for Catullus, and such instances
as *nescĭŏ* and *Pollĭŏ* in Horace are well known. But the argument from the *io* termination is not strong enough to support
fĭĕrĭ; it seems to have been specially liable to shortening, for
(*ĭ*)*ŏ* became the normal scansion in later Latin, and even in
the Augustan age other poets did not share Vergil's objection
to it. Catullus x, again, in which *commodă* occurs, is a poem
of peculiarly colloquial tone and therefore stands close to
comedy in its prosody. We cannot argue from it to formal
composition like the *Annales*.

pauum: this second declension form is found also in Varro
(ap. Gell. vi. 16) and in the late Latin of Tertullian and
Arnobius. The tradition of Ennius' descent from Homer is
fully given by the Scholiast on Stat. *Theb.* iii. 484, who,
though he makes Pythagoras older than Homer, nevertheless
preserves a genuine tradition of the Schools: cf. Ovid, *Met.*
xv. 160 ff. and Hor. *Od.* i. 28. 9 ff.; cf. also on the question
of Ennius and Homer, Porph. ad Hor. *Ep.* ii. i. 50 and
Schol. in Pers. *Prol.* 2. The Orphics taught that the human
soul might pass into other animals, or even into plants: cf.
Procl. ad Plat. *Rep.* ii. 338. 10 and Empedocles, Fr. 117 in

Diels, I.³ 268. 9. In Lucian the soul of Pythagoras passed
into an ordinary barn-door cock, and Tertullian's *De Anima*
mentions the passage of Euphorbus' soul into Pythagoras,
and that of Homer into a peacock. The peacock seems to
have been one of the many objects which could be used as
a symbol of apotheosis or resurrection, and as such appears
sometimes in the decorations of tombs and sepulchral
chambers. Echoes of this ancient superstition are not wanting
in our own literature, for Sir Thos. Browne quotes among his
'vulgar errors' the belief that the flesh of peacocks is incor-
ruptible.

Ennius' interest in philosophy is an important legacy from
his early environment. Born at Rudiae in Calabria, he was
educated at Tarentum, no very great distance from Metapontum, a town which cherished carefully its memories of
Pythagoras. It is natural, therefore, that among the many
distinctions of Ennius should be that of having introduced
both Pythagoreanism and Epicureanism into Latin literature.
According to the flesh, Ennius claimed descent from the
legendary king Messapus: cf. Sil. Ital. XII. 393 and Servius
(ad *Aen*. VII. 691).

Considerable difficulty was caused to some of the ancient
grammarians by the use of the present infinitive in phrases
like the present: see, for example, the note of Donatus on
Ter. *Andr*. II. 5. But the present seems to be the regular
tense in early Latin, and is always used when the experience
recalled is that of the speaker himself: the perfect is very
rare, and is found only with reference to the actions or ex-
periences of others.

FR. 6. The opening of the poem proper. It is impossible
to decide whether Ennius gave any detailed account of the
Sack of Troy, though if he wished to do so he would find a
certain amount of material ready to his hand in Latin no less

than in Greek. There can be little doubt that the *Bellum Punicum* contained some description of the last scene of Priam's tragedy, and we hear from Varro (*L.L.* VII. 28) of a *Carmen Priami* (cf. Excursus II).

ueter: *senex* is a constant epithet of Priam in later verse; *e.g.* Ov. *Trist.* III. 37 and *Met.* XIII. 409.

FR. 7. For the subject-matter editors compare *Il.* XX. 239. The epithet *pius* applied to Anchises strikes the modern reader as strange in view of its association with Aeneas in Vergil; but cf. *Aen.* III. 690 (the prayer of Anchises). In Naevius also, Anchises is called *senex fretus pietati*, but the word may be deliberately chosen in our passage because Ennius followed a form of the legend in which Anchises was in reality the rescuer (see later on Fr. 9).

FR. 8. One of the most difficult passages in the *Annales*, and one in which the unexplained disagreement of our two authorities (see sources) makes it almost impossible to arrive at any certain conclusion. Fleckeisen's correction of the first two words appears certainly right, and I follow him again in reading *pulcherruma dium* at the end of the line. This termination is practically that of *Schol. Ver.*, involving nothing but the substitution of *diū* (= *dium*) for *diu*: but in the second line I unhesitatingly follow Probus. *Fari donauit* (= ' gifted with speech ') is not a phrase that is likely to be due to a faulty memory; and had the original been anything so simple as *fata docet fari* (Bernays' widely accepted suggestion), or *fari fata docet*, so difficult a variant would never have arisen. It is true that *fari fata* is redolent of antiquity. Still, *fari* might be glossed *scilicet fata*, and *fari fata donauit* be adapted to the metre. Or the reading of the Verona Scholia could also be due to the intrusion of the gloss *fata docet*, explaining *fari donauit*. *Fari* is used in an almost technical religious sense, and means 'to speak as a prophet,' as did the *Fauni*. *Fatua*, the name by which Faunus' wife or sister was known *in pontificum libris*, is clearly connected with *fari*: cf. Lactantius, I. 22. 9. As defined by the grammarians, e.g. Varro, *L.L.* VII. 52, *fari* means 'to utter articulate sounds'; but Varro himself suggests the other meaning, and Servius (ad *Aen.* VII. 47) puts it in a sentence—*Dicti autem sunt Faunus et Fauna a uaticinando, id est fando*: cf. *id.* ad *Aen.* VIII. 31 and II. 54; Mart. Cap. II. 167. The usage of Greek cognate words like φημίζειν supports this meaning, and the noun *fatum* is so used in both prose and verse. Vergil preserves the meaning in the verb also, as in the phrase *fandi doctissima Cymodocea*, and again in the prophecy of Jove in Bk I. In the latter passage there is a conscious differentiation between *dehinc talia fatur*, which means simply 'speaks,' and the *fabor* of five lines later, which must obviously mean 'I will utter prophecy,' and which is explained by the emphatic *fatorum arcana mouebo* following.

In our present line the second infinitival phrase is more or less explanatory of the other. The two infinitives play the part of nouns: cf. Plaut. *Bacch.* 158. The double accusative with *donare* may be paralleled by Ter. *Hec.* 849 (where, however, the second object is a neuter pronoun). Though the infinitive construction with *donare* found in later poetry seems always to be accompanied by a dative of the person, yet in it also the infinitive is an accusative governed by the verb, as in the Horatian *Diuinare etenim magnus mihi donat Apollo.* The augural science of Anchises' was evidently famous in early tradition. It is mentioned also in the *Bellum Punicum* of Naevius—*Postquam auem aspexit in templo Anchisa?* For Anchises' association with magical powers in general, we may remember that it is he who, in the underworld, reveals the future history of Rome, and he who after death appears in warning visions to Aeneas: cf. *Aen.* IV. 351 ff. For the length of the final *a* in *Anchisā* cf. Lindsay, *Early Latin Verse*, p. 152.

Fr. 9. This line certainly refers to an appearance of Venus; and probably Frs. 10 and 11 form part of the same description. The word *caliginis* is sometimes taken to mean darkness, as if the goddess appeared at night, and for this reason *Quom superum lumen nox intempesta teneret* (Fr. 32) is usually placed close to our line. I, however, place it before the description of the auspice-taking for reasons stated in the note ad loc. Here I suggest that *caligo* does not necessarily or even probably refer to the darkness of night. Its proper meaning is, like that of the Greek ὀμίχλη, a cloud-like vapour, mist, or fog, which may be present by day or night: it is instructive to examine the Vergilian usage of the word. In three passages (*Georg.* II. 309, *Aen.* VIII. 253, XI. 187) it is used of smoke, in three of a cloud of dust, in one of fog, and in one of gloom (of the underworld), but it never means 'the darkness of night.' The usage of Lucretius corresponds to this: a good instance of what he understood by the word is found in VI. 476, a description of the thick white mist to be seen in marshy bottoms and water-meadows. It is quite clear then that, without some defining word such as *noctis*, *caligo* cannot properly be used to mean 'the darkness of night.' The following interpretations of our line might seem possible:

(*a*) She passed swiftly through the smoke (of the burning city).

(*b*)   „   „   „   dust (of battle).

(*c*)   „   „   „   delicate airy clouds.

(*d*)   „   „   „   insubstantial air.

Either (*a*) or (*b*) would in itself be both appropriate and accurate in view of the Vergilian passages mentioned above. But the adjective *tenerae* seems to make them both impossible; we should expect a word like *nigras*, *densas* or *piceas*. I suggest

that (*d*) may be correct. As stated above, *caligo* resembles
ὁμίχλη in meaning; ὁμίχλη in turn comes very close to ἀήρ
(indeed the two can be used side by side as practical synonyms
as in *Il.* XVII. 649), and the specialised meaning of 'lower
atmosphere' which ἀήρ bears in Homer and Hesiod is well
known. So far as we can judge Ennius did not use *aer* in this
specific contrast to *aether*: in *Ann.* III. fr. 2 it is used as a
synonym for *uentus*, and this reappears in the *Epicharmus*
where *Aer* is personified and identified with Jove. If Ennius
preferred not to use *aer* in this special sense he may well have
fallen back on *caligo*; and some expression of the idea would
be almost inevitable in a passage like the present. With this
interpretation the whole phrase would very closely resemble
such Lucretian lines as I. 207, but, if it be not accepted, our
line must be understood as (*c*) above. Colonna understood
the reference to be to the *umbra* of Homer rising up from the
underworld; Merula, quite without justification, changed *cita*
to *citus* and explained the line as a description of the apotheosis
of Romulus. Modern editors, however, rightly refer it to
the descent of Venus; and, with this reference, it must be
explained in some such way as above.

FR. 10. The appearance of Venus. It is generally assumed
that the person to whom she came was Aeneas, because it is
so in Vergil. But the plural *sos* clearly suggests that there
were at least two men present, and it is natural to suppose
that the second was Anchises. Our fragment and the next
seem to refer to the legend preserved by Dionysius, and
evidently used by Sophocles in the *Laocoon*, that Aeneas withdrew to Mt Ida on the advice of Anchises, who had been
instructed to urge him to do so by Venus. Venus herself is
probably the speaker in Fr. 11, and Anchises and Aeneas
are both with her. We must recognise here one of the many
features in which the Vergilian legend of Aeneas differs from

that current in earlier times; and certainly there is no suggestion in Ennius, as he survives, of the rescue of Anchises
from the fallen city. In Sophocles, and perhaps in Ennius,
Aeneas and his party withdrew from Troy as a result of the
portent of the two serpents sent to devour Laocoon and his
sons.

The phrase *inde loci* is found once again in the *Annales* and
once in the Satires, and is used several times by Lucretius.
It is difficult to determine whether the meaning is temporal
or local.

sos pro eos, as Festus says; other forms from the same stem
found in the *Annales* are *sas*, *sum*, *sam* and *sapsa* (= *ea ipsa*).
All the examples given by Festus are from Ennius except
one from the *Teucer* of Pacuvius. From this demonstrative
stem we must distinguish the reflexive-possessive stem (cor-
responding to Gk *$\sigma F o \varsigma$—$\H{o}\varsigma$) also used by Ennius and giving
forms *sam = suam*, *sis = suis*, *sos = suos*. The similarity of
these two stems created a good deal of confusion (cf. note
on Fr. 38 below), but the distinction is clear. More doubtful
is whether Ennius employed this form as a mere spelling of
monosyllabic *suam*, *suos*, *suis* pronounced with synizesis.

dia dearum: though we should not be too ready to speak of
Graecisms in early Latin syntax, this phrase seems to be a
direct imitation of the Homeric $\delta \hat{\imath} a \ \theta \epsilon \acute{a} \omega \nu$. There are two
other similar phrases in the *Annales*—*sancta dearum* and
magna dearum, both of Juno, but no other examples elsewhere
in the early period.

Fr. 11. Venus urges Aeneas to obey his father's suggestion.

face is of course the old Latin for *fac*: the form was
already obsolescent in the earliest literary period.

orare pro agere, as Festus says; the meaning is 'plead' or
'urge.'

Fr. 12. The first mention of Italy. Our line is quoted to

illustrate *Aen*. I. 530. It is probable that, as Pascoli suggests, Ennius proceeded to give the name by which Italy was known to the gods: cf. *Il*. II. 811 ff. As Valmaggi remarks, the central group of the *Tabula Iliaca* shows the flight of Aeneas, and bears the inscription Αἰνήας σὺν τοῖς ᾽Ιλίοις ἀπαίρων εἰς τὴν ῾Εσπερίαν. Naturally Italy was 'the sunset land' to the Greeks.

FR. 13. The primitive history of Italy. The chiastic arrangement *prisci casci populi Latini* is to be noted. Probably *prisci Latini* is to be regarded as a noun-adjective compound of the sort familiar in Plautus in such phrases as *mala res*, *mala crux*. *Cascus* is itself a very ancient word, of Sabine derivation according to Varro (*L.L.* VII. 28: cf. Oscan *casnar = senex*). The *Prisci Latini* were regarded as the aboriginal inhabitants of Italy (*qui prius quam conderetur Roma, fuerunt*).

FR. 14. The arrival in Latium. *Laurentis etiam pro Laurens dicebant*: Priscian. For the supposed origin of the name see *Aen*. VII. 59 ff.

FR. 15. The early history of Latium. Evidently the arrival of Aeneas in the district was made the occasion for a description of its primitive condition, which Vergil may have used for *Aen*. VII. The genealogy of Saturn is introduced because he is represented as the founder of the royal family. That the name *Saturnia* or *mons Saturnius* was regarded as belonging to the Capitol appears from Varro, *L.L.* v. 42: cf. note on next fragment.

FR. 16. It seems clear from Varro that the word *late* belongs not to Ennius but to Varro himself, who uses it to describe the extension of a name originally limited to the Capitol.

FR. 17. Events after the death of Aeneas: the dream of Ilia. It is abundantly clear that, for Ennius, Ilia was the daughter of Aeneas; and, despite the Augustan 'official recension' of early history, his influence kept this form of the story alive. In the well-known passage in *Aen.* VI, after the list of Alban kings from Silvius to Capys, Numitor and Silvius Aeneas, there follows the remarkable prophecy, *Quin et auo comitem sese Mauortius addet | Romulus Assaraci quem sanguinis Ilia mater | Educet.* The note of Servius, ad loc., shows that he was much puzzled by the word *auo* and found it impossible to refer it to Numitor as editors usually do; cf. *id.* ad *Aen.* I. 237. It should not be overlooked that in the first passage, as well as in the prophecy of Jove in Bk I, Vergil introduces the name Assaracus, which inevitably throws the mind back to the genealogy given by Ennius (Fr. 7).

anus: hardly the unnamed sister of Ilia, but a nurse or slave.

artubus: for the neglect of final *s*, due to the slight pronunciation of the consonant after a short vowel, cf. the important passage in Cic. *Orat.* XLVIII. 161. The fashion survived in pronunciation till the Ciceronian age and makes its last literary appearance in a line of Catullus.

Eurydica: Eurydice is not elsewhere mentioned as the wife of Aeneas. Besides Lavinia, we hear of Tyrrhenia (cf. Alcimus ap. Fest. p. 326 Lind.), but evidently Eurydice was the mother of Ilia's sister, though not of Ilia herself. The word *germana* by which Ilia twice addresses her sister properly means born of the same father and mother, as in Plaut. *Men.* 1102; but it is often used in a looser sense, and need imply no more than that they were both daughters of Aeneas.

corpus meum: the Homeric caesura is to be noted; though rejected later in favour of the 'triple caesura,' the type was nevertheless accepted by Ennius.

homo pulcher: the vision fell into two parts, and Aeneas did not appear until after the departure of the unnamed guide. For a similar magical landscape cf. *Aen.* VI. 638.

sorŏr: the final syllable shows the original quantity; no doubt Ennius felt that there was 'metrical justification' for retaining it, in the fact that the syllable bears the *ictus metricus* and stands before the main caesura. We have, however, one example (Bk XVI. fr. 40; cf. note, ad loc.) where this does not hold good and are therefore probably correct in concluding that *ŏr* was the only scansion which Ennius allowed: cf. Lindsay, *Early Latin Verse*, p. 125.

Corde capessere, corde cupitus: in both these *corde* is a locative ablative of place. Such figurative usages are rare in early Latin, but examples are found both in comedy and satire, *e.g.* Lucilius (190) Marx, Plaut. *Capt.* 420. The effect of the caesuraless line (on which cf. note on Fr. 2 above), expressing rapid and giddy motion, is to be noted.

compellare uoce: the phrase should not be called a mere 'pleonasm' with Pascoli. *Compellat uoce* appears in *Aen.* V. 161.

Aerumnae: according to Charisius, Ennius declared that this word might be spelled either *aer* or *er* to suit one or other of two fanciful derivations. If so, the statement probably found a place in the Satires, where it would be a precursor of the orthographical discussions of Lucilius.

resistet = restituetur: cf. Cic. *Pro Mur.* XXXIX. 84, *ubi lapsi resistamus*, seemingly the only other example.

multa: 'accusative of the inner object,' used with adverbial force affecting the three verbs *lacrumans, tendebam* and *uocabam*. The idea of repetition is strengthened by the accurate contrast of imperfects with perfects in the sentence. Ennius' carefulness in the use of language is frequently praised by such writers as Varro and Gellius, and was probably one of the grounds for his own boast that he was *dicti studiosus*, a finished artist in contrast with the looser, rougher style of his predecessors.

cum: the MSS. vary between *cum* and *tum*; accepting the

former, we have an instance of the seemingly unnecessary preposition which we find elsewhere in Ennius, *e.g.* Bk XIII. fr. 1.

FR. 18. The fate of Ilia. *Sancta* is clearly right. Some of the suggested changes, such as the *sale nata* of Vahlen 1, are unsatisfactory from the elaboration of the phrase produced, for in such an emotional crisis only the simplest epithet would suggest itself, and others are entirely inappropriate. Colonna's *nunc* commends itself by its simplicity, but we might read *te, te sancta*.

cognata: the relationship is the ground of the appeal.

parumper: on the meaning of this word cf. note on Bk VI. fr. 16.

FR. 19. Norden makes Aeneas the speaker here as he is in Vergil's imitation (*Aen.* VIII. 72). Servius (ad loc.) states that *Adesto Tiberine cum tuis undis* was a regular formula in prayers. According to Porphyrio ad Hor. *Od.* 1. 2. 18, Ennius explicitly stated that Ilia was thrown into the river by order of King Amulius. The latter is thus a fundamental person in the story, but in what relationship did Ennius suppose him to stand to Ilia? It has been suggested that a mutilated form of his name appears in a passage of Apollodorus preserved in Festus, which gives Mayllis, Mulus and Rhomus as the sons of Aeneas. Others suppose him to be the same as Aemylus, said to be the son of Ascanius (cf. Festus, p. 22 Lind.—on the name of the *Gens Aemilia*). But the original tradition seems to have been that Ascanius died childless: cf. Serv. ad *Aen.* VI. 762. The information there is almost certainly derived from Cato, and I should therefore prefer the first explanation which makes Amulius at least the half-brother of Ilia. It is not reasonable to suppose that Ennius, coming a stranger to Rome, would run counter to the authority of such a man as Cato on the question of the identity of Amulius. Ascanius, as the founder of the *Gens*

Iulia, seems to have no place in the native form of the legend, and there is little room for him in Ennius except perhaps as the founder of Alba. In Cato we are probably dealing with an early attempt to blend the cycle of Alban legends with those of Rome; those legends, in common with others of the earliest period, must have received much fuller literary treatment than is generally recognised (cf. Excursus II), and possibly Ennius followed Naevius in taking over the character of Amulius from some such source. But the language of Porphyrio quite clearly suggests that Ennius was the earliest authority known to him for the king's proceedings against Ilia. We may therefore conjecture that Ennius did his share in the work of harmonising by identifying Amulius with some brother of Ilia, perhaps with the Silvius mentioned by Servius (from Cato), perhaps with Ascanius himself. There seems to have been some confusion between them, to judge from Cato's statement (reported by Servius) that Silvius was also called Ascanius; and to make the king of Alba the son of Aeneas would be a natural method of rough adjustment when the founder of Rome was still the grandson of Aeneas. The general question of Ennius' chronology, and in particular the date at which he supposed Rome to have been founded, gives rise to many problems. The famous lines *Septingenti sunt*, etc., are quoted by Varro (*R.R.* III. 1. 2) without direct reference, and, though they almost certainly belong to the *Annales*, it is quite uncertain where they should be placed. Varro censures Ennius for inaccuracy, and implies that he was roughly a century out; possibly he was following some Greek historian who, as was often done, placed the founding of Rome well within the ninth century B.C., or possibly he chose, for his own purposes, to identify the Rome of history with such an early settlement as that which appears in Vergil as the 'city' of Evander. In any case, if he knew or cared for the traditional date of the sack of Troy, he cannot have accepted a date anywhere near 754 B.C. But his attitude was that of a creative artist, and his interest was not in scientific chronology, but in the romantic and picturesque features of the legends themselves.

FR. 20. Venus' answer to the prayer of Ilia.

nepos: Valmaggi quotes some examples from inscriptions of this word as a feminine, but it does not seem to be so used elsewhere in literature.

tetulisti: the old reduplicated form.

FR. 21. The speech of Venus continued.

cetera: as in *Aen.* IX. 656.

peperisti: Ennius does not dislike long verbs or verbals at the end of lines; in this book we have already had *perhibebant*, *stabilibat* and *tetulisti*. Of nouns he specially favours *induperator*.

FR. 22. I place this line here, supposing it to belong to Amulius' answer either to the speech of Venus or the entreaties of Ilia. The next fragment marks the conclusion of the speech which this line introduces. It is quoted as an example of the *hexameter minimus*: such lines are naturally rare, but the effect may be intended to convey the solemnity of an authoritative decree.

Albai Longai: cf. note on Bk VI. fr. 9.

FR. 23. *latrones*: the meaning is, as often in Plautus, simply 'mercenary soldiers': by the ancients themselves the word was connected with λάτρον and λατρεία.

facessunt: we should rather translate 'perform eagerly' or 'promptly,' than agree with Nonius that the word does not differ from *faciunt* in sense. There are a number of forms in *ss* which, though used as presents, seem always to convey a special shade of meaning. Such are *lacesso, capesso, incipisso, petesso, quaeso, uiso*.

FR. 24. *reddita*: *more ueteri pro data accipiendum est*. No other example of *reddere nuptum* is quoted.

FR. 25. In this corrupt and doubtful passage, I find the meaning 'the flood goes down and the river flows back into its proper channel': cf. Livy, I. 4. 6. Festus' explanation of *remanant* as *repetunt* can be supported by *Aen.* XI. 793, *patrias remeabo inglorius urbes*. The MSS. *riuos camposque* would imply a second flooding of the fields and may be right.

FR. 26. This fragment clearly describes the falling of the Tiber's overflow, but the text is most uncertain. The corrupt and meaningless *qui sub ciuilia* may probably be removed from the text (cf. critical note), but if it is to be retained, the most attractive hypothesis is that *ciuilia* conceals *Ilia*. A reference to her would be natural at this point; the river deposits the children safely because the mother is now his bride and lives below his waters.

FR. 27. For the general description cf. the Shield of Aeneas, *Fecerat et uiridi e.q.s.*, with the note of Servius, *Sane totus hic locus Ennianus*. On *lupus* as a feminine cf. Quintilian I. 16. 12, a passage which is interesting as indirect testimony to the part played by Ennius in moulding the early legends.

FR. 28. The reference seems to be to the *ficus Ruminalis*. A note in Caper (98 K.) quotes the second conjugation form *lactentes*, but there is not evidence enough to warrant the introduction of it into the text of the present fragment.

FR. 29. *omnis*: the shepherds or *latrones* of the king.

permensa parumper: the phrase is found again *Inc. Sed.* 76, a line which Pascoli places next to the present fragment. *Parumper* here clearly bears Nonius' secondary meaning— *cito et uelociter*, but cf. note on Bk VI. fr. 16.

FR. 30. The sport of the brothers with their shepherd-followers: cf. Ov. *Fast.* II. 365.

ludicrĕ: actually the (3rd decl.) neuter adjective, though the force is fully adverbial. The adverb itself could not stand except as an instance of 'cretic shortening' (for which see note on Fr. 5 above).

Fr. 31. One of the conflicts with the royal shepherds.

potĭtur: third conjugation form. The verb is one with which the case-usage fluctuates. Of the three possibilities, genitive, accusative and ablative, Ennius has the two first but seems to have avoided the third.

ratus: *pro firmo, certo ponitur*, as Festus says. The phrase *ratus Romulus* has all the air of a popular coinage like 'Ethelred the Unready' or one of the 'constant' epithets in Homer. It is not impossible that we have here a borrowing from a Saturnian poem (cf. Excursus II), and the effect is greatly heightened by the double alliteration which looks like deliberate 'binding.' Indeed, one is almost tempted to find a Saturnian in *Vbi potitur ratus Romulus praedam* as it stands. The unusual cadence is intensified by the neglect of final *s* in two consecutive words.

Fr. 32. The founding of the city. I suggest that this line, with its description of the dead of night, belongs to the auspice-taking. It is a well-known fact that Roman augurs went out after midnight to await the dawn in silence: cf. Varro ap. Gell. III. 2. 10, and also Festus, p. 470 Lind. *Nox intempesta* is the *uox propria* to describe just such a period of the night: cf. Varro, *L.L.* VI. 7; VII. 72. The phrase is repeated in Bk V. fr. 3; it is used by Cicero several times and also by Vergil, in whom *Nox intempesta* is personified as the mother of the Furies.

Fr. 33. The auspice-taking. Apart from minor textual and other difficulties, the chief *crux* of this famous passage is the question of the position of each of the brothers. The one fact that is clear is that *Romulus* stood on the Aventine; we must at the outset admit that here again Ennius is following a different form of the legend from the Augustan. It is but reasonable to recognise further that his must have been the original, for the first authoritative statement that *Remus* was on the Aventine comes from the Augur Messala who was consul in 53 B.C. and who lived to be an ardent supporter of Augustus. He declared that the Aventine was outside the *Pomerium* because Remus' unfavourable omens had made it unlucky. Such a statement is almost certainly 'inspired' and forms part of the deliberate scheme of Augustus to enhance the glory of the Palatine by detracting from that of the other hills. It cannot therefore be allowed to weigh against the text before us. Nor is Ennius' statement unsupported from other sources; the fact that Romulus threw his spear *from the Aventine* to the Palatine after taking the auspices is recorded by Servius, Plutarch and Arnobius. There is, moreover, a distinct probability that Naevius placed Romulus on the Aventine, for he discussed the etymology of the name and connected it with *auis* (cf. Varro, *L.L.* v. 43) because it was a favourite haunt of birds.

Beyond this two other questions remain—what is the special force of *altus* applied to *Auentinus*, and where did Remus stand? The name *Auentinus* seems to have applied originally to the height now called *Santa Sabina* only, and as it is certainly some ten feet higher than *Santa Saba*, Hülsen understands Ennius in this restricted sense. This is probably correct, though others doubt whether, even assuming the levels to have been relatively the same in antiquity, the difference is great enough to justify the emphatic *alto*; but the meaning 'on the summit of the Aventine' which they give to the words would require not *alto* but *summo Auentino*. Most editors assume, as Mommsen did (see *Hermes*, XVI. 15), that Remus must have stood on the Palatine, and attempts have been made to introduce the name into our text. But the natural suggestion is that of Vahlen, that he was on his own *Remuria*

or *Remoria*. Festus, Plutarch, Dionysius and Stephen of
Byzantium all declare that Remus stood on the *Remuria*,
but its exact position is a matter of dispute. Festus calls
it *locus summi Auentini*, Plutarch χωρίον τι τοῦ 'Αβεντίνου
(the lack of a word to correspond to *summi* is important and
supports the explanation of *alto* given above, as it suggests
that *Remoria* may have been the name of the second and
lower crest). According to Dionysius and Stephanus, however, the *Remuria* was another hill outside Rome altogether;
and it has even been identified (by Niebuhr) with a hill close
to San Paolo Fuori. Very possibly the suggestion of Mommsen, that the early annalists placed it at some considerable
distance from Rome, and that its localisation on the Aventine
was a later development, is correct; but we may fairly assume
that Ennius placed Remus on the Remuria, whether he supposed it to be on the Aventine or not. On the whole it seems
most likely that both brothers were on the Aventine: as
indicated above *alto* seems necessarily to imply comparison
with some lower part of the hill. The presence of the name
Remuria or of *Remurinus* in the text might easily cause the
loss that has taken place.

auspicio augurio: from the number of technical terms in
the passage and the accuracy with which they are employed,
it would seem that Ennius intended some distinction between
these two and did not merely use them side by side as a
consecrated formula. If so, the distinction made by Nonius
was probably in his mind (see p. 693 Lind.). It is to be
noticed that the omen actually observed is the flight of the
birds and that after it has been given the word *auspicium*
is used alone, which agrees with Nonius' definition. This is
much more likely than that Ennius accepted the distinction
which Servius seeks to establish, ad *Aen.* I. 398, really that
between *augurium impetratiuum* and *oblatiuum* (see Serv. ad

Aen. VI. 190); the emphatic repetition *dant operam, se deuouet, seruat, quaerit, seruat* shows that both *auspicium* and *augurium* were deliberately sought. Evidently Romulus' omen was in two parts, first a single bird (*longe pulcherrima praepes*, 'the best omen'), then twelve birds together.

seruat: the technical word for 'to watch for omens,' as in the common *se seruare de caelo*, which appears in Lucretius as *seruare caelum*.

seruāt: we find also *dederāt, memorāt, uersāt, manāt, ponēt* (the last in the 'fall' of the foot); similarly *ēt* in *iubēt, essēt* (in the 'fall'), *faciēt, tenēt, fierēt*, and *īt* in *constituīt, fuerīt, uelīt, cupīt, nictīt, infīt* (in the 'fall') and, in a doubtful line, *uoluīt*. There are, however, many examples of *ăt, ĕt* and *ĭt*; the shortening of a long vowel before *t* probably began earlier than the similar shortening before *r*, and Ennius seems chary of preserving the long vowel except where there is 'metrical' excuse: cf. note on *sorōr* in Fr. 17. Cf. Lindsay, *Early Latin Verse*, p. 137.

The next few lines are of great importance for the history of the indirect question construction. The following examples are found: (*a*) ...*Romam Remoramne uocarent*, (*b*) ...*uter esset*, (*c*) ...*quam mox emittat*, (*d*) *utri sit data*. In Ennius, or at least in the extant fragments of the *Annales*, the 'paratactical' indicative construction has disappeared; but, if the mood is regulated, the tense-usage has not yet fully developed. (*a*) is clearly a 'dependent deliberative' out of which the entire construction is often said to have developed. (*b*) however is a question of fact with future reference ('which was going to be') like *expectans si mussaret* (Bk x. fr. 8). This type is commoner with primary tenses (as in (*c*) below) than with secondary, but both are found: in many instances the idea of futurity is readily deduced from the meaning of the verb, in others it is helped by some adverb such as *mox* (as in (*c*) again). But there are others in

which we may see a survival of the simple future meaning
of the I.-Eur. subjunctive; and to this type our (*b*) seems to
belong. (*d*) is a curious combination of tenses. Bennett
(*Syntax of Early Latin*) calls *sit data* 'a kind of *repraesen-
tatio*,' but he does not explain his meaning, nor is his parallel
(Plaut. *Aul.* 550) satisfactory, for there the primary *accusem*
expresses a purpose still existing, while the secondary *medi-
tabar* deals with a preliminary process already complete. He
himself points out that the perfect subjunctive can be used
as a historical tense in a secondary sequence as in Plaut.
M.G. 262, *Amph.* 745. Probably *sit data* is to be explained
in the same way, as in reality an aorist. The general type of
the question resembles (*b*).

Remoram obviously connected with Remus.

esset: for the quantity cf. note on *seruat* above. The simile
is interesting. Ennius is fond of comparisons drawn from
horses, but the present is remarkable as a specifically 'Roman'
allusion of the kind so common in Plautus. The phrase *carceris oras* does not mean more than 'at the barriers.' Literally
ora is the edge or boundary and the spectators look at the
outside surface of the yet unopened gates: cf. notes on Bk II.
fr. 1 and Bk VI. fr. 1 (*luminis oras* and *belli oras*). The *carceres*
(earlier *oppidum*) marked the starting-point in the races. The
singular in this sense is mostly poetical, though it is found
also in Suetonius and Auctor ad Herennium.

pictis faucibus: from Livy VII. 20. 1 we learn that the
carceres of the *Circus Maximus* were originally of wood, which
naturally made painted decorations more appropriate. Valmaggi suggests that the reconstruction in stone, referred to
in the damaged text of Livy XLI. 27, took place in 176 B.C.
If so, our present passage may be of importance for the date
of the composition of the *Annales*; certainly the only decorations of the *carceres* which seem traceable later are the Hermae
at the angles of the gates.

populūs: such a scansion is called a purely 'metrical' lengthening: for a discussion of the question see Vollmer in *Transactions of the Bavarian Academy* (1917).

uictoria regni: the genitive resembles that in *auspicio regni* above. With *uictor* a genitive is common in the Latin of all periods.

sol albus: I retain this line where it appears in the MSS. We are not justified in changing *sol albus*, as there is no variant in Cicero; strange as the words may seem at first sight, it is possible to understand them of the moon as Merula did. There is a very careful choice of epithets in the passage, and the contrast between *albus* ('dead-white'), *candida* ('brightly shining') and *aureus* ('golden' or 'glowing') is true and vivid.

icta: this should not be changed to *acta* as is often done. *Foras*, which seems to have occasioned the alteration, qualifies *dedit*, and *icta radiis* taken together mean hardly more than 'illumined by light from the sun'; the actual form of the expression may be due to an imperfectly conceived metaphor, as if the Far Darter smote Lux with the rays that are his arrows.

pulcher and *praepes* are religious words: *pulcher* means sometimes 'without blemish' (as in descriptions of animals for sacrifice; see *Comm. in Lud. Saec.* I. 106), sometimes 'lucky.' In this sense it appears three times in Horace. *Praepes* is an augur's technical term, meaning 'of good omen'; cf. Gell. VII. 6. 8.

Laeua: of good omen for the Roman augur, who faced the south and therefore had the east on his left hand; outside the religious sphere, the meaning is the exact opposite of this. The three monosyllabic terminations *lux*, *sol* and *dant* are noteworthy as being typical of Ennius' usage in this particular. Unless specially emphatic, the words he chooses for this position are normally either verbs or words ending in two consonants or a double consonant, or else parts of *res* or *uis*. Such an ending as Bk XIV. fr. 8 (first line) is extremely rare.

quattuor is scanned as two syllables. The form *quattor* is sometimes suggested here; it is actually found in certain late inscriptions, but we cannot safely admit a form for which the sole authority is 'vulgar' Latin. A further possibility would be *quāttŭŏr* (by 'cretic shortening'); but see note on Fr. 5 above.

Auium: two syllables, *i* becoming a consonant.

propritim: cf. Lucr. II. 975. I doubt *proprīam*.

stabilitā: before *sc* of *scamna*.

scamna regni = 'throne': in itself *scamna* means simply 'seat.' *Regni* is constructed with all three nouns *auspicio*, *scamna* and *solum* as with *auspicio*, *augurioque* and *cupientes* above.

FR. 34. The contemptuous words of Remus.

Iuppiter: as an exclamation also in Catullus I. It seems to be a colloquialism, intended, in our present line, to give the speech an air of actual talk.

quamde: an old form of *quam* found in Livius and also in Lucretius (I. 640).

FR. 35. The reply of Romulus. *Hic* refers to the speaker himself.

toruiter: compared by Pascoli to the Homeric ὑπόδρα; but that word is never used except with ἰδών, and *toruus*, though properly applied to the expression of the face, is not uncommonly used of the voice, as here and in *Aen.* VII. 399. Nonius who quotes the line gives another example of the form *toruiter* from Pomponius.

increpuisti: again the polysyllabic termination is a verb.

FR. 36. The suggestion of Vahlen's first edition *astu non ui* was most attractive and has been widely accepted; but its author rightly withdrew it, pointing out that the MS. reading can be explained as *at tu, non ut eum decet rem summam seruare, sic simili cura premeris*.

sum = eum as before, answering to the *hic* of the previous fragment.

FR. 37. *animatus = anima praeditus*, 'alive': the word is normally used with reference to a particular state of mind (*animus*), but I cannot accept Vahlen's suggestion that *impune* qualifies it, in the sense of 'incorrigible.'

calido sanguine: the adjective suggests the idea of *life* blood, but the phrase may be used with a secondary meaning also, such as it bears in Hor. *Ep*. I. 3. 31 f., as if the sin were to be expiated by the very thing which caused it.

FR. 38. The sole fragment which can be referred definitely to the episode of the Sabine women. Owing to the metrical difficulties involved, *uirgines* is often 'emended,' sometimes very violently, but there is no justification for any change; Festus and Verrius both accepted the text and there is no variant in our tradition. The first foot then must be *uirgines*, but it is quite uncertain whether it is a dactyl, or a spondee. As a dactyl, it would be an instance of 'cretic shortening'; and a better case can certainly be made for its admission here than elsewhere: but cf. note on Fr. 5. As a spondee, it would be a daring case of syncope but one which is not impossible. Ennius was a pioneer working in a none too tractable medium; he may therefore have experimented with contracted forms even if they had no philological justification. And it must be admitted that syncope in Latin is very capricious. Possibly, again, there may be simply a 'metrical' as opposed to a linguistic reason, and we might find a parallel for the suppression of the *i* in the famous and puzzling *semine oriundi* of Lucretius, where the *i* simply disappears for metrical purposes. The difference of opinion as to the meaning of *sas* which Festus reports is due to the confusion of the possessive and demonstrative stems.

FR. 39. The treaty between Romulus and the Sabines. The speaker is almost certainly Hersilia. The strong alliteration should be noted.

FR. 40. The suggestion *alternum* for *aeternum* is at first sight attractive; but there is no authority for the idea that Romulus and Tatius held power on alternate days, nor is it clear what the meaning of *serere* would be with Colonna's interpretation. The phrase *diem seritote* would normally be *diem e die seritote*, 'add day to day,' i.e. 'pass your days,' which is a meaning readily derived from the literal sense of the verb, and is one of the most familiar of its metaphorical uses. *Aeternum* can be understood as an adverb, and thus no change is needed.

FR. 41. Hersilia's speech continued.

bene = ualde (cf. Porph. ad Hor. *Od.* III. 24. 50): the line, another remarkable example of alliteration, must however stand elsewhere if we accept Macrobius' order (see my Preface).

FR. 42. *reique*: scan *rēïque*, as often in Plautus.

FR. 43. I place the fragment at this point, supposing the reference to be either to the settlement of the Sabines on the Aventine (Serv. ad *Aen.* VII. 657), or to a general gift of land to all the citizens: cf. Cic. *de Rep.* II. 26.

Here Martia was worshipped in connection with legacies and inheritances (Paul. e Fest. 89. 4 Lind.).

FR. 44. The council of the Gods. Juno and Mars were both speakers, and the question discussed was the deification of Romulus, though Jove gave a promise which included the future greatness of Rome and the overthrow of Carthage: cf. Varro, *L.L.* VIII. 6; Ov. *Met.* XIV. 812, *Fast.* II. 485; Hor. *Od.* III. 3. 16 ff.; Serv. ad *Aen.* I. 20 and 281. On the question whether there was more than one council see note on Bk VIII. fr. 18. Lucilius seems to have parodied the present passage (cf. Serv. ad *Aen.* x. 5 and 104) with a full-dress debate on the fate of the rascally Lupus, and the lines *Consilium summis hominum de rebus habebant* and *Quo populum atque urbem pacto seruare potis sint*, survive. I have placed the council later in the book than is usually done, because the words of Ovid (l.c.) suggest that it was held when the power of Rome was fully established.

cenacula: quoted by Tertullian with the suggestion that Ennius used the phrase *quia Iouem illic epulantem legerat apud Homerum*.

FR. 45. A description of Jove. The beautiful phrase *stellis ...aptus* recurs in Bk III. fr. 11 and Bk x. fr. 6. It is possible to see in the word a trace of its literal meaning, and we may translate 'tangled in a skein of shining stars.' The same metaphor with a slightly different application is found in *Trin.* 658. The literal meaning appears in Bk x. fr. 9, and the word is sometimes found even in prose in the sense of 'fastened together.'

FR. 46. Servius gives no exact reference, but I place the line here as it seems to introduce the speech of Juno granting assent to the deification of Romulus.

sancta dearum: cf. note on *dia dearum* in Fr. 10 above.

FR. 47. *Hora*: the name of the deified Hersilia; cf. Ov. *Met.* xiv. 829 ff. The difference of quantity (*Hŏra* for our *Hōra*) led Baehrens to propose *Quirine pater ueneror, Hora, teque Quirini*: but there is no necessity for such a change. A certain amount of liberty was natural in the difficult matter of proper names, and Ennius' treatment of them was sometimes a problem to the grammarian. Cf. Gell. XIII. 22, on the prosody of *Nerienem*, which he supposed to be *Nĕrĭĕnem*, but which is, of course, *Nĕrĭēnem*.

FR. 48. *genitalibus*, 'the gods who gave him birth': cf. *genitabilis* in Lucilius I. I (Marx).

APPENDIX TO BOOK I

FR. 49. Quoted without exact reference or author's name by Fronto and therefore placed by me in the Appendix, though matter and style alike suggest Ennius as the author.

FR. 50. The fact that Varro opens his discussion of poetic diction (*L.L.* VII. 6) by quoting this line makes it only reasonable to suppose that it is by Ennius. But it cannot be placed in the body of the text, for, famous as it evidently was, the author's name is never mentioned.

BOOK II

FR. I. I restore this fragment to the book to which Priscian assigns it: to place it in Bk I, as is usually done, is to rob *diu* of all meaning. The exact length of the fragment is a matter of uncertainty, but it is clear that the generally accepted expedient of separating *post optimi regis obitum* (which is assigned to Cicero) from *pectora diu e.q.s.* is impossible. From the arrangement of the words it must be concluded that the two belong to the same source. Again, *post optimi regis obitum* cannot qualify the parenthetical *sicut ait Ennius* as Valmaggi seeks to make it by a mere misrepresentation of a plain passage. Müller, indeed, removed both phrases from the text and supposed the quotation to begin at *simul*; and this is the only logical possibility unless everything from *pectora* to *obitum* (except of course the parenthesis) is to be admitted to the text. At least one serious difficulty would be removed by following Müller, for the problem of *diu* (for which see below) would no longer arise. There is, however, a decided rhythmical run about *pectora...desiderium*, and I hesitate to assign the words definitely to Cicero. Moreover there always remains, as we must recognise, the possibility that Ennius may have admitted *optimi* to a hexameter as he did not hesitate to admit *uirgines*. Hence, in default of any solution which I can accept as completely satisfactory, I have prefixed the words *pectora...obitum* exactly as they stand in Cicero.

diu of the Cicero MS. must be kept. There is no real variant, as the *dia* of the second hand is an obvious scribe's emendation. No alteration should be admitted, least of all any that introduces a form so doubtful as the *pīa* of Havet. The *i* was, no doubt, originally long, but it does not follow that Ennius could have scanned it so. It is short in the only example of the word in the whole of the extant fragments.

luminis oras: a very famous phrase. It is found no fewer than nine times in Lucretius, and actually appears thrice in the first 200 lines of Bk I. In Ennius himself it is used literally in Fr. 13 below.

FR. 2. *effugit*: the subject is Romulus and the word suggests the supernatural mode of his passing, resembling that described in Livy and Ovid.

speres: accusative governed by some word now lost; the same plural form is found in Bk XVI. fr. 13.

FR. 3. *Et qui se sperat*: I accept without hesitation these emendations of C. O. Müller and Salmasius; no more than the correction of a single letter is involved. The line describes the difficulties of settling the succession after the death of Romulus; cf. Livy I. 17.

regnare: this use of a present infinitive for the correct future is not uncommon in early Latin; cf. Fr. 12 below.

Romae Quadratae: not used, of course, in the technical sense of the *Mundus* of the city (cf. Festus, p. 310 Lind.), the shaft of which is now visible on the Palatine, but to include everything within the fortifications of Romulus. There are clear traces still to be seen of walls of *cappellaccio* (grey tufa), which may go back to the sixth century. Grammatically, the words are locative; not genitive, though Valmaggi calls them genitive governed by *regnare*. But he has no parallel except Hor. *Od.* III. 30, and indeed there seems to be no instance of such a construction in the early period, though *potior* with a genitive is not uncommon. *Romae quadratae*, another noun-adjective compound; cf. note on *Prisci Latini*, Bk I. fr. 13.

FR. 4. The reign of Numa and his intercourse with Egeria. The traditional meeting-place was close to the *Porta Capena*, though there was another grove and spring sacred to Egeria at Aricia. Possibly Ennius represented her as teaching Numa to overcome Faunus and Picus, and even to guess the riddles of Jove, as she does in Ovid.

FR. 5. The religious institutions of Numa.

Mensas: probably a reference to the tables called *Curiales*, on which offerings were made to *Iuno Curetis*. A reference to her would be specially in place, as Numa was traditionally a native of Cures.

ancilia: for the story see Ov. *Fast.* III. 329 ff. We cannot determine whether Ennius knew of Mamurius and his connection with the *Ancilia*, but the probability is that he did not. In Ovid and Festus (p. 117 Lind.) he is the maker; but Propertius speaks of him only as the artist of the first bronze statue of Vertumnus, and Varro knows nothing of his name in the Salian hymn. Ennius may have thought Numa himself the originator of the device.

Liba: the sacred pancakes for which Cato (*R.R.* 75) and Athenaeus (III. 125) give recipes. The *placenta* was more elaborate, though Horace identifies them in *Epp.* I. 10. 10.

fictores: the persons who made the cakes. All our terms

are defined by Varro, *L.L.* VII. 43 ff. The ancients themselves were at a loss to explain the origin and meaning of the ceremony of the *Argei*. For three conjectures see Ov. *Fast.* v. 621 ff.; to these Festus (p. 250 Lind.) adds two more, quoting the authority of Sinnius Capito for preferring a reference to the *pons* of the voting *saeptum*; cf. also Festus, p. 66 Lind. and Varro ap. Non. p. 523 Lind. The rite must, of course, have a religious origin. For a recent discussion of it cf. Rose, *Roman Questions of Plutarch*, p. 98 ff.

tutulatos: to Varro we may add Festus, p. 484 Lind.

Fr. 6. Numa's appeal for the preservation of his institutions.

It is a matter of dispute whether *me* is ablative or dative, and Festus' words are capable of either meaning. Valmaggi argues strongly in favour of the dative, suggesting that *te* also is dative in Ter. *Phorm.* 180 and Plaut. *Asin.* 481 (*uae te!*). This *me* he calls a by-form of *mi* (standing for an original **moi̯* or **mei̯*) with *e* to represent *ei*. But it seems safer to suppose that Festus is reporting a syntactical difference.

Fr. 7. The exact form of the proper name is uncertain. Quint. 1. 5. 12 compares the *vitii geminatio* which it shows to that committed by Tinca Placentinus in writing *precula* for *pergula*. *Precula*, however, contains two faults, the substitution of *c* for *g* (*immutatio*) and the metathesis of *e* (*transmutatio*). Both must therefore appear in Ennius, though Müller explains *vitii geminatio* as 'the commission of one fault twice over.' The dative form in *oi* is not an 'error' but an archaism; cf. Mar. Vict. 17. 20 K. The fragment probably deals with the appointment of Mettius to the Dictatorship as Pascoli suggests.

Fr. 8. *Quamde*: cf. note on Bk 1. fr. 34. The line is from a speech made during the parley described in Livy 1. 23.

Fr. 9. The episode of the Horatii and the Curiatii.

ningulus = nullus: cf. 'Marcius Vates' quoted by Festus with our line. The formation resembles that of *singulus*. Ennius' description of the combat seems to have been famous: cf. Propertius IV. 2. 7.

Fr. 10. *occasus*: 'opportunity,' as Festus says. The meaning of *saltu* is difficult to decide, but, as Valmaggi suggests, we may be dealing with the beginning of a simile. He aptly quotes *Aen.* IX. 550.

Fr. 11. *mǐs*: stated by Priscian to be genitive of the personal pronoun. A corresponding *tīs* (though with long vowel) also occurs: cf. Lindsay, *Early Latin Verse*, p. 158. The line is generally assumed to belong to the survivor of the Horatii, who debates whether he can rival the exploits of his brothers. This suits *aequiperare* well (and we might suppose that *uirtutem* stood at the beginning of the next line), but it is not so appropriate to *concordibus*. The line might mean 'I have a great desire for harmony among friends.' Horatius might still be the speaker, though some of the older proposals, such as that of Merula, which refers the fragment to Julius Proculus, are not impossible.

Fr. 12. Horatius defends himself against the reproaches of his sister.

Adnūit: cf. the remarks of Priscian, and also the very important passage in Varro (*L.L.* IX. 104) on the pronunciation of such forms.

decernere: for the present infinitive cf. note on Fr. 3.

Fr. 13. The reference is plainly to the mother of Horatius. To represent her as making the appeal for her son's life would accord with Ennius' instinctive dramatisation of every situation.

Fr. 14. The appeal continued. I suggest that the line contains a protest against the utterance of the *lex horrendi carminis* of which Livy speaks (I. 26) and which, in the view of the ancients, compelled the *Duumuiri* to condemn the accused, whether guilty or not (see Livy I. 26, Cic. *pro Rab.* IV. 13).

quam = potius quam: a well-known usage.

tolerare: '*patienter ferre*' Festus.

FR. 15. I leave this line incomplete, in default of a satisfactory addition. *Tota ui* is a very doubtful phrase for 'with all their strength,' and the other suggestions are quite arbitrary.

tuditantes: '*negotium agentes*' Festus. The word is a frequentative form from *tundo*.

FR. 16. The punishment of Mettius Fufettius.

FR. 17. Another line in which we are faced with unexplained differences in our authorities. The MSS. of Priscian give *in siluis*, those of Servius vary between *in siluis* (A, S, M), *in campos* (R) and *in campo* (H, F, C); Charisius (MS. and *Editio princeps*) *in spineto*. Charisius and Servius (H, F, C) have *miserum* for *supinum*. There is evidently inaccurate quotation, but I prefer *in siluis*. Koch's *in spinis* has been widely accepted, but the Vergilian passage on which he relies, *Raptabat...per siluam et sparsi rorabant sanguine uepres*, does not support one reading more than another; and Charisius' *spineto*, which is probably a gloss, might have been an explanation of *siluis* just as well as of *spinis*. There is, moreover, no authority for *spinae* in the sense of *spinetum*: the nearest parallel is Propertius IV. 5. 1, but even here the sense of 'sharp thorn' is prominent.

homonem: the form *hemonem* is also found; cf. Festus, p. 89 Lind.

FR. 18. The line may stand here if it refers to the destruction of Alba Longa by Tullus Hostilius. The Vergilian reminiscence is well known—*At tuba terribilem sonitum*, etc.

(*Aen.* 503); but Vergil did not venture to repeat what is probably the boldest onomatopoeic coinage in Latin. The old play *Wily Beguiled* has 'Where trumpets sound tantara to the fight.' On the general question of the treatment of the Sack of Alba in early poetry cf. Excursus II.

FR. 19. The lack of caesura is no doubt due to the difficulty of the proper names. Note *Ancŭs* but *Marciŭs*.

FR. 20. The foundation of the port of Ostia, the first 'maritime colony' of Rome.

The phrase *munda facit* is regularly interpreted as *instructa facit*, yet no indication is given of the real meaning of a phrase so extraordinary, and no parallel for *mundus = instructus* is quoted. Surely the meaning must be 'he *cleaned out* the mouth of the Tiber': that is, the line describes dredging operations which were necessary if the water-way was to be preserved. This sense of *mundus* is readily derived from the literal meaning and is supported by Cicero's use of *terra pura* in the sense of 'freed from stones and weeds.' Festus' first quotation of our line is to illustrate the meaning of *mundus*, but his text is badly damaged; Paulus however supports my explanation and gives as synonyms *lautus* and *purus*, both of which mean 'freed from dirt or foreign admixture.' With this interpretation, *nauibus* and *nautis* are, of course, dative, not ablative as the editors say.

celsis: may be a 'stock' epithet (Eng. 'tall' ship) or may be intended to suggest the characteristic build of the deep-draughted cargo-boat. *Quaeso* is not an old Latin variant for *quaero*, as the note of Festus might suggest, but a different word derived from **quai-s-s-o* with double *ss*. *Quaessentibus* would be Ennius' spelling, or *quaissentibus*.

FR. 21. The description of Ostia continued.

Isdem: Cicero discusses the form of this word in *Or.* XLVII. 157, but modern editors have much confused his statements. I adopt the following reading: (1) *Isdem campus habet, et in templis* (2) *isdem. At* (3) *eisdem erat uerius, nec tamen probauit ut opimius: male sonabat* (4) *üsdem: impetratum est a consuetudine ut peccare suauitatis causa liceret* (the 'corrected *mutilus*' version with transposition of *probauit*). With this reading, the following facts are clear:

textrinum: 'arsenal'; cf. the definition of Servius.

1. The two examples of *isdem* stand on the same footing: both must be dat.-abl. plural or nominative singular.

2. Cicero does not state which they are.

3. The form *üsdem* cannot be nominative singular. Therefore, if it is admitted to the text, we must conclude that in both quotations *isdem* is dat.-abl. plural. This is the most natural assumption in the second. In the first, all difficulty vanishes when we take the line as a whole. *Isdem* is dative, parallel in construction to the *nautis* and *nauibus* of the previous fragment. The meaning is 'And for them there is also an arsenal on the plain,' that is, the harbour works are contrasted with others further inland.

FR. 22. It is very uncertain what should be supplied to remedy the damaged quotation, but Scaliger's ⟨*pont*⟩*i* is perhaps simplest.

ponti: the ⟨*camp*⟩*i* of Reichardt may be right, as the phrase *caerula prata* is certainly applied to land in *I.S.* fr. 18. The much mutilated quotations which accompany our present fragment in Festus (see sources) should not be placed here, as Festus seems to distinguish quite definitely between them and it by his specific mention of Bk II only in the case of the fragment which comes between the other two; in the case of the last he actually adds *alibi*, and the first, which seems to be described as 'a joke,' probably does not belong to the *Annales* at all. Lindsay's ⟨*cael*⟩*i* suits the Festus-paragraph, if it collects examples of the *figura etymologica* or 'punning epithet.'

BOOK III

FR. 1. The omen to Tarquin.

Olim = tum: this, the original meaning, is found quite commonly in Plautus. The word is connected with the pronoun stem *ollo* (**ol-so*).

laeuum: 'favourable'; as before. Cf. *Georg.* IV. 667, a *scholium* on which is the source of Fr. 3. Ennius never uses the word in the sense of 'unlucky,' though he has it in the literal meaning.

inclutŭs: as before. The word, applied here to Jove, is used by Ennius even of things. Cicero has an interesting note (*Or.* XLVIII. 159) on the pronunciation of such words, which really describes the phonetic process of nasalisation. As has been often remarked, Greek transliterations exactly illustrate Cicero's point: *e.g.* πότηνς (*potens*))(κεντυρίωνες (*centuriones*).

FR. 2. Tarquin's omen continued.

aquilā: the long *ā* is unique in early Latin poetry, as all other examples are Greek words, mostly proper names, *e.g.* Bk VI. fr. 3 (*Aeacidā*). On the case of *I.S.* fr. 47 cf. comm. ad loc. *Aquilā* has 'metrical' excuse for lengthening (cf. note on Fr. 17 *sorōr*), but Ennius may have been aware that the 'lengthening' was in reality a restoration of the original quantity. The case of *Aen.* XII. 648 is complicated by hiatus. But both Ennius and Vergil seem very occasionally to lengthen a naturally short syllable by the *ictus metricus* only. Or perhaps we should say they allow a short syllable to stand in place of a long one.

pinnis: this with *penna* forms one of those pairs of doublets which has never been properly explained. The variation cannot be due to the natural change of *ĕ* to *ĭ* in unaccented syllables, nor to the rustic pronunciation of which Cicero speaks (*de Or.* III. 12. 46). Nor does the grammarian's distinction that *pinna* means 'sharp point,' *penna* 'wing' or 'feather,' hold good for Ennius, for, if we can trust our tradition, he consistently uses *pinna* in the latter sense.

uento obnixa: 'breasting the breeze.' Ennius' explanation of *uentus* and ἀήρ is strictly correct philologically; the Greek root is ἀϝ corresponding to Sanskrit *vâ*, 'blow,' etc.

aera: the correct Greek form is to be observed; in the *Epicharmus aerem* is used, a form which Charisius (85 K.) notes as archaic.

FR. 3. I refer these words to Tarquin's omen, but there must have been many occasions on which favourable omens appeared.

rite: 'duly'; in the general sense given by Varro, *L.L.* VII. 88.

probatum: 'accepted as good or true,' perhaps by Tanaquil; cf. Livy I. 34. 9. On the importance of the quarter of the sky cf. Cic. *de Div.* I. xxxix. 85, where *ratum* means the same as our *probatum*.

FR. 4. The death of Ancus.

sis = suis: Festus calls the case dative; the construction must be explained as a slight extension of the usage common with verbs like *aufero*, *adimo*, etc. In its literal meaning *liquit lumina* comes very close to 'he deprived his eyes of light'; but the phrase is remarkable inasmuch as the doer of the action is also the person affected by it. The Lucretian imitation (III. 1025) is well known; *Il.* XVIII. 14 is a familiar parallel, and the phrase *liquerunt lumina* is used by Cicero (*ex Iliade*, II. 303): cf. also *linquant lumina* from Naevius, *Lycurgus*.

FR. 5. The accession of Tarquin.

For the phrase *sola regni* cf. Bk I. fr. 33. The subject of *dedit* is probably *populus*. On the caesura cf. note on Bk I. fr. 2.

FR. 6. The death and burial of Tarquin.

Again it is difficult to decide between the variants of our authorities. I prefer Servius' *Tarquinii corpus* as a phrase that is at once better and moreover appropriate to the style of Ennius, who uses similar periphrases with *corpus* both of persons and of non-human creatures. *Corpus* may be used in the sense of *cadauer* simply as in Ov. *Fast.* III. 833; or it may be intended to suggest the physical beauty or striking appearance of the living man as in *Aen.* VII. 650. The effect desired may be that of the Homeric κεῖτο μέγας μεγαλωστί, or of Vergil's description of the dead Priam: *iacet ingens litore truncum*, etc.

bona femina: despite suggestions to the contrary we cannot refuse to accept the statement of Servius that the person intended is Tanaquil. Müller's conclusions from the Vergilian imitation cannot be accepted; its real importance for us is that it suggests a possible source for Servius' *corpus*, if Donatus is to be preferred (see *Aen.* VI. 222).

FR. 7. The funeral of Tarquin; cf. *Aen.* XI. 142 ff. with the note of Servius ad loc.

Varro, quoted by Servius (ad *Aen.* I. 727), distinguishes the *candela funalis* (wax candle with a wick) from the *candela simplex* (taper). The epithet *candida* is carefully chosen to point the contrast with the smoky flame of torches.

Prodinunt: cf. *redinunt* (Ennius), *danunt* (Plautus and Caecilius), *nequinont* and *inserinuntur* (Livius). Other similar forms are *ferinunt, obinunt, explenunt* and *solino* (= *consulo*).

FR. 8. The reference is probably to the Etruscan wars of Servius Tullius, which seem more important and better attested than those under Tarquin: cf. Livy I. 42. According to Livy there was no war with Veii between the time of Ancus (I. 33) and that of Servius. But see Dionysius III. 57 f., where it is stated that Tarquin engaged in hostilities with Veii and Etruria in general.

Fr. 9. The speech of a general, probably an Etruscan, on the eve of the battle briefly described by Livy i. 42.

Note the use of *noctu* as a feminine noun: cf. the remarks of Macrobius (i. 4) on Bk iv. fr. 4 below. It is properly a *u*-stem locative (without *i*), and we occasionally find *nox* (genitive of νυκτός, German *nachts*) used in its stead as in Bk xvi. fr. 228 below.

Fr. 10. The description of the battle.

The syntax of the line is noteworthy. The infinitive is used as a verbal noun in the ablative case to express the means or cause; cf. Plaut. *Epid.* 197, *Merc.* 805, *Trin.* 75. Cf. also the examples of this infinitive usage in practically every case given by Lindsay (*Syntax of Plautus*, p. 72). Ter. *Phorm.* 885 is especially instructive, as it shows infinitive and gerund side by side in an identical construction.

Hastis ansatis: the weapon called *amentata*, a javelin to the middle of which a strap (*amentum*) was attached to give greater force in hurling; cf. Serv. ad *Aen.* ix. 662. Our line describes the passage from volleying at a distance to hand-to-hand fighting: hence *ansatis* is used with technical correctness, as the *amentata* was the specific weapon of the *ueles*: cf. Cicero, *Brut.* lxxviii. The operations first described are those of the *rorarii*: cf. Nonius, p. 887 L.

Fr. 11. I agree with Vahlen that the reference is to Lucretia.

I retain the mss. *prospexit*, suggesting that the meaning is 'looked out over the expanse (of heaven).' The word is so used in such passages as *Aen.* xi. 908, Hor. *Od.* iii. 25, Lucan i. 195, Livy xxi. 49. 8, and the meaning is always to look out over or at something from a high point. So in Ennius we may imagine Lucretia on a flat roof gazing towards the horizon.

stellis...aptum: cf. note on Bk I. fr. 45 above.

FR. 12. This fragment is usually referred either to the foundation of the temple of Diana on the Aventine by Servius Tullius, or to the construction of the *Area* of the temple of Jupiter Capitolinus by Tarquin. But there is no evidence to suggest any connection with a temple, and a much more probable explanation is that we are still concerned with Lucretia and her preparations for death.

super esse: should be written as two words; cf. Gell. I. 22. 16.

BOOK IV

FR. 1. The siege or storming of a town, probably Anxur (406 B.C.).

scalae: a regular part of the siege train, often mentioned by historians.

summa...opum ui: repeated in Bk XVI. fr. 4 and used by Vergil, *Aen*. XII. 552.

FR. 2. *Vulsculus*: the diminutive form, not found elsewhere, may be intended to express contempt.

Anxur: the native (Volscian) name for the town of Terracina. On the derivation of the name see *Aen*. VII. 799 with the note of Servius ad loc.

FR. 3. The eclipse of June, 400 B.C.; see the remarks of Cicero *de Rep*. I. 16. 25. [For a contrary view see Soltau in *Woch. für kl. Phil*. III. 979 ff.; his arguments are accepted by Valmaggi.] Cf. also Beloch in *Hermes*, LVII. 119 ff. This eclipse was afterwards largely used in calculating dates: cf. Cic. *de Rep*. I. 16. The careful record of the present line may be a trace of the personal influence of Cato, who, as is well known, was interested in chronology and may well have been helped in his researches by his contemporary, C. Sulpicius Galba. For the latter's work in astronomy cf. Pliny, *N.H*. II. 13.

Information regarding eclipses would be derived originally from some such source as the *Annales Maximi* (cf. Cato, ap. Gell. ii. 28).

Iunis: apparently the only undoubted instance of a dat.-abl. plural from an *-io* stem with a monosyllabic termination. It is probably an experiment made *metri causa*.

nox: Pascoli is probably right in explaining this word as forming a kind of hendiadys with *luna*, in which the first noun (*luna*) gives the cause, and the second (*nox*) the consequence.

FR. 4. Macrobius assigns the fragment to Bk VII, where some modern editors retain it, explaining it as a reference to some episode in the war with the Gauls which arose out of the operations in Illyria (see Polybius ii. 23 ff.). I agree, however, with those who, finding no reference to the capture of any *arx* by the Gauls in those operations, place the lines in Bk IV, and refer them to the events of 390 B.C. Ennius' description of the assault upon the Capitol was included by Propertius among the special glories of the *Annales*.

Qua noctu: as *hac noctu* in Bk iii. fr. 9.

concubia: 'the sleep time,' the period usually described as *intempesta nox*.

FR. 5. I follow Müller in placing this line here and referring it to the Gauls encamped before Rome.

duellis: the only certain example of the form in Ennius. It is often assumed that the three-syllable scansion which later poets took over from Ennius, is due to error or misapprehension and that the *u* of this word was always consonantal. Plautus, however, uses the trisyllabic form once (*Amph.* 189), and it was probably the original.

BOOK V

FR. 1. *tenet*: probably means something like 'holds him to his purpose.' The line may, as the editors suggest, describe such a single combat as that of T. Manlius and the Gaul (Livy VII. 10. 2).

occasus: *occasio* Festus; as in Bk II. fr. 10, Bk VIII. fr. 25.

FR. 2. A fragment of quite uncertain reference, though a possible occasion for such an appeal might be the capture of Fregellae (313 B.C.), after which 200 of the leaders of the national party were publicly beheaded in the Forum. Our line may describe the scene in the town with the women appealing for the captives before their removal.

FR. 3. Quoted by Acro without exact reference; but, as the editors agree, the line must belong to Bk IV of the *Annales*. Probably it is concerned with the battle described by Livy X. 12. In Horace the long-drawn battle appears as a popular, almost proverbial, illustration; and his archaism *duello* may be intended to suggest the early annalists or Ennius himself.

FR. 4. Siege operations.

Ansatas, sc. *hastas*: cf. note on Bk III. fr. 10.

turribus: wooden towers erected by the besiegers, technically called *falae*; cf. Bk XV. fr. 1. The word is said to be derived from the Etruscan word for sky (cf. Paul. e Fest. p. 78 L.), and gave its name to the *telum maximum* (*falarica*) discharged from it: for a description see Servius ad *Aen.* IX. 702, and cf. *I.S.* 70.

FR. 5. The river in question is almost certainly the Liris, the 'quiet flow' of which was famous. Cf. Sil. IV. 348 ff. and the universally known Hor. *Od.* I. 31 with the note of Porphyrio ad loc. But there are two objections to the generally assumed identification of the town with Minturnae:

(1) The difficulty of understanding the force of *quod*.

(2) The presence of *amoenam*. The exact meaning of this word is admirably illustrated by Horace's line: *Hae latebrae dulces* ('dear to me') *etiam si credis amoenae* ('pleasing in themselves'). It is correctly used of the *amoena salicta* in Bk I. fr. XVII, the only other instance in the *Annales*; and it seems impossible that a native of a mountainous country could have applied it to *Minturnae*, situated as the town was in close proximity to very extensive marshes. Both these difficulties are removed by supposing the town to be *Interamna Lirensis*. Being higher up the river, Interamna was far enough removed from the marshes to be called *amoena*; and *quod* may be explained as introducing one of those etymological remarks of which Ennius was fond; cf. Varro, *L.L.* v. 28. The territories of the town were laid waste in 294 B.C.; hence a reference to it would be natural.

agmine: a bold phrase in Latin, though *pes* used of a river is not uncommon in poetry.

FR. 6. I retain the line in the book to which Nonius assigns it. The actual narrative of the war with Pyrrhus opened in Bk VI, but some preliminary matter may have been dealt with in Bk V. A very likely occasion for a first mention of Pyrrhus would be his occupation of Corcyra (295 B.C.) which brought him for the first time into direct relations with Tarentum, and was therefore a remote cause of the war with Rome. Ennius had been educated in Tarentum, and his interest in the town coupled with his enthusiasm for Pyrrhus may have led him to introduce the episode.

Burrus: the form is attested by Cicero as correct (*Or.* 160). *Burrus* = 'red,' is a rustic adjective; cf. Paul. e Fest. p. 22 Lind.

BOOK VI

FR. 1. The war with Pyrrhus was treated on a scale of unprecedented elaboration; it occupied the whole of Bk VI and extended into Bk VII (cf. Excursus I). It is to private and personal motives, the attraction of the chief character, the poet's interest in the scenes in which the fighting took place and his attachment to Tarentum, the part played by his own tribe, possibly by his own immediate kinsfolk, that we must look to explain this somewhat excessive elaboration; we must look to them also for the reasons that led Ennius to distinguish Bk VI by a special prologue, and not to any theory of 'separate editions' or 'composition in parts.' All such theories are necessarily the merest conjecture; we know practically nothing of the chronology of Ennius' works, and the *Thyestes* is the only one that can be definitely dated (169 B.C.). The *Annales* cannot have been begun before 204 B.C., probably not until considerably later; and all we know about its composition is that there was a break after the completion of Bk XV; cf. Pliny, *N.H.* VII. 10, and see later on Bk XVI. But we have no information on the composition of Bks I–XV: the nearest approach to a definite date is derived from Varro ap. Gell. XVII. 21, where Ennius is said to have declared that he wrote a certain book of the *Annales cum septimum et sexagesimum annum haberet.* But:

(1) It is not clear whether this describes the year 173 or 172 B.C.

(2) The MSS. give XII as the number of the book, but most editors reject this, declaring that six books cannot have been produced in between three and four years, more especially as the dramatic and miscellaneous output was continued at the same time. We have no means of determining what bulk six books would represent, but Ennius may have been, indeed

probably was, a very rapid worker, and is certainly hardly less remarkable for the fecundity than for the versatility of his genius (see further on Bk xv below). Our special prologue, then, marks the special importance of the coming narrative as in Bk x. It is possible, moreover, that the passage was not a prologue in the strict sense but was introduced into the body of the narrative as in *Aen.* IX. 525 ff. (a passage with a famous reminiscence of our line).

potis, sc. *est*. Like the neuter *pote*, this form is used freely for any number and gender in the sense of 'able' or 'possible.'

The metaphor in *ingentis oras* seems to be from unrolling a manuscript but it is difficult to define exactly the meaning of *oras*. Any metaphorical use of the word is rare, and seems largely, if not wholly, derived from Ennius himself. Servius' note on Vergil's line takes the meaning to be 'from beginning to end'; this is possible, but I suggest that it is rather 'even in outline,' a meaning readily derived from the literal sense of *ora* = 'outside edge'; cf. note on Bk I, fr. 33. This interpretation would, moreover, add greatly to the force of the rhetorically stressed adjective *ingentis*. The fragment preserved in the Berne *schol.* on *Georg.* II. 43, *Non si lingua loqui superet*, etc., may possibly belong to the present passage, as the connection of thought would well suit the Homeric original (*Il.* II. 484 ff.); but the matter is uncertain, and I have therefore left the fragment among those *incertae sedis*: cf. comm. ad loc.

FR. 2. Bk V. fr. 6 is usually united into a single fragment with the present line. Festus (p. 168 Lind.) has a remarkable note on the word, but other grammarians understood its meaning better; see Mar. Vict. VI. 9 K.

FR. 3. One of the most widely quoted lines in Ennius, cited usually as a typical example of oracular *amphibolia*.

Aeacidā: with *ā* as a Greek proper name; cf. note on Bk III. fr. 2.

On the spurious line *Pemonoe Burro*, etc., accepted by Valmaggi, cf. note ad loc.

FR. 4. The stormy voyage of Pyrrhus: cf. Excursus I.

FR. 5. Description of Pyrrhus' ship.

stlat(t)aria: a very rare word, found elsewhere only in Juv. VII. 134. It is derived from *stlat(t)a*, a kind of ship very broad in the beam; cf. Paul. e Fest. (p. 411 Lind.). Similar forms are *stlembus* (= *lentus*, Lucilius) and *stloppus* (Persius V. 13). Quintilian (I. 4. 16) mentions *stlocus* and *stlis*, which survived down to Cicero's time in the phrase *Decemuiri stlitibus iudicandis* (*Or.* XLVII. 156).

FR. 6. The resentment felt in Tarentum, as described by Plutarch and Zonaras.

mussabant: a favourite word with Ennius to describe discontent among the rank and file of an army; sometimes, however, the meaning seems to be not *murmurare* but *tacere*; cf. Varro, *L.L.* VII. 101.

FR. 7. Macrobius quotes the line specifically from Bk VI, but it is with considerable hesitation that I place it at this point, as the reference is extremely doubtful. On the whole, it seems best to understand it as a description of 'cattle-lifting' operations carried out in Tarentine territory.

quatit: may bear the meaning of 'drives ahead with blows,' as in Ter. *Eun.* 3. 58; Verg. *Georg.* III. 132; Sil. XII. 204, and especially *poeta* in Cic. *de Nat. Deor.* II. 42, *Arctophylax prae se quatit Arctum*. For a contrary suggestion, accepted by Valmaggi, see Havet, *Rev. de Phil.* IX. 166 ff.

FR. 8. Most probably from the description of the battle of Heraclea, the first occasion on which the dreaded *Lucae boues* were seen by Roman soldiers. The rout, due entirely to the elephants, must have been worthily described; and we may perhaps see a hint of Ennius' picture of the elephants themselves in two Lucretian passages, II. 536–7 and V. 1302 f.

taetros: *tetrum pro fero*, Isidore.

elephantos: Ennius' own spelling would be *elepantos*. Aspirated *ch*, *th*, *ph*, were represented by simple *c*, *t*, *p*, and such a form as *adelpus* is found on an inscription which may be as late as 81 B.C. The aspiration was introduced during the lifetime of Cicero (cf. *Or.* XLVIII. 160), and there was for a time a craze which is ridiculed in the Arrius of Catullus, and of which Quintilian speaks (I. 5. 20). The second declension form of our word is to be noted; *elephas* and *elephans* also occur; cf. Prisc. I. 216 H. The note of Isidore on the meaning of *taeter* is repeated a number of times; the *Excerpta ex codice Cassiensi xc* (= *Corp. Gl. Lat.* V. 581. 14) adds the words *ad inguinem*, which were first attributed to Ennius by Landgraf (*Arch.* IX. 446). It is tempting to see in them a corruption of *anguimanus*; but the evidence is weak, and probably we should recognise in them a fragment of some other gloss erroneously attached; cf. Goetz in *Corp. Gl. Lat.* VII. 330.

FR. 9. The preparations for burning the dead after the battle of Heraclea. For the general effect cf. *Il.* XXIII. 114 ff. (funeral of Patroclus), and *Aen.* VI. 179 ff. (funeral of Misenus). There are a number of other similar scenes in Latin poetry: *e.g. Aen.* XI. 134 ff.; Sil. X. 52 ff. It is instructive to glance at the elaborate version of Statius (*Theb.* VI. 90 ff.) and observe how the Ennian tradition persists even when Imperial false taste has altogether overlaid the directness and simplicity of the original.

arbusta: properly the n. pl. of the adjective *arbustus*. The formation resembles that of *salictum*, etc., and is said by Claudius Quadrigarius (ap. Gell. XVII. 2. 25) to be *nobilius* than *arboretum*. The use of the plural *arbusta* = *arbores* is common in the poets, and the word is so used here; the corresponding use of the singular, however, is very rare, but, unless we can assume it for the last line of the passage, it is difficult to see any distinction between *arbustum* and *siluai*. The reference given by L. and S. for this usage (*Ecl.* III. 10) is clearly mistaken.

The elaborate use of alliteration and internal assonance in the next few lines, one of the most striking instances in Ennius, is intended to reproduce the sounds of rustling and crashing among trees.

fremitu: a strong word, used elsewhere by Ennius (in a tragic fragment) of a downpour of rain.

siluai frondosai: the termination has its full value as two long syllables. All told, there are seven examples of *ai* as against five of *ae* in the *Annales*, a fact which indicates that the transition from one to the other was actually in progress while the poem was being written. In the non-hexameter fragments the form in *ai* is found once only (*Medai*), so that its later association with the epic measure seems due to the influence of Ennius. It is found in Lucilius, Lucretius, Cicero, Vergil and others of the Classical period, and, in the case of Vergil, is noted as a conscious archaism by Quintilian.

FR. 10. The finest and the most famous single speech preserved from Ennius, and one which fully deserves the eulogy of Cicero. Pyrrhus stands revealed in it as the chivalrous foe, the ancient Saladin and, *quia non carebat uate sacro*, is remembered side by side with Scipio for the sake of the poet who honoured them both. The occasion of the speech was the embassy of Fabricius to treat for the ransom of the prisoners taken at Heraclea.

mi: represents *moi* (Gk μοι), resembling a locative and should not be called a contraction of *mihi*. For the form of the double question *ne...an* cf. Plaut. *Persa*, 33.

cauponantes: cf. Aesch. *Septem*, 526. Ennius has, however, changed the application of the phrase.

uitam cernamus: *i.e. certemus certamen de uita*; the accusative is an extension of the 'accusative of the inner object.' The use of *cernere* in the sense of 'to decide an issue by fighting' is not common, and is noted by Seneca as obsolete. Nonius (p. 398 L.) has a long note on the meaning of the word; Varro (*L.L.* vi. 81) tries to derive all the various senses from the one 'to see,' but its original force seems to have been 'to set apart.'

era Fors: *fortuna*, standing so close to these words, would inevitably turn the Roman reader's mind to the goddess *Fors Fortuna*, but here *fortuna* is not personified and the reference to 'Lady Chance' is quite general: *fortuna* is constructed with *belli* as several times in Caesar.

experiamur: 'let us make trial' (and so find out which, etc.). *Eorundem*, three syllables, as so often in Plautus.

Dono, ducite: the absence of caesura should be noted. The impressive monosyllabic termination is echoed twice by Vergil (*Aen.* iii. 12 and viii. 679): of the speech as a whole it may be said that it would be difficult to have a finer illustration of the truth of the ancient criticism, that Ennius produced some of his loftiest effects by means of words *non nimis ornata*. Throughout the vocabulary is that of the simplest prose.

FR. 11. Cicero implies that the fragment is from the famous speech delivered by Appius Claudius Caecus against making peace with Pyrrhus after the battle of Heraclea: cf. Ovid, *Fasti*, vi. 199 ff. (June 3rd); Plutarch, *Pyrrhus*, xix. This speech was long extant, as Cicero says, and was remembered as the first attempt at artistic prose composition in Latin.

flexere: on this form cf. Cicero, *Or.* xlvii. 157; Quint. i. 5. 42, and Servius ad *Aen.* ii. 1. In the early writers the

-ere termination is used at pleasure and does not differ from *-erunt*.

mentes...dementes: as Valmaggi remarks, this is the only 'oxymoron' in the extant fragments.

Lambinus' *uiai* is clearly right: grammatically the genitive is constructed with *quo*. Such usages are found in early Latin with adverbs of quantity, place and time. Cf. note on Bk I. fr. 10; for the form cf. note on *siluai* above, p. 143.

Fr. 12. The speech continued.

quid: 'to what purpose?'

animo: *uenuste additum animo*, Donatus. The ablative best explained as locatival in force, though such figurative uses are rare in early Latin. Pascoli compares the Homeric ὀλοφύραο θυμῷ (*Od.* XI. 418).

Fr. 13. The return of Cineas after his unsuccessful mission to Rome.

Orator: 'envoy' or 'ambassador'; see Festus (p. 196 L.) and Paul. pp. 17 and 197 L. The meaning survives into classical times and is found several times in Vergil; cf. note on I. 11. The strong alliteration on *r* should be noted.

rem: the nouns *res* and *uis* are most commonly used by Ennius for monosyllabic terminations.

Fr. 14. The MS. reading is *Aut animos* (or *animas*) *superant atque asp...rima..fera belli spernunt*. A possible reconstruction would be: *Ast animis superant atque aspera prima duelli Mortiferi spernunt*. The form *duelli* actually occurs in Bk IV. fr. 5; it is introduced by Pascoli into his text. *Animis* is supported by the fact that Vergil (*Aen.* V. 473) uses the plural though his line refers to a single individual, which suggests that the whole phrase came straight from Ennius. Keil's *aspera prima* is an easy and obvious addition, and gives an appropriate sense, as the mission took place very early in the war.

However we complete the line, the general sense is clear enough: 'the courage of the Romans rises superior to all disasters.' The Vergilian line already mentioned (*Hic uictor superans animis*, etc.) suggests that here too *superant* is intransitive and that the meaning is 'are high of heart.' Such a sense is an easy transference from the common meaning 'to be abundant.'

aspera prima: either 'the disastrous beginnings' or 'the first disasters.' *Aspera* is used as a noun in Prop. I. 18. 13, and *prima* of the opening campaign of a war in Livy VIII. 3.

FR. 15. As Valmaggi points out, the present *sunt* makes it necessary to suppose that the criticism was made by a contemporary. I suggest that the complaint, which is really one of a lack of psychological insight, is made by a friend of Pyrrhus who yet censures him, and so belongs (like the previous fragment) to Cineas. We know that he was very powerfully impressed by what he saw in Rome, and his admiration has already appeared in Fr. 14. The words probably belong to a soliloquy as they are rather bold from a courtier to a king.

stolidum: 'senseless,' a very strong word; cf. Bk I, fr. 39, where it is used of *sues*.

Bellipotens: is taken over by Vergil as a name for Mars (*Aen*. XI. 18), and appears occasionally in later epic. The polysyllabic terminations of both lines should be noted.

sapientipotentes: a coinage of Ennius' own; the force of the first part is clearly that of σοφία, wisdom got by special study and training, perhaps with specific reference to the art of rhetoric: cf. Cic. *de Or*. III. xv.

FR. 16. The self-devotion of Decius Mus (the third of that name) in the battle of Asculum: cf. Cic. *Tusc*. I. 39. 89; *de Fin*. II. 19. 61. Ennius is the only early authority for this third sacrifice, but he must have drawn on sources of informatjon now lost to us, perhaps on 'non-literary' sources and oral tradition.

parumper: the meaning is defined by L. and S. as *cito et uelociter* in all the Ennius passages, but this is incorrect. Besides the present it appears in the following lines: Bk I. frs. 18 and 29, and *I.S.* frs. 42 and 76. The meaning preferred by L. and S. is given as secondary by Nonius, and is appropriate only to the second and third: in the others, as in the present line, Nonius' primary meaning should be accepted (*interim et paruo tempore*), as appropriate in itself and as agreeing with Festus, who gives *paulisper*. This is the ordinary meaning of the word; the other seems to be an experiment on the part of Ennius, and Nonius' secondary meaning is an inference derived from his usage.

Vt: L. and S. are again wrong in explaining this as *quomodo*: it is clearly temporal (*quo tempore*) and is used to define the meaning of *parumper* as *dum* is both in prose and verse.

prognariter: the MSS. reading should be retained. Nonius explains the meaning as *strenue, fortiter et constanter*, and again as *audacter*, but the editors who retain *prognariter* assume without discussion that Nonius is wrong and give the meaning as 'knowing beforehand,' *i.e.* as a mere repetition of *prudens*. But *prognariter* must qualify *certando*, and therefore others correct to *praegnauiter*, explaining Nonius' assertion as due to an already corrupted text which foisted the correct meaning upon the wrong word. But this argument is invalidated by the fact that in the second place Nonius quotes only a passage from Plautus (*Persa*, 588), where the text is undoubtedly sound; and there is not the difference between *audacter* and *strenue, fortiter* and *constanter* which Valmaggi postulates. The meaning seems in reality to be 'with knowledge gained beforehand,' *i.e.* 'with mind fully resolved because aware,' which readily passes into 'with resolution.' The very fact that *gnarus* and *gnauus* are cognates shows how easy the transition is.

animam mitto: the strong word emphasises the voluntary nature of the sacrifice; so Vergil uses *animam proicere* (*Aen.* VI. 435).

FR. 17. Not a council of the gods, as the editors assume, but a soliloquy of Jove; cf. *Il.* XVII. 200 ff.

diuum pater e.q.s.: like the Homeric πατὴρ ἀνδρῶν τε θεῶν τε. Slight variations of the phrase occurred at various points. Varro (*L.L.* V. 65) quotes *diuomque hominumque pater*, *rex*; and Cicero (*de Nat. Deor.*), *patrem diuomque hominumque*.

Effatur: a specially religious word. Cf. Cic. *de Or.* III. 38. 153.

FR. 18. The coming of dawn. The reference is probably to the second day of the battle of Asculum, when Pyrrhus was early on the move to secure favourable and commanding ground that would enable him to retrieve the previous day's disasters.

Vertitur: the whole vault of heaven carries round the stars as it moves. The theory is Epicurean (Fr. 92) and appears in Lucretius V. 510 f.

FR. 19. The break of day.

indalbabat: shows the old *indu* (*endo*) as in *indotuetur*, *induperator*, *indupedio* (Lucretius), etc. There is a reminiscence of our line in Apuleius, *Met.* VII.: *Vt primum tenebris abiectis dies inalbebat*. The reference is to the second day of Asculum.

FR. 20. The damaged condition of Festus' text has led to many different interpretations of these words, but I suggest that they describe the device of cutting the traces of the horses in the Roman war chariots, which was adopted by the numerous escort of Pyrrhus' elephants on the second day of Asculum, and which was the first move towards breaking the Roman front.

scitus: the connotation is shown by the collocation in

Plautus, *Pseud.* I. 3. 151; it would be appropriate in describing such a device.

agaso: properly a driver, is used specifically of a groom attending horses, but might serve for the mahout of an elephant. However the line should be interpreted the gap is too great to make suggested completions profitable.

FR. 21. This fragment should be retained in Bk VI to which Macrobius assigns it. There is no need to read into it a reference to the Punic wars. I suggest that it describes an incident in the concentrated attack on Syracuse made by Carthage and Rome both by land and sea as a step in the aggressive campaign which followed the death of Agathocles (289 B.C.). It was this attack which led Syracuse to call on Pyrrhus for help; and the Numidian scouts of our line may well belong to the land army conducting the siege.

EXCURSUS I

There can be no reasonable doubt that the universally accepted view, that the *Annales* detailed the events of the *First* Punic war, is entirely mistaken. Cicero's statement (*Brutus*, XIX. 76) that the war was deliberately omitted because Ennius feared to enter into rivalry with Naevius is ignored, misrepresented or explained away. But, till we have definite proof of its falsity, we must believe it to be true: there could have been no conceivable motive for falsehood, there must have been every motive for avoiding error in a matter so easily tested as the contents of the most famous poem in Latin literature. Eight fragments have been, by universal consent of the editors, included in the supposed narrative of the First Punic war: but an impartial examination of them will show that in some cases the identification cannot be correct, and in all the rest is by no means the only possibility. I therefore suggest that we must take Cicero at his

word; and that to do so, the easiest and best way is to refer
the doubtful fragments to the war with Pyrrhus. This war,
for personal reasons already suggested, was treated on a scale
so elaborate that it occupied part of the seventh book as
well as the whole of the sixth. A natural assumption is that
the break was made at the Sicilian expedition, and it should
be noted that none of the fragments surviving from Bk VI
need refer to anything later than the battle of Asculum.
Bk VII probably opened with the *Primordia Carthaginis*: such
a digression would be even more natural at that point than
as a prelude to the First Punic war, as it was Pyrrhus' operations in Sicily which brought Rome and Carthage into close
touch, and made the later struggle inevitable. There is no
difficulty in supposing that the narrative was, like that of
the *Second* Punic war, carried over more than one book; and,
indeed, it is an open question whether Ennius was himself
responsible for the division into books. Suetonius (*de inl.
gram.* 2) makes a statement which to us contains a real am-
biguity, and it is possible that he meant that Vargunteius
not merely lectured on the *Annales*, but also divided the
poem, as Lampadio did the *Bellum Punicum* of Naevius.
However, for our present purpose, it is enough to examine
the actual fragments themselves:

1. *Appius indixit Karthaginiensibus bellum* (Bk VII. fr. 21
Appendix).

2. *Mulserat huc nauem conpulsam fluctibus pontus* (Bk VI.
fr. 4).

3. *Et melior nauis quam quae stlataria portat* (Bk VI. fr. 5).

4.   *tonsam ante tenentes,*
    Parerent, obseruarent, porticulus signum
    Quom dare coepisset (Bk VIII. fr. 23).

5. *Poste recumbite uestraque pectora pellite tonsis* (Bk VII.
fr. 10).

6. *Pone petunt, exim referunt ad pectora tonsas* (Bk VII.
fr. 11).

7. *Denique ui magna quadrupes eques atque elephanti
Proiciunt sese* (Bk VII. fr. 13).

8. *Alter nare cupit, alter pugnare paratust* (Bk VII. fr. 12).
The first line obviously refers to the outbreak of the First
Punic war. But its attribution to Ennius, though probably
correct, is purely conjectural, and Cicero (see sources) gives
no author's name. Even admitting its genuineness, it need
be no more than a 'time note' or cross-reference (with *post
quam* at the end of the line before). As a 'date' I suggest
that its most probable place is the end of Bk IX, to indicate
the length of the whole struggle between Rome and Carthage
('Scipio finished the conflict sixty years after Appius began
it'). Another possibility is that it belongs to the *scripsere
alii rem* passage, and is in effect a parody of Naevius and the
narrative style which Ennius affected to despise. (2) and (3)
I place together as describing the effects of the storm which
Pyrrhus encountered on his voyage to Italy, and the excellence of his own ship which enabled him to weather it for a
time: see Plutarch, *Pyrrhus*, XV. The comparison in (3) gains
in point as we can refer it to the other ships which carried
the *impedimenta* and animals. A change in the number of
the book to which (2) belongs is involved (Priscian gives VII.),
but numerals are notoriously easy of confusion. We might,
however, retain it in VII. and refer it to some incident of the
naval engagement during Pyrrhus' return voyage to Italy.
(4) plainly refers to the *Second* Punic war: it is quoted from
Bk VIII, and nothing is gained by refusing to accept the
number. The reference is to the 'sham fights' described by
Livy XXV. 51; cf. XXXV. 26. [This possibility is admitted by
Vahlen alone among the editors.] (5) and (6), I suggest,
refer not to the famous drill of 260 B.C., but to orders given to

Pyrrhus' pressed rowers, either when they were first enrolled, when they must have been drilled, or during the encounter with the Carthaginian fleet referred to above; cf. Plutarch, *Pyrrhus*, XXII. It should be noted that there is nothing to indicate the special feature of the 260 B.C. drill, namely, that it was carried out on land. (8) probably belongs to the moment when Pyrrhus decided to concentrate all his efforts on breaking through to Italy (*ibid*. ch. XXIV.). The meaning has been much disputed; but the words can be understood quite simply and literally to mean, 'One side [Pyrrhus] is eager to advance upon its way, the other [Carthage] is ready for the fight.' *Nare* means simply to move over or through the water. Our remaining fragment (7) can be referred to a disorderly retreat as well as to an advance; and the most striking event of the battle of Beneventum was the panic caused among τὰ θηρία of Pyrrhus by the Roman fire (*ibid*. ch. XXV.). But whether these individual ascriptions be right or wrong, it is at least clear that the First Punic war need not have formed any part of the narrative of Ennius. *Note:* The bulk of this excursus was written in 1919 (see *C.Q.* for October of that year) and my conclusions were fully formed before I saw Norden's *Ennius und Vergilius*. The support it lends to my theory is naturally welcome.

BOOK VII

FR. 1. The book opened with a prologue which, I suggest, was somewhat elaborate, and which fell into two parts. The first was a kind of *apologia pro se*, containing the portrait of Ennius himself in the present fragment, and possibly with other personal and artistic details which not merely served to mask the gap in the narrative but also led naturally on to the contrast with Naevius which I believe was elaborated at

the end of the prologue, and which occupied the end of the
Primordia Carthaginis, the résumé of Carthaginian history
with which the prologue closed. The self-justification of
scripsere alii rem served as an apology for the omission of the
natural climax. I retain our fragment in the book to which
Gellius assigns it, though the editors for the most part
transfer it to Bk VIII, on the ground that the Servilius mentioned is to be identified with Cn. Servilius Geminus, who
was consul in 217 and commanded the Roman centre at
Cannae. There is no proof of this, however, and so I follow
the explicit statement of Gellius. Gellius further asserts on
the authority of Aelius Stilo, that the 'friend of Servilius'
is in reality Ennius himself (XII. 4).

bene saepe: 'very often'; cf. Porph. ad Hor. *Od.* III. 24. 50.

Mensam sermonesque suos rerumque suarum: the genitive is
governed directly by *inpartit* (cf. Frobenius, *Syntax des
Ennius*, p. 34, where δόμεναι σίτου, *Od.* XVII. 4, is compared). Cf. Cato, *Agr.* 74, *aquae...addito*; Plautus, *Poenulus*,
641. The genitive is really partitive in sense and is quite
natural with *inpartit*, the meaning of which is *participem facit*.
There are many verbs in early Latin which govern sometimes
an accusative, sometimes a genitive; and the only difficulty
in the present line is that the two constructions are combined.
But this is probably done *metri causa*. Certainly the explanation, which is accepted by Vahlen in his second edition, re-
moves any necessity for alteration in the text, and is greatly
preferable to Valmaggi's suggestion, which makes *rerum
suarum* an objective genitive depending on *sermones* ('i
discorsi suoi e delle cose sue').

lassus has a predicative force; 'had spent a great part of
the day (and so grown) weary.'

triuisset: I accept Baehrens' emendation for *fuisset* which,
apart from the difficulty of the quantity of the first syllable,

does not give a reasonable sense nor explain the force of *magnam partem diei*.

indu: found in composition (cf. Bk VI. fr. 19) as well as alone, as in Bk XVII. fr. 4.

se cura: I accept *se* (= *sine*) *cura* from Hosius for *et cuncta*, which, with slight and unimportant variations, is the reading of all the MSS. The form is well attested: cf. Festus, p. 374 Lind., Paul. p. 453 Lind.; and is preserved in a number of laws, in phrases like *se fraude* and *se dolo malo*. *Se cura* is closer to the MSS. than *cuncta simul*, the generally accepted reading, and gives a more satisfactory meaning and a better-balanced sentence.

qui = quo: the form is most probably an instrumental or true ablative, but its frequent use in an instrumental construction suggests the former. Here it is adverbial, resembling *quo modo* ('if by any means'): the phrase *qui fit ut* survives into classical times.

tuto: masculine ('to a person who would not betray him'): for the meaning cf. Hor. *Od.* 1. 27. 18.

uolup: the MSS. vary between *uolup, uolup...*, *uoluptas* and *uoluptatem*. The form is probably an adverb, shortened from *uolupe*, neuter of **uolupis*, though it may be a noun (cf. Nonius, 187. 6 Lind.) as it is in the *Carmen Nelei*. Our construction resembles that in Plaut. *Amph.* 994.

Ingenium quoi, etc.: the MSS. reading should be retained. *Nulla sententia* is the subject of *suadet*, which governs *ingenium*, *malum* agrees with *facinus* in the next line, while *leuis* and *malus* are used predicatively with the subject of *faceret*, a masculine pronoun understood out of *quoi*. The use of *suadeo* with an accusative, though rare, is well recognised; the best and clearest parallel is from Apuleius— *Vxorem eius tacite suasi...*, but there are others, *e.g.* Cic. *Prou. Cons.* 17. 42. Servius is troubled by the possibility of the same construction in *Aen.* x. 10, but his note is most valuable as providing us with the fragment *quis te persuasit* from Ennius himself. Pascoli suggests that *ingenium* is governed by *suadet*, but quotes no Latin parallels, contenting himself with *Il.* xvii. 842 and xxii. 78.

sententia: 'inclination,' as in the common *ex sententia* and *praeter sententiam*.

facinus: simply *factum*, as commonly in Plautus. Throughout the early period an adjective seems necessary to supply the specific sense.

leuis aut malus: 'from caprice or malice.' *Leuis* cannot be a complimentary word as applied to a person, and it seems therefore necessary to accept *aut* for *haut*.

malŭs, doctŭs: it is unusual to find final *s* neglected so often as it is in this passage (nine times in eighteen lines). This is perhaps a sign of somewhat hastier writing than usual, and suggests that Ennius may, like Vergil, have left some parts of his poem unrevised. The suggestion is strengthened by the unusual amount of repetition (*malum malus, tenens tenens, ueteres ueterum*).

doctus: perhaps in a quasi-technical sense as so often in the Augustan age. Ennius may have been the first to give the word its meaning of 'poetic.'

facundus: means 'a good talker,' and is therefore not inconsistent with *uerbum paucum* (= 'not a babbler'); cf. the distinction in Sallust ap. Quint. v. 22.

verbûm: on the gen. pl. in -*ûm* cf. Cicero, *Or.* 155, where the usage of Ennius is discussed, Varro, *L.L.* viii. 71, and Quint. i. 6. 18.

Quae facit, etc.: I adopt the reading of Vahlen's first edition, and also his *prudenter* in the line below. The increasing conservatism of his second edition, though sometimes justified, seems sometimes a mistake.

Prudenter: the tact of Ennius is the justification of the confidences of Servilius.

inter pugnas: with the identification of Servilius with the Consul of 217, these words might naturally be understood of fighting in the Second Punic war, and may have given rise to the late tradition, which appears in Claudian and Petrarch, that Ennius actually accompanied Scipio to Africa. But without such identification the reference may be to metaphorical *pugnas*.

Fr. 2. An anticipation of criticism arising out of the dream-picture with which the poem opens (see Hor. *Ep.* II. 1. 50 f., Persius, *Prol.* 1 f.), and therefore part of the *apologia*. For the etymological note cf. Bk III. fr. 2.

perhibere: a favourite word with Ennius.

In somnis: a clear reference to the vision of Homer.

sam = eam: from the demonstrative stem as before.

Fr. 3. The beginning of the *Primordia Carthaginis*: the founding of the city.

Sar(r)a as a name for Tyre is mentioned by Servius ad *Geo.* II. 506, and also by Gellius, XIV. 5. 6. But, while the name is more correct than *Tyros*, the notes of both Probus and Servius (l.c.) contain serious errors. Probus implies that the name is found in 'Homer,' but he does not mention 'Tyre' or 'Sarra' at all, and the only occurrence of Sara in Greek seems to be in 'Pseudo-Scylax,' 104. Even here it is usual to emend to Σάραπτα. Nor is it possible that Sarra can be connected with any Semitic word for 'fish'; it is clearly a transliteration of the native name (Hebrew *Sōr* or *Tsōr*, Phoenician *Tsur*, Assyrian *Sunu*, Egyptian *Da-ru*), and the difference is in reality merely that between two representations of the Hebrew and Phoenician letter *V* (*Ts* or *S*). The Latin form is closer to the correct Phoenician pronunciation, and is very probably derived from the Cartha-

ginians in the Mediterranean, whereas the Greek form, closer
to Egyptian, suggests that the Greeks made their early contact with Tyre by way of Egypt and Crete. *Sarranus* is not
uncommon in Latin poetry in the general sense of 'Tyrian,'
and is used several times by Silius for 'Carthaginian.'

FR. 4. The worship of Moloch. A sketch of national
customs may well have formed part of the *Primordia Carthaginis*: but it is possible that our fragment should be placed
in Bk VIII and referred to the embassy sent to Hannibal to
demand his own sons for sacrifice; cf. Silius, IV. 763 ff.

sŭos: scanned as a monosyllable.

puellos: Nonius quotes examples of this form from Lucilius, Varro and Lucretius, as well as our present line.

FR. 5. The prologue concluded: Ennius and his predecessors.

The textual difficulties of this famous passage are matters
of disarrangement and omission rather than corruption, but
there are certain points of interpretation which affect the
other problems vitally. The word *superarat* was introduced
in the edition of 1536, and since that date it has been assumed that *Musarum* and *scopulos* should be taken together
as referring to some holy place of poetry. But I submit that
this interpretation is entirely unwarranted. *Scopulus* means
a detached crag or point of rock, usually in the sea; it may
describe part of a hill, but cannot mean the whole of it. The
nearest approach is the use of *Mauortis scopulus* by Ovid
(*Met.* VI. 70) for the Areopagus; but against this we must
set many other passages, like Sil. x. 239, Stat. *Theb.* x. 665,
Val. Flacc. VI. 633, and the Vergilian description of the cave
of Cacus. We cannot interpret *Musarum scopulos* of Parnassus
or any other hill; and I suggest that *scopulos* is used metaphorically in the sense of 'difficulties' or 'dangers,' exactly
as Martial uses *salebras altaque saxa* in reference to early

poetry (XI. 90). *Musarum* must be constructed with some word now lost. This explanation seems to underlie Pascoli's suggestion *auxilio*, but he does not state it even in the briefest form. His idea is quite possibly right, but I cannot accept his line—*Cum neque Musarum auxilio scopulos superarat*; the metre is unsatisfactory, and further *superarat* is not appropriate to the metaphor. We should expect some such word as *fugere* or *euitare*, either alone or with *discere*. However, I have made no attempt to supply words and have merely given Cicero's text unaltered save for the position of *quisquam*, which I place before *nec dicti*. In *Or.* 171 *ante hunc* and *nos ausi reserare* are mentioned together in a way which clearly suggests that they both 'began new paragraphs' in the complete passage, that is, with the prevalence of end-stopped lines, that they stood at the beginning of their respective lines. With *ante hunc* at the beginning of a line, *nec dicti studiosus quisquam erat* becomes unmetrical, but is restored to metre by placing *quisquam* first. If *quisquam* were omitted in its proper place and then added after *studiosus*, this would cause the loss of the word or words following *erat*.

scripsere alii rem: for the importance of the plural *alii* see Excursus II.

rem: the First Punic war, the subject of Naevius' poem; cf. Cicero, *Brutus*, XIX. 76.

Versibus: the Saturnian metre. For its connection with the *Fauni* cf. Varro, *L.L.* VII. 103.

uates: 'seers,' like the so-called *Marcius Vates* and the other mentioned by Livy (v. 16). Our passage probably played the largest part in the discrediting of the word which lasted till the Augustan age.

dicti: 'style.'

Ante hunc: probably introduced a description of the early

state of Latin poetry and contained the new metaphor introduced by *reserare*.

FR. 6. The narrative of the war resumed: the protests of Pyrrhus' Italian allies of Lucania, Samnium and Tarentum, who bitterly resented his proposed withdrawal to Sicily. The present line probably belongs to the spokesman of Tarentum, and voices his recognition of the fact that his appeal has had the opposite effect from what was intended: *flexa est*, *i.e.* 'contrary to our desires.'

quianam: in the sense of *cur*; cf. Servius ad *Aen.* x. 6. The usage is found both in Plautus and Naevius.

FR. 7. The reply of Pyrrhus to the threatening tone of the Tarentine speaker. It is a generalised statement, but the thought is, 'Attempts at coercion make me the more resolved'; such a reply would be thoroughly in keeping with Pyrrhus' haughty and imperious temper.

censent: as often, carries with it the suggestion of error in the opinion entertained; cf. Plautus, *Amph.* Prol. 122.

ibi: answers to *dum* at the beginning of the line, as in Plaut. *Ep.* 595 to *ubi*, and Cic. *Pro Caec.* 27 to *cum*. The usage is mostly ante-classical and poetic but is common in Livy.

sos = eos: as before.

FR. 8. Pyrrhus to the Samnites and Lucanians.

euertit, perhaps an intentional colloquialism for the logically necessary future, to distinguish speech from formal narrative. *stat*: 'stands beside you as a helper'; in the normal prose construction *ab*, *cum* or *pro* is required. *Iuppiter hac stat* is found in *Aen.* XII. 565.

FR. 9. The speech continued.

data est: 'has been assigned,' *i.e.* 'is the prerogative of.' These four fragments are not explained as above by any of the editors.

FR. 10. Operations in Sicily. For the interpretation of Frs. 10–13 see Excursus 1.

tonsis: 'the oars'; the *portisculus* who gives the orders is described by Silius (VI. 360 ff.). His name is derived from the *malleus* he used; cf. Festus, p. 266 Lind. and Nonius.

FR. 11. *Pone*: a derivative from *post*, used even in the classical period, but considered archaic by Quintilian, VII. 3. 25; cf. Festus, p. 292 Lind.

FR. 12. Cf. Excursus 1.

nare: to move over the water.

FR. 13. Cf. Excursus 1.

eques: on the correctness of this form see Gellius XVIII. 5. The meaning 'horse' is attested by other grammarians, *e.g.* Macrobius VI. 9, Non. p. 152 Lind., and is found in Lucilius and Vergil (*Geo*. III. 110 f.); cf. the note of Servius (D.) ad loc. The actual significance, however, seems to be 'man-and-horse,' and *eques* could not be used for *equus* in the case of a riderless animal (cf. the somewhat similar use of 'a troop of horse,' etc. in English). For an opposite view see Haverfield, *C. Rev.* XIII. 305 ff. Valmaggi, quoting Wölfflin, gives examples of the usage from prose also; *e.g.* Auct. *Bell. Hosp.* III. 3, Minuc. Fel. *Oct.* VII. 3.

FR. 14. The minor events between the two Punic wars: the Illyrian pirate war (231 B.C.).

sica: a large curved knife.

sibyna: the Illyrian name for a short, broad spear (see Paul. e Fest. p. 453 Lind.). Ennius is careful, wherever possible, to give a touch of local colour by introducing native names for non-Roman weapons.

fodentes should be retained; the form, as well as *effodentes*, is found in Gregory of Tours (Wagener in *Neue* III³. 244).

FR. 15. The manufacture of weapons.

deducere: the metaphorical use is derived from weaving

and is perhaps due to the presence of *filo* in the immediate context, *filum deducere* being such a common phrase. The only other passage in which the word seems to be used for metal-working is Juv. VII. 54–5, where the whole passage is figurative.

habiles: predicative, 'to make them handy.' We cannot, despite the references in Livy VII. 10. 5 and XX. 11. 46, both of which contain the word *habiles*, have in our line a reference to the Spanish sword which was short and thick. Probably the Gallic sword is described: Livy (l.c.) specifically contrasts it with the Spanish.

filo: seems to be used for *forma*; cf. Lucretius V. 571, Plautus, *Merc.* 755, Varro, *L.L.* x. 4. *Filo gracilento* describes a slender blade with a fine edge.

FR. 16. The text of this fragment, like that of the next, is very uncertain, nor is it altogether clear whether we are dealing with one fragment or two. Since the time of Spangenberg it has been assumed that there are two. The text of Nonius actually runs—*Legio †redditu† rumore ruinas, Mox auferre domos populi rumore secundo*, but Lindsay now inserts *et* between *ruinas* and *mox*. It seems clear:

(1) That if the double *rumore* is correct we must have two quotations.

(2) With two quotations *secundo* must be inserted with the first. *Rumore* alone could not bear the meaning required.

(3) With *secundo* thus inserted, *ruina(s)*, which is clearly genuine, must be the only surviving word of another line now lost. To assume two quotations involves less change in the MSS. reading than to attempt to produce a single line; hence I read as shown in the text. Vahlen returns to a single fragment, reading *murumque* for *rumore* in the first place.

FR. 17. I accept Müller's *ruina* for the MSS. *ruinas*. He suggests a reference to the outcry against Sp. Cassius, when accused of aiming at a tyranny, but a more probable explanation is that the language is really sarcastic and describes exaggerated reports of the boldness of the Illyrian pirates.

FR. 18. The river Nar was famous as draining off the sulphurous waters of the Veline Lake: cf. Pliny, *N.H.* III. 12. 17, Verg. *Aen.* VII. 517, with the note of Servius ad loc., where it is stated that *nar* is the Sabine word for sulphur. Ennius seems to have attributed fatal powers to the exhalations; cf. *Aen.* VII. 563 with Servius. The phrase *posuit spiramina*, curious as it is, seemingly means 'died.' *Spiramen* can be used in the sense of *spiritus*, and the phrase *spiritum posuit* for 'died' is actually found (Val. Max. VII. 8. 8). The occasion for mentioning the river may have been the extension of the *Via Flaminia* from Narnia to Spoletium.

FR. 19. There is nothing to indicate the exact subject of either this or the next fragment.

To the present Valmaggi adds *populeae* from Ausonius, *Technop.* 161, arguing that had Ennius ever used the singular *populea fruns*, Charisius would have quoted it instead of the plural which he actually gives, as the immediately following passage is concerned with the singular forms of *fro(n)s*. This is somewhat arbitrary reasoning, however, and I prefer to suppose that Ennius used both singular and plural of such an exceedingly common word. On the interchange of *u* and *o* before a nasal cf. Prisc. I. 26. 35 H., where the *u* forms are said to be due to old-fashioned country pronunciation. Cf. also Vel. Long. 49. 15 K.

FR. 20. *rectis foliis*: with *cupressi* ('stiffly upright leaves').

amaro: as honey made from box flowers was bitter, and as Pliny (*N.H.* XVI. 16. 70) mentions this peculiarity in the honey of Corsica, it is possible that the present line may be from a description of the occupation of Corsica.

buxum, n.: usually the 'wood,' here the 'tree' as in

Pliny, *N.H.* XVI. 43. 231. For the substitution of *B* for
II (πύξος = *buxus*) cf. the proper name *Burrus*, Bk v. fr. 6.

APPENDIX TO BOOK VII

FR. 21. For a discussion of this line cf. Excursus I. Even
granting that it is genuine Ennius, I cannot, however, feel
certain that it really belongs to the *Annales*, much less to
this particular book. It may have found its place in the
Scipio, which, to judge from its fame in later generations,
was a much more elaborate work than is generally supposed.

FR. 22. This line has all the air of genuine Ennius, but
must be placed in the Appendix, as Cicero gives no author's
name. The person referred to is M'. Curius Dentatus, and
the line is an excellent epigrammatic statement of his two
great claims to glory; cf. Val. Max. IV. 3. 5.

Excursus II

On the existence of a school of native ballad poetry in
Rome. (For general support of some of the views put forward here cf. de Sanctis' history of Rome.) The once famous
theory of Niebuhr has fallen into discredit; but it is beginning
to appear, to historians and students of literature alike, that
epic poetry was in full process of evolution at Rome long
before Livius translated the *Odyssey*. We need not speak of
the *Naeniae* and *Cantus Conuiuiales*, nor of Saturnian epi-
taphs and *Tituli*; but there are other very ancient poems which
must be briefly considered. Some were quite short, no doubt
of a ritualistic or religious character; but others show the
secularisation of the style and its development in the direction
of the narrative lay. In his discussion of the name *Saturnius*,
Charisius (*G.L.K.* 1. 288) suggests that it may have arisen
quod eodem (sc. *Saturno*) *defuncto apotheosis eius hac dictione*

sit celebrata, cuius exemplum *adhuc in linteis libris reperitur*.
Here is a definite statement that in the fourth Christian
century there was still extant a poem (presumably one of
many *cuius exemplum* above) on the glory of a mortal who
became a god. Festus (p. 325 M.) attests the widespread use
of the metre; and we may see a faint trace of the activity
referred to in scattered single lines like *Occursatrix artificum
perdita spinturnix* and another *uersus antiquus*, as Festus calls
it, with a regular epic simile *Quasi messor per messim unum-
quemque spicum*. We may further remember the phrase used
by Dionysius of Halicarnassus in reference to Coriolanus;
ᾄδεται καὶ ὑμνεῖται can mean only 'songs of praise are
in circulation about him.' The last instance to be considered
here depends on a very fragmentary and much restored passage in Festus (on the *Corona naualis*): *Item alii* (sc. *adepti
sunt*) *inter quos M. Atilius* (*Atillus* Thewrewk) *bello ⟨quod
gestum est contra Poenos, ut scrip⟩tum est in car⟨mine Saturnio⟩*
(Lindsay, following Thewrewk, supplies *car⟨mine⟩* only).
Broken as the passage is, it nevertheless proves that a poem
of some kind existed. The reference cannot well be to the
Bellum Punicum, which was for Festus the stock example of
the Saturnian metre, and would therefore most probably be
introduced under its own name. Is it too much to suggest
that Festus had in mind an episode of a separate poem on
Regulus, an *Aristeia* in fact, dealing with his personal exploits
in the First Punic war and possibly the source of the legend
immortalised by Cicero and Horace? The point is important
for the student of Ennius; and I suggest that in the famous
lines Bk VII. fr. 5, *scripsere alii*, *alii* is a real and not merely a
rhetorical plural and that this very Regulus poem may have
been before Ennius as he wrote.

Lastly, we may consider the evidence for the existence of
poems on Romulus himself. Again the question is one of

special interest for our present purpose, for if such poems
existed, Ennius was not the man to ignore them. It is even
possible that one of his lines preserves a fragment from such
a source; cf. the note on *Ratus Romulus* (Bk I. fr. 31). But,
apart from such speculations, Cicero (*Tusc.* I. 12) shows quite
clearly that the deification of Romulus came to Ennius from
early legend. More important still are the Greek authorities,
such as the well-known passage in Dionysius (*A.R.* I. 79)
... ὡς ἐν τοῖς πατρίοις ὕμνοις ὑπὸ Ῥωμαίων ἔτι καὶ νῦν
ᾄδεται (the divine and royal birth). With this we may compare Plutarch, *Numa*, v. ... Ῥωμύλον ... παῖδα θεῶν ὑμνοῦσι
φήμαις κ.τ.λ. Here we have evidence which shows beyond
all reasonable doubt that poems on the Romulus legend were
actually in existence in Imperial times. It is hard to believe
that the categorical statement of Dionysius is untrue, for,
whatever he was as an archaeologist, in literary matters his
authority is very much greater than that of any other ancient
historian. He is a real literary critic, possibly the author of
the *de Sublimitate* itself, certainly a man of wide reading and
sympathetic understanding, specially interested in poetry.
The reference to the 'traditional lays' is a quite characteristic
transference of this interest from Greek to Latin literature,
and it would not be in keeping with his known tastes to suppose that his statement is taken over *verbatim* from some early
annalist. This, however, seems to be the opinion of the
critics. Again, it is unreasonable to argue that such valuable
evidence must be ruled out of court as a contradiction of
Cic. *Brut.* XIX. 75 (*utinam exstarent*, etc.). There is no real
discrepancy, for the two refer to different things. Cicero
speaks of mere κλέα ἀνδρῶν, songs of the earliest and most
primitive type, but Dionysius' poems belong to the second
clearly marked stage in the evolution of epic poetry. They are
narrative lays and not mere κλέα, and the features to which

special attention is drawn by both Dionysius and Plutarch imply narrative on a fairly elaborate scale. Moreover, the poems are definitely stated to have Romulus for their hero, but Cicero nowhere suggests that his *carmina* had any particular reference to the first king. The words ὕμνοι and ὑμνοῦσι in this connection offer no difficulty; the precedent of the *Homeric Hymns*, if nothing else, shows that they could be applied to long poems narrative in all but name. Incomplete as this evidence may be, it nevertheless suggests that if a school of native ballad poetry did exist, its work developed on lines which we might expect. Beginning with short quasi-lyrical κλέα and θρῆνοι, it passes to poems of a mythological-religious character, thence to half-legendary, half-historical lays, and finally to poems on well-authenticated historical characters. Such a background would have the advantage of making Naevius much more readily understandable; he would no longer be an isolated figure without real literary ancestors, for the *Bellum Punicum* at least, as he is without successors. He would be the last of a line of poets who had been steadily developing native themes in the native manner; his poem would be the swan-song of those *Veteres Casmenae* whom the unnamed author of the *Carmen Priami* invokes. Yet another fact tells in the same direction. Livius Andronicus was in his day an even greater pioneer than Ennius; he was, moreover, a South Italian Greek, and came to Rome a prisoner of war. He had, therefore, nothing to prejudice him in favour of things Roman, and yet, while he began the work of naturalising Greek metres for his dramas, his translation of the *Odyssey* was in Saturnians. We may, therefore, conclude that he considered the Saturnian a not unworthy representative of the metre of Homer; and in this we have one of the strongest possible indirect proofs of its development. For had it not been employed for fairly long poems it would not have seemed fit to bear the weight of the whole *Odyssey*. Again, Naevius used Saturnians for the *Bellum Punicum*, and that at the very end of his literary career. He had behind him his dramatic experience, in the course of which he had produced some elaborate metrical effects. Yet for narrative he preferred the Saturnian. Finally, I bring forward two named poems to represent the work of the ballad school in its latest or transitional period. Neglected or misconceived as they have been, they are of the utmost importance for the present purpose. For the first, the *Carmen Priami*, we have the authority of Varro (*L.L.* VII. 28), who quotes the title and one line, presumably the first. The words missing after *quod est* in Varro's text may have conveyed invaluable information as to authorship and text. Very significant is the single line we possess—*Veteres Casmenas cascam rem uolo profari* (the reading is that with the best MSS. authority and is accepted by the latest editors of Varro); it serves to crystallise for us the whole conflict between the old and the new. The author does openly what we infer that Livius did, and his deliberate choice of the *Veteres Casmenae*, the ancient native manner and metre, does not a little to indicate the vigour and vitality of the Saturnian tradition, which was thus able to impose itself on some part at least of the sacred tale of Troy.

The second poem, the *Carmen Nelei*, is known to us only from the references and quotations of Festus and Charisius. It is usually called a tragedy, on the ground that the fragments, five in number, must be iambic *senarii*. Were this the fact, the question would not admit discussion, for Baehrens' theory of a narrative poem in iambics deserves no credence. But that it is a narrative poem is plain from the title (exactly like *Carmen Priami*), as indeed Baehrens says; cf. *F.P.R.* p. 53. I do not stress the word *carmen*, which is a term so wide as to include even prose formulae; it might be applied

to a tragedy, though the regular word is *fabula*, and Cicero
actually uses it of a tragic *canticum*; nor do I stress the fact
that the name is *Neleus*, though critics tell us that the work
is an imitation of the *Tyro* of Sophocles. Such changes of
name, though comparatively rare, are not unknown. But
the form seems decisive. When the name of the principal
character appears in the title it is regularly in the nominative
case, and it is inconceivable that any play imitated from the
Tyro could bear any name but *Tyro* or *Neleus*. Cannot we
conclude that the poem really was what its title would imply,
and what we might infer from the fact that it is nearly always
mentioned in company with the *Odyssey* and the *Bellum
Punicum*, namely, a narrative poem—in Saturnians? The
fragments show that this is not impossible:

(1) *Nunquam numero matri faciemus uolup.*
(2) *Foede stupreque castigor cottidie.*
(3) *Strigores exerciti.*
(4) *Saucia puer sumam.*
(5) *Topper fortunae commutantur hominibus.*

The first is too short for a *senarius*, but is as it stands a
perfectly good Saturnian of Lindsay's type A with less common
variant of the second hemistich (see *Am. J. P.* XIV. 1893).
Mere fragments like (3) and (4) prove nothing. Of the first
half of (2) we may say that *Foéde stupréque castígor* is equivalent to *Quáre lubéns-te in-grémium* (allowing the 'half elision'
tĕ in and the resolution of – into ◡ ◡ which makes *castigor*
equivalent to the word-group *in-gremium*); the addition of
a two-syllable word such as *miser* would give a conclusion of
a familiar type like *fortissimos uiros*. If we could suppose a
possible *four*-syllable second colon no addition would be
required. And the possibility is suggested by two lines in
Livius—*Carnís uinúmque quod-líbant | ánclabátur* (which
seems a better division than *carnis uinumque quod | libant*

anclabatur with its separation of the natural word-group
quod-libant); and *Átque éscas habeámus | méntiónem* (where
rursus is usually supplied on the supposition that the line is
a translation of *Od.* IV. 213). But it may equally well be from
Od. X. 177, where there is no ἐξαῦτις. The first of these is
practically identical, both accentually and quantitatively, with
our (4). No. (5) is also Saturnian if we recognise it as the
end of one line and the beginning of another. The conclusion
is like *Eorum sectam sequontur | multi mortales*, the beginning
like *Aut in Pylum deueniens | aut ibi ommentans*. The generally
iambic run of the lines is no bar to their being in reality
Saturnian. In fact, the opening half of the line nearly always
gives an effect quite definitely iambic; and in the few cases
in which we have consecutive lines preserved, there is an
actual majority where the end of one line read continuously
with the beginning of the next will give an iambic at least as
good as *Topper fortunae commutantur hominibus*. Some lines,
indeed, are actually iambic as they stand: *e.g. Transit Melitam
Romanus insulam integram*; and a very large number become
trimeters if they are shorn of a single word or a single syllable.
Indeed Diomedes defines a Saturnian as an iambic trimeter
plus an extra syllable. There is then no good ground for
declaring that these fragments must be iambics; and so the
only justification for calling the poem a tragedy disappears.
As a narrative poem, even if it were translated from some
Greek original, it would stand on the same footing as the
Latin *Odyssey*; if it was in truth inspired by the *Tyro*, the
conception of turning a tragedy into a narrative poem would
be so bold as to make it essentially an original creation. One
last suggestion may be appended. In Servius' note on *Aen.*
II. 486 it is stated that the whole passage is taken over *de
Albano excidio*. The editors assume the reference to be to an
episode of the *Annales* of Ennius. The sack was, of course,

described by him (cf. note on II. 18); but I suggest that Servius is speaking of an independent poem. The form of his note is very unusual; we should expect his ordinary *Ennianus est locus* or *de Ennio* if the original were really the *Annales*, and *Albanum Excidium* looks like a title. Moreover, there is no traceable imitation of the *Annales* in the passage; the only Ennian reminiscence is of the famous lament of Andromache. Hence it is possible to see in 'The Sack of Alba' another product of the ballad school.

BOOK VIII

FR. I. The magnificence of the tribute paid by Horace to the first two lines of our fragment is universally realised; but we must not forget what a large body of heroic verse was already in circulation when the first book of the *Satires* was produced. Gallus must have been busy at the time, and Varius was already famous as a master of epic (*Sat.* I. 10. 55), so that, apart from minor writers, there was much material on which to draw. Yet Horace turns to the *Annales* for an illustration of the essential qualities of great poetry. I follow Norden (*Ennius und Vergilius*, pp. 8 ff.) in adding the last two lines (which are generally referred to Minerva or left uncertain) and understanding them as a description of *Discordia*; as he rightly argues *par* is the emphatic word. The 'four elements' of Empedocles are all present, but in a monstrous and unnatural combination, for ὑπερβολή, 'the excess of one over another,' is the essential condition of separate existence. *Discordia* is thus not that Νεῖκος or Ἔρις which is the real creative force of the universe; she is an incarnation of chaos, and her coming wrecks the world. In this conception Norden sees the influence of Pythagoreanism and neo-Platonic ideas; but its boldness and its truth combine to commend it to the poet. I further agree with Norden that, after the fine and impressive opening, the vivid but homely realism of the *pellitur e medio sapientia* passage, which is usually placed immediately after our first two lines, is intolerable; and that *Discordia* must be emphasised as a personal agency. Hence the elaborate description in the two lines which Norden adds. I differ from him, however, in retaining the fragment in Bk VIII, where most editors place it, and in arranging the lines as I have shown them. I suppose the picture to be of *Discordia*, who has been confined *within* the gates during the interval of peace, suddenly breaking out and leaving them flung open wide: cf. *Aen.* I. 293 ff.

taetra: 'horrible,' from the unnatural manner in which the *corpus Tartarinum* is built up.

Belli...portas: the traditional name of the two doors of Janus' temple in the Forum; cf. Plutarch, *Num.* xx. For the legend see Ovid, *Fasti*, I. 252 ff., Macrobius I. 9. 17. The specific reference is to the opening at the outbreak of the Second Punic war, after the gates had been closed for the second time in Roman history.

Corpore Tartarino: Festus quotes the explanation of Verrius Flaccus—*horrendo et terribili uult accipi*.

paluda: dressed in the *paludamentum*, *i.e.* equipped for war; cf. Varro, *L.L.* VII. 37. For the form cf. the use of *citus* beside *citatus*, *praetextus* beside *praetextatus*, etc.

FR. 2. The civil population in time of war.

In Cicero's *pro Murena* the quotation is introduced by the words *proeliis promulgatis* which I place in the text, believing (with Baehrens) that they belong to Ennius. I do not, however, accept his *si sunt proelia promulgata*, for it is at least possible that *proeli(i)s promulgatis* can form the end of a hexameter without change. *Proeli(i)s* may appear as a spondee as *Iunis* does in Bk IV. fr. 3 (cf. note ad loc.); in that case we

should probably write *proelis*. The meaning of the phrase
seems to be 'when news of battle is received.' *Promulgare*
is a publicist's term, used constantly with *legem* and *roga-
tionem*, and the literal sense is 'to make known publicly.'

orator bonus: the adjective is emphatic; it is not merely
the *orator odiosus...et loquax* who is despised when the man
of action alone is valued.

horridus: the meaning is 'blunt' or 'uncouth.'

doctis dictis: the elaborate rhetoric of the courts.

inimicitiām: note the quantity which is not reduced by the
hiatus. Probably the *ām* is due to the incidence of the *ictus
metricus*, though the *ā* of the accusative in *a* stems naturally
had the long vowel of the nominative originally (on the
general question cf. note on Bk III. fr. 2). Hiatus is undoubtedly permitted in Ennius, though we do not know the
rules which govern it, and therefore I retain the MSS. reading;
for an opposite view see Valmaggi.

ex iure manum: Gellius praises Ennius for accuracy in the
use of legal technicalities: the phrase is derived from the
'joint seizure' employed in property cases, and is found in
the Twelve Tables as well as in legal formulas in Cicero and
elsewhere: cf. also Varro, *L.L.* VI. 64.

consertum: the supine construction is due to the thought
of the regular phrase *uocare consertum*.

Rem repetunt: because the legal process was used especially
in cases of disputed ownership.

regnumque petunt: means little more than 'try to get the
better of others.'

solida: the meaning is akin to that of Horace's *solida mens*
(*Od.* III. 3. 4), 'determined.'

FR. 3. I accept Baehrens' *duplex* for the meaningless *dubius*
of the MS.; but I arrange the words as parts of two hexameters. This seems the simplest remedy, and the fact that

duplex and *dubius* may be synonyms in some senses probably caused the corruption. The subject is evidently Hannibal as contrasted with Pyrrhus, and the present passage may have done much to create the legend of his *perfidia*.

duplex: 'treacherous' or 'wily' as in Catullus LXVIII. 51: cf. the note of Robinson Ellis ad loc.

FR. 4. The line is usually referred to the expedition of Hamilcar Rhodanus which is described in the text of Orosius; it is therefore made part of the *Primordia Carthaginis*, and placed in Bk VII. This is not impossible, but the episode seems hardly one that Ennius would describe (unless indeed he made it the occasion for a character sketch of Alexander himself, which is unlikely). I suggest therefore that the reference may be either to Pyrrhus or Hannibal and so place the fragment here, supposing it to have stood near the last. They are quoted very close together in the St Gall Orosius.

potesset: the old Latin form which was ousted by *posset*, a form that seems to have arisen from the analogy of *possum* (*pot(e)sum*) beside *potis sum* and *possim* beside *potis-sim*.

FR. 5. The attempts of Aemilius Paullus to dissuade Varro from accepting battle: cf. Livy XXII. 44 ff., Sil. IX. 38 ff. The time is the eve of Cannae.

I accept Müller's *praecoca*, as the words of Nonius clearly suggest that he is illustrating the use of the form *praecocus* beside the ordinary *praecox*.

praecoca: *immatura* Nonius; regularly the word means 'ripening early.'

FR. 6. *abnueo*: the opposite of *adnueo* used of Curiatius.

FR. 7. *conficit*: 'brings to accomplishment'; the meaning is 'success can be rapidly achieved.' The Vergilian reminiscence has *rettulit in melius* (*Aen.* XI. 425 ff.). Probably Varro is the speaker.

FR. 8. The battle of Cannae. For the cloud of dust cf. Livy XXII. 46.

puluīs: a 'metrical' lengthening due to the *ictus*, as in *Aen.* 1. 478.

FR. 9. A charge of heavy cavalry (*summo sonitu*), perhaps the main Carthaginian body under Hasdrubal which charged early, and chased the weak Roman right wing up the river.

FR. 10. *obstipum*: *obliquum* Festus. Livy too speaks of *sol...obliquus*, and, as he states that the position of the sun was convenient (*peropportune*) for both parties, *exaugere* must describe a good result. Perhaps Valmaggi's conjecture of *uires* for the object may be right.

FR. 11. The infantry engagement.

Hastati: in its technical sense of 'front-line troops.' Verg. *Aen.* VIII. 596 is modelled on our line.

FR. 12. *Densantur*: cf. the notorious line *Sparsis hastis longis campus splendet et horret*, itself, perhaps, a description of Cannae. The reference of this and the previous fragment is probably to the stand of the Roman infantry under Servilius. They had penetrated deep into the enemy centre but were caught by a double attack from the Libyans (after defeating Gallic and Spanish troops) and so compelled to stand in a dangerously crowded mass.

FR. 13. The mutilation of the wounded on the field; cf. Livy XXII. 51. 7.

perna: for the regular *poples*, does not seem to be used elsewhere of human beings.

superbia Poeni: a more emphatic form of *Poeni, homines superbi*, as in Livy's familiar *montium altitudines* of the Alps. The use of the singular in a collective sense is characteristic of Ennius. *Superbia* is coupled with *inhumanitas* by Cicero (*de Or.* I. 22. 99) and with *crudelitas* by Livy (VIII. 33. 11).

The quality was especially odious to the Roman from its association with the typical *rex*.

FR. 14. The fourth consulship of the Cunctator.

pater: a title of honour belonging properly to gods and heroes of antiquity. Gellius again praises Ennius for accuracy in preserving the distinction between *quartum* (for the fourth time) and *quarto* (in the fourth place). To judge by Pompey's perplexity over *tertium* and *tertio*, and Cicero's advice to write *tert*. and so be safe, the distinction was not always appreciated.

FR. 15. The siege of Capua.

The form *Opscus* (or *Obscus*) has not yet been 'reduced' to *Oscus* by the loss of the first consonant (due to the difficulty in pronouncing the group).

FR. 16. Hannibal's night march on Rome, a ruse to relieve the siege.

Ob: its range of meaning is much wider in early than in classical Latin: *circum*, *ad* and *iuxta* are attested.

noctu: used simply as an adverb here.

FR. 17. The fall of Capua.

Summus: evidently the two magistrates were not equal, but stood in the relation of Consul and Praetor (*Imperium maius* and *minus*).

meddix: the native name of the chief magistrate of the Campanians (cf. Livy XXVI. 3, where the full title *Med(d)ix Tuticus* is given). The word is a Latinisation of the Oscan *Meddiss*, root *med madh*, 'to be wise'; for the meaning cf. *med-icus*, *med-eri*, μέδοντες. The second element represents *dic* (*dicere*) as in *iu-dex*; cf. Conway, *Italic Dialects*, II. 633. With reference to the fall of Capua, the *Meddix* who was captured was Seppius Lesius.

FR. 18. I agree with those editors who place the fragment here. Evidently the Second Punic war marked a crisis in the divine attitude towards the growing power of Rome; in particular its latter stages brought to an end the hostility of Juno. This change must have been described by Ennius; cf. Servius ad *Aen.* I. 281 and also Propertius III. 29. But I cannot accept the suggestion that there was a formal 'Council of the Gods' in this book. There is no real evidence for anything more than a single council, and that must be placed in Bk I. The speech of Jove recorded by Servius (ad *Aen.* I. 20) contained, indeed, a promise of the destruction of Carthage, but it need not therefore belong to Bk VIII; the example of Vergil shows that there is no difficulty in the combination of a promise, which is to take immediate effect, and a prophecy referring to the remote future. In Bk I Juno so far relents as to agree to the deification of Romulus; but active co-operation does not begin till the period of the Second Punic war: *Coepit placata fauere* as the result of a special plea to her alone (see further below). The insistence of the editors that there must have been two councils at least seems to rest ultimately on the idea that (1) Jove's promise of destruction to Carthage must have been more or less contemporary with the event, (2) Juno's consent to the deification of Romulus was in reality the same event as that described by Servius. The first of these conceptions has been already briefly discussed. With regard to the second we may observe that even in Horace (*Od.* III. 3), our capital text on the matter of Juno's speech, her promise deals with the deification only, and, far from indicating the direct protection implied by *fauere*, holds out a clear threat of reprisals should there be any attempt to restore Troy. Moreover, the language throughout makes it plain that the sack of Troy is only just accomplished (*Nec iam Lacaenae e.q.s.*). There is further more than a hint that Romulus himself is still the grandson of Aeneas (in the emphatically placed *nepotem*, still more in *Troica sacerdos* and *auitae...Troiae*); yet his deification is to take place *protinus*. We are therefore still close to the sack of Troy. The second part of the speech does no more than permit the growth of Rome with the very emphatic proviso indicated above. The extraordinary emphasis placed upon the condition has been explained by the suggestion that Augustus actually entertained a scheme for refounding Troy. But there is little doubt that the condition was traditional, and Ennius' narrative may have led up to the change in Juno by a description of some incident which showed that Troy would never be reborn. The small expedition against Istria, undertaken in 221 B.C. with the object of destroying the last lurking-places of the pirates and linking up Roman possessions on both sides of the Adriatic, was bound to involve operations passing right through the district called *pagus Troianus* (see Livy I. 13). A possibility, therefore, is that some town bearing the name of Antenor's *Troia* suffered or was destroyed at that time, and its fate may have 'appeased the wrath of Juno.' This is, however, very problematical; but our general conclusion may fairly be that our line introduces, not a speech in a formal council, but a prayer to Juno, one of the *pia uota* of which Propertius speaks. We may further find in it and the next fragment a uniquely interesting reference to the hymn composed *Ad Iunonem Reginam* in 207 B.C. by the veteran pioneer Livius Andronicus[1]. In this attempt to expiate the evil omens which had terrified the people, literature was for the first time officially recognised and poets for the first time received a substantial reward in the foundation of the famous but little understood *Collegium Poetarum*. In his description of the events of 207, Ennius can hardly have failed to refer to the work of his brother poet who may have died in the very year in which he came to Rome, and with whose *Collegium* his residence on the Aven-

[1] If he was really the author of the Hymn, which has been doubted.

tine must have familiarised him. Hence, I suggest that the next fragment has the hymn of Livius for its subject (cf. note ad loc.).

Saturnia: used also as a name for Italy, Bk 1. fr. 16.

magna dearum: cf. note on Bk 1. fr. 10.

FR. 19. The hymn of Livius. The words themselves may well form part of the prayer introduced by the previous fragment, the unique service offered at the moment being put forward as an additional claim to Juno's favour.

Tibia: because the hymn was sung *cum tibicine* like the ancient songs at banquets.

Musarum: depends on *melos*, not, as all the editors seem to take it, on *tibia*. Pascoli mistranslates *Il.* 1. 602 ff. to support his view that the line describes a banquet on Olympus; and, apart from Euterpe, the Muses when they play use a *barbiton* or some other form of the lyre.

pangit: usually of the author, here by a natural transference of the instrument that marks the tune.

melos: is a transliteration of the Greek μέλος; it does not occur elsewhere in Ennius, but Nonius quotes it from a number of early writers including Naevius, Accius and Pacuvius: the phrase *Musarum m.* means simply 'melodious song.'

FR. 20. I accept this line from Hug who restores it by a very slight re-arrangement of words from Servius ad *Aen.* 1. 281.

FR. 21. Scipio's camp in Africa. I suggest that the change of scene was made the occasion of a further discussion of the antecedents and character of the Carthaginians, to which I refer both this and the next fragment. They may be the remains of a speech from Scipio to his men, the connection of thought being 'the stock springs from Dido'; therefore the people are effeminate (*tunicata*) and will never endure a war in their own country. Or the picture may be that of the exultation among the civil population in Rome.

Didone oriundi: the gerundive is used in a purely adjectival sense.

FR. 22. The contemptuous sense attested by Gellius shows that the garment in question was the *manicata* (long-sleeved tunic): cf. the contrast elaborated by Vergil, *Aen.* IX. 603 ff.

FR. 23. The 'sham fights' by which the Romans kept themselves in training: cf. Excursus I.

FR. 24. I suggest that the reference is not to the incident described by Livy (XXII. 30. 4), but to the attack made by Scipio in the spring of 203 on the two camps of the Carthaginians and Numidians (under Syphax). His previously-made insincere proposals of peace had lulled the enemy into temporary security, hence perhaps the relaxed discipline of *uino domiti*; the attack was made at night, hence *somno sepulti*. That very strong phrase is repeated by Lucretius V. 974, and also by Vergil, *Aen.* II. 265.

FR. 25. *occasus*: *occasio* Festus; as in Bk V. fr. I and Bk II. fr. 10.

audere: used as a noun (= *audaciam*) governed by *repressit*.

APPENDIX TO BOOK VIII

FR. 26. The words of Cicero make it practically certain that Ennius is the author, but he is not named. Hence I place the fragment in the appendix. The speaker is Hannibal, and the occasion either the battle of the Ticinus (where a similar speech is made in Livy) or Cannae (as in Silius Italicus).

I retain the *erit...siet* of the MSS. and punctuate with a strong stop after the second *erit*[1]. The widely accepted *siet... siet* of Merula assumes that the clauses are parallel in construction; but the first (*erit*) is taken closely with the first line and the tense is accommodated to *feriet* and *erit* there. *Siet* is an

---

[1] This reading is retained also in Vahlen's second edition.

indirect question depending on some verb now lost. The connection of thought is '(I will not stop to ask) of what country he be: all have an equal chance.'

quoiatis: introduces an indirect question in Plautus, *Men.* 341 and Accius ap. Non. p. 427. 17 Lind. The suffix *atis* appears in words like *optimatis*, *Arpinatis* (later *Arpinas*) and *sanatis* quoted by Festus from the Twelve Tables and meaning revolted allies who returned *quasi sanata mente*.

BOOK IX

FR. 1. The assumption of uncertainty with which Cicero introduces the lines was one of the reasons which led Müller to place them in Bk x, supposing, as he did, that all the events of the Second Punic war after the death of Hasdrubal belonged to that book. His arguments were:

(1) The account of the Second Punic war must have been much fuller and more detailed than anything which preceded it, not merely from the importance of the war itself, but because of the admiration felt by Ennius for its leading personalities, especially Scipio.

(2) If we place the Macedonian war in Bk x there is no material for Bk xii.

(3) None of the surviving fragments of Bk x need refer to the Macedonian war.

(4) The lines *Aegro corde comis passis late palmis pater* and *Et simul erubuit seu lacte et purpura mixta*, which certainly belong to Bk x, must refer to Sophonisba. The only one of these arguments which carries any real weight is (1). But the division which I suggest, that Bk viii included everything up to the recall of Hannibal to Africa, would allow the admiration which Ennius undoubtedly felt for Scipio even greater scope to display itself. Bk ix could then be devoted

entirely to the triumph of Scipio in Africa and his victorious
return, the hero's *Aristeia* in fact, covering much the same
ground as the *Scipio* and serving, perhaps, as a rough draft
for it. In support of this view I may suggest the interpretations of Bk VIII. frs. 23 and 24 already given, which carry
the contents of Bk VIII certainly down to the last stages of
the war. Further Cicero's *in nono, ut opinor, annali* implies
no real uncertainty but is merely a dramatic touch to give
the dialogue the air of real conversation. With regard to (2)
we may note that Bk XII is one of the most fragmentary books
and we know practically nothing of what it contained (see
further in notes ad loc.). In any case, individual books may
have varied as much in length as do the books of the *Aeneid*.
(3) is untrue, as *Leucatam campsant* refers to the expedition
of M. Valerius Laevinus; and the fragments mentioned in
(4) may be explained in other ways: cf. notes ad loc. I assume,
therefore, that Bk IX began with, or immediately before, the
recall of Hannibal. I accept Müller's transposition *Tuditano
conlega* for the MSS. *conlega Tuditano*, which involves not
merely the scansion *conlegā*, but also the wrong quantity
Tŭdĭtano for *Tūdĭtano*. In any case the line has a defective
caesura, excused, perhaps, by the difficulty of dealing with
proper names. The two men mentioned were consuls in 204;
here the reference seems to be to some legation or mission,
perhaps in connection with the peace negotiations entered
upon in 203.

Corneliŭs Marcŭs: for the postponement of the *praenomen*
cf. Bk x. fr. 3.

Tuditanus: the name is derived from *tudites*, an old word
for *mallei*; cf. Ateius Philologus quoted by Festus, p. 480.
1 Lind. Like so many other Roman names it is derived from
a physical peculiarity.

ollis: for the form cf. Varro, *L.L.* VII. 42, where *olla cen-*

turia and *ollus leto datus est* (used at funerals) are quoted: cf. Macrobius III. 9. 10 (*ollis legibus*). Cicero uses *olli ollis olla ollos* in the *de Legibus*, doubtless owing to their legal associations. Lucretius has *ollis*, Vergil and later epic poets *olli, ollis* (the only forms found in Ennius). *Olli* is mentioned by Quintilian (VIII. 3. 25) with *quianam, moerus, pone* (all from Ennius) and *porricerent* as words which lend an antique grace and dignity to the style of Vergil.

Suadaeque medulla: 'the marrow of persuasion'; a fine descriptive phrase, despite the strictures of Seneca which so roused the wrath of Gellius. *Suada*, for the more ordinary *Suadela* (Πειθώ), is really the feminine of the adjective *suadus*.

FR. 2. It is most probable that the reference is to the Roman army after Zama.

undat: used for *abundat* as the Scholium says; cf. also Val. Fl. 1. 539.

FR. 3. The fragment is best referred to the resumption of Italian agriculture, one of the most obvious and important manifestations of the national relief at the withdrawal of Hannibal.

dentiferos: I accept this for the meaningless *dentefabres* of the MSS. The *rastrum* was a heavy rake called *quadridens* by Cato.

capsit: either the (sigmatic) 'aorist optative,' or, more probably, a real future perfect: cf. Paul. e Fest. p. 57 M. We find also *accepso* and *incepsit* as well as *axim* (see next fragment), *taxim, insexit*, etc.

causa poliendi agri: suggests that the fields were *non politi*, i.e. rough and overgrown from neglect. *Polire*, properly meaning 'to rub smooth,' is the *uox propria* for 'to put into a state of (high) cultivation.' Varro uses *politus cultura fundus*, and Cato *politio*.

FR. 4. The textual problem of this line is greatly complicated by the uncertain reading in Nonius himself. Accepting

Lindsay's *perpetuassit, sit perpetua, aeterna*, I follow him in reading *perpetuassit* for the usual *perpetuassint* of the editors, which has been accepted owing to a failure to realise that Nonius is illustrating the *intransitive* use of the word which, rare in any case, is usually transitive. *Perpetua* is fem. sing., not neut. pl. as Müller seems to have thought, and is due to the gender of *libertatem*. *Libertatem* itself is governed by some word now lost. On the form *axim* cf. previous note. The whole fragment may well be from Scipio's prayer at the ratification of peace.

Fr. 5. Evidently a fragment of a speech, but our knowledge is not great enough to determine either the speaker or the occasion.

quid: 'to what purpose.'

Dictum factumque: *Prouerbium celeritatis* Donatus ad Ter. *Andr*. 381. It corresponds to the Greek ἅμ' ἔπος ἅμ' ἔργον or the English 'no sooner said than done,' and the colloquialism is probably deliberately introduced to give the effect of real speech.

frux: *pro frugi homo* Priscian. Cf. Bk XVI. fr. 7 for another meaning.

Fr. 6. The famous reminiscence in Lucretius (III. 1032) suggests that here too the reference may be to Scipio. But any reference to the death of Scipio, which is the subject in Lucretius, is quite impossible here from the date no less than from the tragic circumstances in which it took place. Ennius cannot have darkened the picture of his hero's triumph by any hint of what was to come. If there is any reference at all to Scipio, the only possibility is that the line forms part of a speech addressed by Hannibal to him, warning him not to rely on the permanence of fortune's favours. This seems to be the view of the editors (except Müller), but against it I suggest the difficulty of the tense of *reddidit* (unless, indeed, we suppose it to be a 'gnomic perfect'). A further difficulty is the exceedingly strong phrase *e summo regno*. I therefore suggest that the reference is to the plight of Hannibal, either after Zama, or more probably after the negotiations of 195, when the man who had been practically dictator was compelled to withdraw from his native city, his property was confiscated, his house razed to the ground, and he himself became a hanger-on at the court of Antiochus, to all appearance as dependent on his whims as was the lowest of his slaves. Ennius may have included the episode from a feeling that the removal of Hannibal was the real end of the war; or he may have referred to it by anticipation as a proof of the fine character of Scipio, who made an indignant protest in the Senate against the hounding down of his great adversary.

famul: a latinisation of the Oscan *famel* (= *fam-las*), 'a dweller': cf. the note on Bk VIII. fr. 17.

oltimus: should certainly be read; the correction is very slight, and, though the form is not elsewhere found, it is but another instance of the interchange of *ŏ* and *ŭ* before *l* combined with another consonant.

FR. 7. It is impossible to do more than state that the fragment describes fighting. Valmaggi very curiously prints it twice, once in its proper place in Bk IX with Dousa's reading, which is that given by me, once in Bk VII with Havet's *Illyria*.

FR. 8. For the gender of *puluis* cf. Bk VIII. fr. 8. Again the reference is too vague to make discussion profitable.

FR. 9. I place this fragment here, supposing the reference to be to the indemnity paid by Carthage. Varro does not imply that the meaning is 'made payment to the mercenary troops,' as is sometimes assumed. His point is merely that the use of the word *stipendia* in the sense of money payment shows its derivation from *stips*.

Fr. 10. It does not seem possible to determine the reference of this and the next fragments.

Debil: may be another case of Oscan influence, and the form may be modelled on such words as *aidil* = *aedilis*.

Fr. 11. It is possible that we should read *lucinorum* here as Ritschl suggested. Such 'parasitic vowels' were a marked feature of Oscan and may therefore have come with special readiness to Ennius; the insertion of *i* in the group *c(h)n* can be exactly paralleled by such instances as *tec(h)ina*, *cucinus* and *Procina*.

Fr. 12. Hug rightly calls this curious simile *non adeo uenusta*, but it is impossible to guess to what it was applied.

BOOK X

Fr. 1. The Hannibalic war was in a sense the climax of the *Annales* and the centre of interest for Ennius. The new war, therefore, was introduced with a certain amount of elaboration to prevent any flagging from being apparent to the reader; hence the separate prologue with which the book opened.

Insece: imperative of the archaic *inseco(-quo)* which shows the same root as *inquam* (*in-s-quam*); cf. Greek ἔννεπε from ἔν-σ-επε (cf. ἐνισπεῖν). Paul. e Fest. p. 111 Lind. attributes to Ennius the form *inseque*, but Gellius quotes the authority of Velius Longus in support of the form *insece*.

manu: tempting as Müller's *mihi* is, we must retain the MSS. *manu*. There is no variant and the word can be translated and explained. Probably both *manu* and *induperator* are constructed with *Romanorum*, 'the deeds each Roman general did with his citizen band.'

Fr. 2. The best MSS. of Priscian give the specific reference to Bk x.

Leucatam: Vahlen is undoubtedly correct in restoring the latinised form, which is regular in such names in Ennius. The reference is to the expedition of M. Valerius Corvinus, one of the incidents of the First Macedonian war: cf. Livy XXVI. 26.

campsant: the word may be an actual Greek derivative as Priscian suggests, belonging to an early Mediterranean *lingua Franca*, but it is best regarded as an intensive form from the root *camp*. Greek κάμπτω would naturally become **campto*, not *campso*. In any case, the word belongs to sailors' *argot*.

FR. 3. The Sextus Aelius here mentioned was consul in 198.

cordatus: does not seem to occur elsewhere except in Seneca (*Apoc.*)—*pulchre cordatus*. Lactantius uses *cordatior* and Plautus has *cordate* several times. The meaning is derived from the use of *cor* for the seat of the intellect.

catus: the meaning of this word was disputed even in the time of Varro. He insists that the meaning is not *sapiens* but *acutus*, which he illustrates by *I.S.* fr. 31. He is strictly correct etymologically; the word is from the root $k\bar{o}$ (cf. *cos*). Other writers, however, accept the meaning *sapiens*; *e.g.* Pliny, *N.H.* VII. 118 and Plutarch, *Cato*, I. That Ennius' description suits the character of the man appears from Cicero, *de Rep.* I. 18.

FR. 4. The fact that the number 8000 appears in the fragment has led most editors to refer it to the landing of Flamininus in Corcyra: cf. Livy XXXII. 9. But the great stress laid on the picked character of the troops and their special equipment rather suggests that they were life-guards attached to the person of Philip.

Insignita: either 'wearing a special uniform' or 'with special badges.' Caesar (*B.G.* VII. 45) speaks of *insignia militaria*, which seems to mean badges on the helmets of the officers; cf. Bk XVI. fr. 22, where the singular *insigne* is used.

militum octo: the hiatus bears out the remark of Priscian that syllables ending in *m* were not always elided; cf. Bk VIII. fr. 2.

tolerare: = *patienter ferre*; as before.

FR. 5. The night march of Flamininus. Evidently the nights were especially bright while it was in progress; cf. Livy XXXII. 19.

apta: Ennius' favourite and beautiful description of the night sky.

FR. 6. The second *horitur* of Diomedes is clearly wrong, hence I accept Hug's *horitatur*, rather than the ordinary *hortatur*, which could not have been so corrupted. From the form **horiri* we should naturally expect the iterative *horitari* corresponding to *factitare* from *facere*, *uentitare* from *uenire*, etc. Valmaggi's arrangement of the words should be followed, as to place them together at the end of the line would involve *horitatūr*, the only case of *ūr* without 'metrical justification.' The line refers to the speech of Flamininus before the battle of Cynoscephalae; cf. Livy XXXIII. 8.

FR. 7. The anxiety of Flamininus before the battle. He may well have had in mind such incidents as the mutiny at Apollonia (199) caused by the widespread resentment at the outbreak of the new war and the failure of the government to keep its pledge with regard to voluntary recruiting.

FR. 8. I accept the *uelox* of Turnebius.

Scaliger's *Sicuti si* was adopted in Vahlen's first edition and may be right; it introduces a simile in *I.S.* fr. 79. Turnebius' *ueluti quando*, however, involves less change. In the next line I retain the MS. *solet* in place of the widely accepted *dolet* of Baehrens, but accept the *feras* added by C. O. Müller. I can, however, feel no confidence that the lines are thus restored to correctness.

nictīt: *leuiter gannit*, 'whines'; *-īt* with 'metrical justification,' as before. The simile most probably belongs to a description of impatient troops.

FR. 9. Another much disputed line. The text of Nonius offers no variant—*Ennius Annalium*, lib. x. *Aegro corde comis passis late palmis pater*: there have been various attempts to make a hexameter of these words but they are all too far from the MSS. or give an absurd meaning like Merula's *comas passis palmis lacerantes*, or Ilberg's *comis late passis palmisque*, which approaches the grotesque. I suggest that the error centres in the word *comis*. A glance at the context in Nonius shows that he has already dealt with the meanings of *passus* (*dispersus, solutus*) in which it might be applied to *comae* and has given two examples; he then passes on to the meaning *extensus, patens*, which applies to *palmae* but not at all to *comae*, and the note after the Ennius quotation shows clearly that it is intended to illustrate this sense only: *Passis ait palmis patentibus et extensis*. I suggest that *comis* should be omitted in this place, as being due to a mistaken reminiscence of the previous section, and that the word it displaced was *pater*, which was added at the end of the quotation when its loss was discovered. I further suggest that *pater* is not vocative as the editors seem invariably to assume, but nominative, and that the reference is to the protests or farewells of a father whose son had been included among the hostages demanded by Flamininus after the battle of Cynoscephalae. We might therefore restore (with *pater* in its proper place where *comis* now stands): *aegro Corde pater passis late palmis ⟨lacrumatus⟩*. Valmaggi, without, however, adducing the above reasons, also suggests that the error lies in *comis*; but his proposed *comes* does not seem readily intelligible. His further remark, however, that with the removal of *comis* all necessity to refer the fragment to a woman disappears, is perfectly sound; and with it also disappears all justification

for Müller's assumption that the line deals with Sophonisba
and that therefore the narrative of the Second Punic war was
continued into Book x.

FR. 10. Müller finds in these words a reference to the
Carthaginian envoys asking for peace either from Scipio or
before the senate. The word *pinso* is, however, ridiculously
strong for any such explanation; cf. Varro, *L.L.* v. 138.
I suggest that the description is of men scrambling over rough
ground (such as was often encountered during the Macedonian wars) on hands and knees.

FR. 11. Yet another fragment of very doubtful reading.
I accept Scaliger's *iam summouere columnam* which seems
closest to the MSS.; this necessitates the change of *uersatum*
(which might otherwise be supine) to *uersatam*. The reference
may be to a general description of the battle of Cynoscephalae
from the Macedonian point of view or, more probably, to a
lament of a Macedonian patriot (perhaps King Philip himself) that the prince Demetrius had been handed over as a
hostage to Rome. The line may have stood close to the *aegro
corde* passage above.

FR. 12. On the form, specifically attested for this place
by Macrobius, cf. note on Bk I. fr. 5 above.

APPENDIX TO BOOK X

FR. 13. Müller is most probably right in referring this
line to Ennius, though Isidore gives no exact reference of
any sort. If so, it must belong to the beginning of Bk x;
cf. Livy XXXI. 5.

FR. 14[1]. This, with the second and third fragments in the
appendix, is to be referred to the episode of the shepherd sent

---

[1] It seems best to place this fragment in the appendix, as the definite
attribution to Ennius rests on the authority of a single MS. of Donatus:
cf. *Mus. Rh.* LII. p. 80.

by King Charopus, in virtue of his private understanding
with Rome, to act as guide to Flamininus; cf. Livy XXXII. 11.
The reference was first established by Madvig (*Op.* II. 291).

adiuero: the same shortening is found in both Plautus and
Terence, and perfects without *u* were frequently used in the
time of Cicero; cf. *Orat.* XLVII. 157.

leuasso: the form corresponds to *faxo* (*fac-so*), etc.; a similar
collocation of future perfect forms is found in Plaut. *Capt.*
695 and *Fr.* 62 W.

coquit: the homely metaphor suits the speaker, but it is
found several times in Vergil and at least once in Catullus.

uersāt: as before with 'metrical excuse.'

FR. 15. This fragment and the next are almost certainly
intended by Cicero as quotations from Ennius and should
be understood of the shepherd guide. The present line may
be part of a speech by the shepherd himself, or it may be the
reply of Charopus to the enquiries of Flamininus; cf. Livy
XXXII. 11. 2. With the latter explanation it should be placed
after the other line.

FR. 16. The speech of the shepherd. The accusative and
infinitive construction may depend on some such phrase as
C(h)aropus compertit, suggested by Vahlen, or it may be used
absolutely as a question or exclamation.

BOOK XI

FR. 1. There is no good ground for refusing to believe that
quippe bears the meaning *quidni* assigned to it both here and
in Bk XVI. fr. 1. The word is formed of the particle *pe* (cf.
nempe) appended to the neuter singular of the pronoun, which
is either indefinite or interrogative. The interrogative force
appears in the Plautine *quippini*, but the shorter form is used
in our line for metrical reasons. The line probably belongs to

some general reflections on the changed attitude and manners which his defeat at Cynoscephalae must bring to Philip.

FR. 2. The speech of the victorious Flamininus, made when he proclaimed 'the freedom of Greece' at the Isthmian games of 196. The text is very uncertain. Festus refers to the passage twice; the second time he gives the first line in full, but with the names *Graios, Graecos* in that order. The first quotation is very badly damaged, but indicates that the names should be in the order given in the text ...*cos Grai*... *memo*...It shows further that we are concerned with a name given by Ennius to the Romans. The natural inference is that the Hellenizing Flamininus chose to represent Greeks and Romans as kinsmen. For the tradition of the Greek origin of Rome cf. the *Historiae Cumanae Compositor* quoted by Festus (p. 328 L.). In the second line the gaps are too great to be filled, though no doubt *ngua* is the remains of *lingua*. Perhaps Ennius introduced some etymological play like that which connected *Roma* with ʿΡώμη.

FR. 3. Macrobius states explicitly that the lines are from a description of Troy. The fragment is generally referred to the Trojan origin of Rome and made part of the speech of Flamininus. But cf. previous note. At such a festival as that of 196 it would be untactful and injudicious in the extreme for Flamininus to claim kinship with the hereditary foes of Greece, and what we know of his Hellenic sympathies and his susceptibility to the subtle appeal of literary and artistic traditions makes it impossible to suppose that either he or Ennius can have blundered so badly. The lines certainly belong to the 'freeing of Greece' and most probably form part of a speech; but I suggest that the speaker was an independent patriot, possibly that Brachyllas who was universally known as the most decided pro-Macedonian in Greece. Our line forms the retort to the claims of Flamininus, and warns Greece to beware of that Troy which, unsubdued by a ten years' siege, was stretching out her power to enslave Greece. From the poet's point of view such an expedient would be almost essential. For dramatic reasons Ennius has, for the moment, adopted one of the many conflicting traditions of the origin of Rome. But the other, which has been elaborated earlier and which is destined, largely owing to Ennius himself, to become an article of official faith, cannot be openly contradicted or ignored. Hence the Trojan origin is effectively restated through the mouth of a speaker hostile to Flamininus.

FR. 4. I agree with those editors who suppose that the *insignes laudes* of Cato occupied a large portion of this book. He is shown active in home affairs (Frs. 4–6) and as a commander in Spain. Our present fragment is, most probably correctly, referred to his speech against the repeal of the *Lex Oppia*.

peniculamentum: *pars uestis* Nonius; the word is used also by Lucilius and Caecilius. Our line seems to be an attack on fashionable luxury in dress.

FR. 5. An outburst against those who have proposed the repeal of the law. For the masculine *malo cruce* cf. Festus (p. 150 Lind.) where the phrase is quoted from Gaius Gracchus.

crucĕ: dative. The form is probably in reality locative or instrumental and is used merely for metrical convenience as in *Aen*. x. 361 and 653 (cf. Servius ad loc.).

FR. 6. I follow Valmaggi in supposing this fragment also to be part of Cato's speech. He seems to have pointed his moral by a historical illustration drawn from the refusal of the women to accept gifts from Pyrrhus; cf. Livy XXXIV. 4. Our line, with its famous picture of a blush, may be from the description of such a scene of indignant rejection.

lacte: this old *i*-stem form is found several times in Plautus, and the intermediate stage *lact*, between it and the finally syncopated *lac*, is used by Varro, *L.L.* v. 104; cf. *G.L.K.* iv. 7. 4.

Fr. 7. Operations after the despatch of Cato to Spain. The reference is probably to the pitched battle which was necessary to overcome the revolt.

Fr. 8. Quoted by Priscian as an example of the archaic third conjugation form *resonunt*: the compound does not occur elsewhere in Ennius but the simple verb is found in both third and first conjugation forms.

clupei: the *scutum* had replaced the *clupeus* by 340 B.C. as the legionary's shield. Ennius is as a rule extremely accurate and careful in such matters; hence we must be dealing with other troops than legionaries.

Fr. 9. Perhaps a fragment of apology or excuse from a Spaniard who has failed to obey Cato's order for general disarmament. I place the fragment here, supposing that a mutilated form of the line appears in Festus (p. 362 Lind.) where it follows a quotation from Bk XI.

Fr. 10. *Alte*: means not 'high,' but 'deep,' and the picture is that of a sheer cliff from the point of view of a person on the top.

delata: should be retained.

petris...: *naturale saxum prominens in mare* Festus.

Fr. 11. Festus' text is so badly damaged at the point at which the quotation is made, that it is impossible to do more than record the single word.

BOOK XII

Fr. 1. One of the most fragmentary books in the whole body of the *Annales*. The present lines are usually, but

without justification, removed to either Bk VIII or Bk IX; but
there is no need to assume that the obvious reference to the
Cunctator was inserted in the narrative of his exploits, indeed
the last line clearly indicates a considerable lapse of time.
There may have been many references to Fabius scattered
through the latter half of the poem; one is actually preserved
in Bk XVI. fr. 24. Hence I follow the authority of Macrobius
and retain the fragment here. The phrase of laudation,
magnificent in its simplicity, was ever afterwards associated
with the great man to whom it was applied; cf. Cic. *de Sen.*
IV. 10, Livy XXV. 26. 7. The first line may well have given
rise to the *cognomen Cunctator*.

Noenum: Lachmann's almost certainly correct emendation
of the MSS. *non enim*: the latter could be explained only as
a case of 'cretic shortening,' which, doubtful in a single
word for Ennius, seems even more doubtful in a word-group
(cf. note on Bk I. fr. 5), and the unfamiliar *noenum* would
be readily corrupted.

ponebāt: a clear case of the retention of the original quantity
without 'metrical justification' for any lengthening.

FR. 2. *curatos*: for the meaning cf. the phrase *cutem curare*.

The use of *acris* (m.) should be noted. We cannot determine
the incident, though the description seems to be of bar-
barians rejoicing over a Roman defeat. If so the reference
may be to a reverse suffered by Rome in one of her annual
incursions among the Spanish tribes, such as the abandon-
ment of a camp (in 191 B.C.) with heavy losses, leading to a
retreat by means of forced marches. A further possibility
is that some portion of the book was occupied by a short
sketch of the history of the Seleucid kingdom, introduced
like the *Primordia Carthaginis* as a prologue to an important
war. Our line might refer to incidents after a victory described in the course of that narrative.

BOOK XIII

FR. 1. Hannibal with Antiochus. He is nowhere else represented as attempting to prevent a rupture with Rome, indeed his efforts were all in the opposite direction. The only possible reference for our lines is to the story told by Gellius v. 5, which, he declares, came *e libris ueterum memoriarum*.

The meaning of the lines was disputed even in the time of Gellius; the error of Casellius Vindex, in taking *quem* as an interrogative agreeing with *cor*, is repeated by Nonius, but Gellius gives the correct explanation (*quem* relative, referring to Hannibal). *Robore* seems to be used as a dative, though the form is really instrumental; cf. Bk XI. fr. 5.

FR. 2. The siege of Pergamum (190 B.C.), begun by Seleucus; cf. Livy XXXVII. 20.

moeros: the form is frequent in the Vergil MSS.; it is mentioned as one of his archaisms by Quintilian, and Servius, ad *Aen.* X. 24, XI. 382, confirms the reading *moerorum*. The well-known *oenus* = *unus* of Plautus is similar; and even when the sound had as a rule passed into *u*, *oe* was still written in certain words; *e.g. amoenus, Cloelius, foedus, moenia, oboedio, poena, Poenus*.

fauentes: is stated to mean *uolentes*.

FR. 3. An attack upon the pretended powers of the *uates* which we might expect from the author of the *Euhemerus*; cf. the well-known passages in the *Achilles,—Astrologorum signa,* etc. and the *Telamo,—Sed superstitiosi uates*, etc.

uates: = 'prophets,' the only sense in which Ennius uses the word.

uerant: *uera dicunt* Gellius.

BOOK XIV

FR. 1. The battle of Myonnesus. The engagement came very much as a surprise (see Livy XXXVII. 29) but resulted in a very decided and useful victory for Rome. Our line describes the hasty departure of the Roman fleet.

flauo: Gellius has an elaborate discussion of the correctness of this epithet in conjunction with *caeruleum* below. The latter word, meaning 'dark,' is applied to the sea-water in its natural colour; when churned up it takes on the colour described by *flauus* (greenish yellow), which is made up, according to Gellius, *e uiridi et albo*; cf. Pliny, *Epp.* VIII. 20. 4, where *albidius* and *uiridis* together are opposed to *caeruleus* in describing the water of a lake.

sale: an example of this (nom.) form is quoted by Nonius (p. 330 Lind.) from Fabius Pictor. Charisius, p. 25 K., explains the formation as like that of *mare* and *lacte*; cf. note on Bk XI. fr. 6.

FR. 2. The enemy are sighted.

ueliuolis: the word is used also by Ovid (*Ex Ponto*, IV. 5. 42) and Lucretius (V. 1442) and is sometimes applied to the sea as in *Aen.* I. 224.

FR. 3. The arrival of the Rhodian auxiliaries, whose ships seem to have been specially swift; cf. Livy XXXVII. 29. In its form and general effect the line closely resembles *I.S.* fr. 44; cf. also Vergil's *Labitur uncta uadis abies.*

uncta: the literal reference is to the caulking of the timbers, but there seems to be an additional suggestion of smoothness and speed.

FR. 4. A general description of waves breaking on the shore, or perhaps of rocks re-echoing to the noise of battle.

sonunt: for the form cf. Bk XI. fr. 8.

Fr. 5. A speech of exhortation, probably before the battle of Magnesia.

si...siue: cf. Plautus, *Stichus*, 119 and the *Rogatio* in Livy XXII. 10. 6.

Both *uiuimus* and *morīmur* are used loosely with a future sense. For the form of the latter word cf. *adgredīmur* (twice in Plautus), *adorītur* (Lucilius), etc.

Fr. 6. The battle of Magnesia.

Horrescit: a favourite figure of Ennius in this connection.

Fr. 7. *Rumpia*: the native Thracian name for a kind of weapon. Thracian auxiliaries served with the Romans at Magnesia; cf. Livy XXXVII. 39.

Fr. 8. Antiochus in defeat.

I retain the MSS. reading in place of Colonna's widely accepted *ferox*. *Fero*, agreeing with *bello*, is a perfectly natural epithet. In the second line I accept *indignum* from I. Mähly; the change is very easy and seems necessary if we retain *fero sic*. I punctuate with a stop after *bello*, and suppose that *acerbo* agreed with some word in the next line; the phrase *munere militiae* would be very appropriate.

Fr. 9. The funeral pyres which consumed the bodies of those slain at Magnesia.

obcensi: = *adcensi*. For this use of *ob* = *ad* cf. Bk VIII. fr. 16.

BOOK XV

Fr. 1. The siege of Ambracia; cf. Livy XXXVIII. 3.

Malos: the corner beams of the wooden siege towers; cf. Caesar, *B.G.* VII. 22.

tabulata: lit. 'floors.' Caesar, *B.G.* VI. 29, speaks of a *turris tabulatorum quattuor*. The word is common in the historians but rare in poetry, though it appears twice in Vergil (*Aen.* II. 464, XI. 672). The passage illustrates Ennius' accu-

racy in the use of military terms in which he had an old
soldier's interest. He was, moreover, as is well known, an
eyewitness of the Aetolian campaign.

FR. 2. The siege continued.

The 'parisyllabic' form of *lapis* should be noticed.

praecipe: an old form, resembling *bicipes* and *ancipes* also
quoted by Priscian.

FR. 3. The MSS. *arcus ubi aspiciunt* cannot be right, as
arcŭs (nom. sing.) will not stand, and *arcūs* (acc. pl.) necessitates some correction to mend the metre.

mortalibus: the construction, dative of the agent with a
present-stem tense, is remarkable at so early a date. The only
parallels are Plautus, *Rud.* 956, and Accius 283.

FR. 4. I suppose this fragment to form part of the *envoi*
of the completed *Annales* according to the original scheme.
It is quoted by Cicero without exact reference, and has been
associated by the editors with the statement in Gellius XVII.
21. 43 on the age of Ennius when he wrote a particular book
of the *Annales*. But there is absolutely no proof of any connection between the two: Cicero does not even state that
the lines belong to the *Annales*, though the style and the
heroic simile seem to make that clear. We are, therefore, free
to place the lines at whatever point seems most appropriate.
That is surely at the conclusion of a great undertaking. When
Ennius reached the end of Bk XV he believed that his poem
was completed, for we know that the last three books were
added as an afterthought. Hence the present lines, if not
actually the last, must have stood very close to the end of
Bk XV.

Vicit Olympia: is literally the Greek Ὀλύμπια νικᾶν. The
construction is a very slight extension of the ordinary 'accusative of the inner object.' This is probably the earliest of the
many references in Latin poetry to the old racer in retirement.

BOOK XVI

FR. 1. It is impossible to determine whether the events filling the interval between this book and the last were altogether omitted or not. The present book evidently opened with a prologue dealing with the claim of contemporary events to be recorded, with the poet's unwillingness to begin again the labour of composition, and with the motives which led him to do so. There is actually an interval of nine years only between the outbreak of the Istrian war (178 B.C.) and the death of Ennius (November 169 B.C.).

Quippe: = *quidni*; cf. Bk XI. fr. 1.

non: goes closely with *est satis*; it is as if the poet asks himself a rhetorical question, 'Why should I refuse to be satisfied?'

moueri: the word means 'depict' or 'touch upon,' as in Livy XXVIII. 11. 10.

FR. 2. I agree with the suggestion of Baehrens, which is, indeed, natural, that the reference is to the old age of Ennius himself. He is weighing the *pros* and *cons* of beginning to work at the *Annales* again; and the present line is an argument against the resumption. At the youngest, Ennius must have been well over sixty when the words were written, and he perhaps shrank from the labour of collecting and testing material. This is the obvious meaning to be taken from the words as they stand, and I retain the MSS. reading. The *scribendi ferre* of Baehrens (though his general interpretation of the line is correct) could not be accepted even if the MSS. reading were obviously corrupt. It is not a question of continuing or abandoning the literary career altogether, for Ennius continued to produce almost up to the day of his death; it is a question of resuming a particular task that has been laid aside as finished.

Post aetate: Valmaggi curiously seems to regard *post* as a preposition; it is of course an adverb and *aetate* is an example of the so-called 'ablative of specification.' The meaning is that of the English 'late in time.' The construction is quite common with verbs and adverbs and is found sometimes with nouns also, but our example differs from the more ordinary ablative construction with *post*, where the ablative expresses 'degree of difference' (*e.g. multis annis post*).

pigret: the form is found also in Accius 32; the verb is not impersonal, and its subject must have been *cor* or some similar word.

FR. 3. A further argument: 'old age has destroyed all capacity for such work.'

dies: genitive. Gellius has an elaborate note on such forms. He quotes *facies* written in the text (*in ordinem*) of a MS. of Claudius Quadrigarius at Tibur (with *facii* in the margin—*contra-*). He also gives *dies* from Cicero, *pro Sest.* XII. 28, where our MSS. have *diei*, and states that the same form was in a *liber ideographus* of the *Georgics* of Vergil (I. 208). He adds further examples, and finally states that Julius Caesar declared the correct forms to be *die* and *specie*. For the phrase *dies aetas* cf. Lucr. I. 557.

FR. 4. An argument in favour of the additional work. I suppose the connection of thought to be 'Kings labour hard to secure fame surviving after death, but I can immortalise myself and others by means of my poetry. Therefore the labour must be faced.' It is a variant of the familiar thought, 'So long as men can breathe and eyes can see So long lives this....'

Aedificant: the MSS. reading should be retained. The metaphor is natural in itself, and, in this context, is very considerably helped by the words *statuas sepulchra*, which could appropriately be used with *aedificare* in its literal sense. These

two are the typical *monumenta* (cf. Festus, p. 123 Lind.), and
I suggest that they are deliberately chosen in order to make
the transition to verse-writing easy: for *monumentum* is often
used in the sense of *scripta et carmina*, and the idea of
building a monument of verse is readily intelligible in
Latin, as is shown by Horace's famous *Exegi monumentum
aere perennius*.

summa...ui: cf. Bk IV. fr. 1.

FR. 5. The narrative of the war. Before this point, however, there must have been a description of the reconciliation
of the personal enemies Fulvius and Aem. Lepidus, made to
enable them to carry out their official duties; cf. Cic. *de Prou.
Cons*. IX. 2.

The text of Festus is damaged and the proper name Epulo
is mutilated; it can, however, be restored from Varro. It
appears as *Aepulo* in Livy (XLI. 11. 1) and *Apulo* in Florus
(1. 26). *Ĕpŭlo*, with Ennius' quantities, is used by Vergil (*Aen*.
XII. 459), but Livy's *Aepulo* suggests that the first syllable
should be long.

cautibus: I accept this from Vahlen's first edition for
contibus. There does not seem to be authority for *cotibus* in
the sense required, but Vahlen reverts to it in his second
edition.

FR. 6. *obstipis*: = *obliquis*; cf. Bk VIII. fr. 10. The reference is uncertain but may be, as Valmaggi suggests, to the
watch kept by the Istrians on the Roman camp at *Lacus
Timauus*; cf. Livy XLI. 2. It is difficult, however, to see the
exact force of *unde oritur nox*, unless as an indication of the
points of the compass.

FR. 7. A description, perhaps, of the Histri *in omnem
occasionem intenti*; or perhaps a fragment of a speech of exhortation.

luci: a locative form. Plautus' use of it with masculine or neuter adjectives shows that it was felt rather as an adverb than as a feminine noun.

nox: seems to be a genitive form which is used as an adverb; cf. the similar use of the genitive *dius*. It has been suggested that *mox* and *uix* are similar formations.

frux: seems here to mean *usus*; for another meaning cf. Bk IX. fr. 5.

FR. 8. The preliminary arrangements for the Istrian attack on the Roman camp. We know that it took place early in the morning.

FR. 9. The same subject continued.

For the meaning of *aethra* cf. Servius ad *Aen*. III. 553. It is used also as a synonym for *aether*, as in *Aen*. XII. 247 (where, as here, it is qualified by *rubra*).

FR. 10. Roman soldiers on the watch and resting.

insidiãntes: three syllables. Cf. Bk I. fr. 33, *aũium*.

uigilant: is emphatically contrasted with *requiescunt*.

scutis: the specific term for the legionary's shield shows that the men are not Istrians.

ore fauentes: the religious associations of the phrase are so strong that Servius (D.) paraphrases the meaning as *cum religione et silentio*. There is, however, no feeling of *religio* and the word is used simply in the derived sense of *tacentes* as in Ter. *And*. Prol. 24.

FR. 11. I agree with the suggestion of Pascoli, that this fragment, as well as the next two, belongs to a discussion between the consul and the tribune Aelius (see below), who alone stood firm in the panic caused by the surprise attack on the Roman camp. In the present line Aelius urges the consul to do his duty; the consul replies that the men are quite out of hand (Livy notes that he could not control them *nec imperio nec auctoritate nec precibus*); Aelius answers, 'I still hope on,' to which the consul retorts, 'To hope in such an extremity means total ruin.' When we read Livy's (XLI. 2) account of the incident we can hardly wonder that Ennius' imagination was fired by the tribune's heroic stand.

Nauorum: an early instance of the construction, which seems in origin a predicative use of the possessive genitive: or it may be explained as an ellipse of *officium* which appears in such a line as *Truc.* 436. *Nauus*, 'a man of deeds'; cf. Bk VI. fr. 2.

imperium seruare:)(*imperium deminuere*, a regular phrase in connection with insubordination or mutiny in the army.

FR. 12. The tribune speaks, 'I will remain here where my duty is indicated.'

sapsa: = *ea ipsa*, from the demonstrative root.

FR. 13. For the plural *speres* cf. Bk II. fr. 52.

potis sunt: = *possunt*. It should be written as two words, not one as Müller wished.

FR. 14. The consul's answer.

sperando: echoes *speres*.

FR. 15. This important fragment was first placed in Bk XVI by Bergk. The MSS. of Macrobius vary between Bks XII and XV; but it is only natural to assume that the tribune is the same officer as that mentioned in the well-known story given by Pliny (*N.H.* VII. 28), in which the heroism of a tribune was the motive which inspired Ennius to add the sixteenth book. That Bk XVI was concerned with the Istrian war is clear from the mention of the Istrian king Epulo, and Istrians figure in the present passage. Again, Livy, in a passage already mentioned, speaks of the heroism of a tribune in face of the surprise attack on the camp. There is unfortunately great uncertainty as to the tribune's name. In XLI. 29 Livy calls him M. Licinius Strabo; Macrobius calls him Caelius, and Pliny speaks of two brothers Caecilii. In XLI. 1. 7 and 4. 3, however, Livy mentions two brothers, both tribunes, T. and

C. Aelius. These references certainly look like the confusion
of one name, and I agree with those who suppose that
C. Aelius is correct. It is the name given by Livy when, like
Pliny, he speaks of two brothers, and it is a very easy correction of the *cęlij* of Macrobius' MSS. As regards M. Licinius
Strabo, we can only conclude that either Ennius or Livy's
source has confused one tribune with another. Both belonged
to the Third Legion and both served in the same campaign,
so that error or deliberate substitution would be easy. Pliny
rather supports Ennius, and I therefore suggest that Licinius
Strabo as the hero originates with C. Licinius Macer, the
father of Catullus' friend Calvus, whose work was certainly
used by Livy and who had a very bad reputation for inaccuracy and the sort of family pride which leads to deliberate
falsification; cf. Dionysius I. 7 and VII. I, and especially
Livy VII. 9.

Macrobius states that our lines are an imitation of the
Homeric passage, beginning Αἴας δ' οὐκέτ' ἔμιμνε βιάζετο
γὰρ βελέεσσι, and further states that the whole of the famous
passage *de incluso Turno* (*Aen.* IX. 806 ff.) is taken over from
the same original. It is not clear, however, whether Ennius
exercised any indirect influence.

galeae: cf. *Aen.* IX. 666.

nec: = *non*; cf. Festus, p. 158 Lind.

pote: sc. *est*. The use of the neuter in reference to a person
shows that the phrase is on its way to becoming the classical
potest.

FR. 16. Probably the description of the death of Aelius.

The line is the original of Vergil's *Corruit in uolnus, sonitum
super arma dedere*, and is perhaps itself a reminiscence of such
Homeric phrases as *Il.* IV. 204.

FR. 17. The rejoicing of the victorious Istrians; cf. Livy
XLI. 2. 12.

iubēt: with 'metrical justification.'

horiturque: for the form cf. note on Bk x. fr. 7.

FR. 18. The flight of King Epulo when the alarm of the Roman approach is given; cf. Livy XLI. 4. 7.

Conuellit sese: 'starts to his feet'; cf. Servius ad *Aen*. XI. 19.

FR. 19. The reference may be either to the massacre of the Istrians by the Romans, or to the scenes which marked the fall of the Istrian capital Nesactum; cf. Livy XLI. 11. 3.

Clamōr: the only instance of *ōr* without 'metrical justification.' Perhaps we should read *clamos*, which is the form actually offered in the next fragment.

uoluendus: the meaning is 'rolling (through the sky),' and grammatically the word seems to be half-way between a passive participle and an adjective.

uagit: is stated by Varro (ap. Gell. XVI. 17. 2) to be the *uox propria* for the cry of young children or animals. Perhaps Ennius chose it to express the shrill sound of women's and children's voices as opposed to those of men.

FR. 20. *clamōs*: proposed by Lachmann (ad Lucr. VI. 1260) is actually offered by Festus.

uagore: *pro uagitu* Festus; cf. Lucr. II. 576. On the meaning cf. note on *uagit* above.

FR. 21. *Ingenio*: the MSS. reading should be retained; the meaning is little more than 'stoutly.'

pertŭdit: Priscian quotes the line as an illustration of this form in *ŭ*.

FR. 22. A battle description like the last fragment.

induuolans: for the form cf. *indutuetur*, *induperator*, etc.

Insigne: the badge on the helmet; cf. Bk x. fr. 4. Vergil calls it *apex summus*.

FR. 23. *manāt*: with 'metrical justification.' We are still concerned with the battle.

FR. 24. In this line I retain the MSS. reading unchanged

except for Merula's *bradys*; and I suppose the reference to be to Fabius Cunctator, who was quoted as an example in some time of difficulty. *Bradys* must be the Greek βραδύς. It cannot be called a metathesis of *bardus* as Valmaggi (following Müller) calls it, supporting it by the comparison of *precula*, *pergula*; *corcodilus*, *crocodilus*; *Trasumenus*, *Tarsumenus*, etc. There is no philological difficulty, but the meaning of *bardus* is entirely unsuitable to the present passage because absolutely contradictory of *peritus*; it is admirably illustrated by Plaut. *Bacch*. v. 1. 2. The whole phrase is a general description of Fabius' policy, 'not over-hasty in his ruling'; *bradys* is literally *tardus*, and *regimen*, as explained by Festus, is equivalent to *regimentum*; cf. Lucr. III. 95.

Fr. 25. It is not possible to determine the exact reference of this line unless it belongs to some general reflections on the passage of time which found a place in the prologue.

Fr. 26. Of this accusative form Charisius quotes one other example from the *Hypobolimaeus* of Caecilius.

BOOK XVII

Fr. 1. Servius (D.) gives *non possunt*, Paulus *non decet*; the *noenu(s)* of Vahlen is almost certainly correct. For the form cf. Bk XII. fr. 1.

mussare: may mean either 'to grumble' or 'to keep silent,' and either meaning would be appropriate here.

Fr. 2. This and the next fragment are evidently battle pieces. It is hardly possible that the insignificant Istrian war can have occupied more than a single book; so Ennius may have entered on the narrative of the Third Macedonian war though he did not live to see its end. If so our present fragment may describe the cavalry charge of the Thracians under Cotys, which was a feature of the first engagement near Larisa (171 B.C.).

Fr. 3. *clamōr*: with 'metrical justification,' as before.

Fr. 4. The similarity of this passage to *Il.* XVI. 765 was first noted by Colonna.

spiritus Austri: cf. the Homeric πνοίας ἀνέμου, θύελλα ἀνέμου, and also *Spiritus Eurorum* from Furius Antias.

Imbricitor: with 'metrical justification,' as before. The word means 'the rainy wind.'

Fr. 5. *uias*: genitive singular. The form occurs more frequently in Saturnian verse than elsewhere: Priscian quotes *escas*, *monetas* and *Latonas* from Livius, and *terras* and *fortunas* from Naevius. Servius, ad *Aen.* XI. 801, holds that *auras* should be read for *aurae*, and further mentions that Sallust may have used *custodias* as a genitive. Even in the classical period, the form in -*as* is regular in *mater*, *pater* and *filius familias*.

Fr. 6. *montē*: if this reading is retained, the quantity of the final syllable is due simply to 'metrical lengthening.' But we should note that *l*, like *r*, *m*, *n*, *s*, is capable of prolongation in pronunciation, and that the effect may have been felt as *montel-late* (cf. Postgate, *Prosodia Latina*, p. 34).

Fr. 7. I retain the MSS. *longiscunt*, though it is hard to see how one word can mean both *longum fieri* and *frangi* as Nonius asserts. A possibility is that the meaning is 'stretch (and so grow weaker).' Hug's *langiscunt* is attractive, but there seems to be no authority for the form.

BOOK XVIII

Fr. 1. This fragment is quoted by Nonius immediately after the last. It describes the return of summer.

Fr. 2. *Degrumare*: to measure with a *gruma*. I accept Vahlen's *degrumare forum* for the *degrumari ferrum* of the MSS. with considerable hesitation. It ignores the words *gruma derigere dixit* which precede the quotation, and which might quite naturally mean, 'Ennius used the phrase *degrumari ferro* (admitting *ferro* for *ferrum*) for the ordinary *gruma derigere.*' The word *degrumari* (or *-are*) does not occur outside Ennius except in a single passage of Lucilius—*uiamque Degrumabis* (*-atus* Onions) *uti castris mensor facit olim*, which Nonius quotes immediately after our line.

Fr. 3. Quoted by Gellius for the gender of *aere*, which he states to be due to considerations of euphony.

INCERTAE SEDIS FRAGMENTA

Fr. 1. Style and subject-matter alike suggest that the fragment belongs to the *Annales*, though there is no means of determining the reference.

manu magna: cf. the common Homeric phrase χειρὶ παχείῃ. The adjective emphasises the river-god's divinity, as μεγάλῃ does in *Il.* xv. 694 (of Zeus).

Fr. 2. The line seems to describe a gradual and secret approach to the wall of a besieged town. For the force of the double *atque* cf. the note of Gellius.

Fr. 3. The first line is one of the few which Horace has preserved; its introduction was intended to give a comic effect (*urbane abutitur Ennianis uersibus*: Porph. ad *Sat.* i. 2. 37). The second was used by Varro in one of his Menippean satires (*Testamentum*: περὶ διαθήκης).

operae pretium: the full phrase which appears in Bk i. fr. 2 in a shortened form *est operae*, which is common in Plautus. Similar phrases with both *operae* and *curae* are familiar in the Latin of all periods.

Fr. 4. The editors agree, most probably rightly, in referring the line to the *Annales*, but none makes an attempt to guess its subject or occasion. I accept Quicherat's correction of the MSS. Baehrens' *Aduersabantur semper ui uostraque nolunt* is plainly impossible in view of Nonius' note which proves the presence of *uulta*. For the gender of the noun cf. Lucr. IV. 1212.

FR. 5. *permarceret*: this form, offered by *Cod. G* (see sources), should be retained. The unusual word was no doubt the cause of the corruptions *permaneret* and *permaceret*. The form is not quoted as occurring elsewhere, but it is a correctly formed intensive, chosen (or coined) for the alliteration. The mention of the *trifax* suggests a siege, hence I retain the fragment in the *Annales*. Vahlen, however, suggests a moral reference (to the corrupting effect of luxury), supporting his conjecture by the line in *Cena Trimalchionis* 55, *Luxuriae rictu Martis marcent moenia*. If this is correct, as it may be, our line should perhaps be removed to the *Satires*.

trifax: a long missile fired from a catapult; cf. Gell. x. 25.

FR. 6. This description of the harbour of Brundisium might perhaps find a place in the narrative of the war with Pyrrhus, but the matter is too indefinite to permit us to place the fragment in Bk VI. Gellius twice mentions it on account of the unusual epithet *praepes*, the meaning of which he discusses elaborately, finding in it a reference to the story of Daedalus. It is probable, however, that Ennius meant little more than 'convenient' (which is a meaning readily derived from the use of the word in augury) and was simply describing the fine natural configuration which makes Brindisi still one of the world's great ports.

FR. 7. The text of Porphyrion is now established as *ergo et Ennius et Lucilius Bruttace bilingui dixerunt*. This form should therefore be adopted rather than the accusative of Paulus which is due simply to the presence of *dixit*.

Bruttace: from a nom. *Bruttax* which Ennius seems to have coined.

bilingui: because in the district both Greek and Latin were spoken.

Fr. 8. From the metrical point of view this is one of the most difficult among the extant lines; the reading too is uncertain, but it is hardly possible to accept the *nutantibus* of Nonius. With the editors I follow Gellius. The problem of the scansion of *Capitibus* is so great that some scholars (Ritschl, Vahlen 1) have been tempted to regard the fragment as portions of two lines; this however is clearly impossible from the note of Gellius—*dixit...hoc uersu*. L. Müller (*De Re Metrica* 1. 138) suggested that the metre was Sotadean (reading *capite*); it is more natural, however, to accept it as a hexameter. The first foot should probably be called a pro-celeusmatic, introduced perhaps as an experiment; cf. *Il.* XIII. 144, ῾Ρέα διελεύσεσθαι. There is no other example in the extant fragments, however, and some editors refuse to admit the foot. *Captibus* must then be read with Valmaggi (following Schneider): on the possibility of this three-syllable form cf. Lindsay, *Early Latin Verse*, p. 308. It is after all by no means certain that, even as a hexameter, the line is correctly placed in the *Annales*, and in the *Satires* a looser standard of versification may have been allowed.

Fr. 9. The line illustrates the correct spelling, *cum* pre-position, *quom* adverb. The reference may be, as Vahlen suggests, to the *Votorum nuncupatio* on the Capitol, and the subject seems to belong naturally to the *Annales*.

Fr. 10. *Volcanus*: = *ignis*; *a superiore re inferior* Festus.

uegebat: transitive as in the *Ambracia Et aequora salsa ueges ingentibus uentis*; but an intransitive use is attested by Nonius (p. 268. 17 Lind.).

Fr. 11. *fossari* should be accepted as the note of Varro makes it clear that he read some such word (*dictum a fodiendo*). The error is a simple case of omission. For the expression

Vahlen compares Bk III. fr. 10; the construction of the infinitives there is, however, different: cf. note ad loc.

FR. 12. *incutit*: for the general meaning cf. *Il.* XI. 291, and also Livy XXIV. 16, XL. 27.

FR. 13. Quoted by Varro immediately after the well-known passage in the *Euhemerus* with the remark, *Quod hinc omnes et sub hoc, eundem appellans dicit*, etc.

FR. 14. *Dum quidem*: for the scansion cf. Bk X. fr. 4 with the remark of Priscian ad loc.

superescit: *significat supererit* Festus. The termination is the 'inceptive' form of the root; *escit* appears alone in the Twelve Tables and even in Lucretius (I. 619), so perhaps we should read *super escit* as two words here: cf. Bk III. fr. 12 and Gell. I. 22. 16.

toga: introduced as typical of Roman life; cf. Hor. *Od.* III. 5. 10.

FR. 15. The line, called *notum illud* by Quintilian, seems to have become a proverb. The original reference was undoubtedly to a helmsman battling with a storm, but Valmaggi curiously understands it of a prosperous voyage, perhaps that of Scipio.

clauum rectum: cf. Aristides Rhod. 13 (II. p. 75. 22 Keil), τοῦτο δὲ τὸ θρυλούμενον 'Αλλ' ὦ Ποτειδᾶν ἴσθι ὀρθὰν τὰν ναῦν καταδύσων.

FR. 16. *cum*: the preposition is seemingly unnecessary; cf. Bk VI. fr. 17. As Vahlen points out, Servius is mistaken in taking *cum* as a preposition in *Geo.* II. 424. Our line is probably concerned with a soliloquy of Jove; cf. the Homeric parallels given on Bk VI. fr. 17.

FR. 17. This fragment is usually placed early in Bk I, and referred to the vision of Homer. Servius, however, gives no reference beyond *Ennii uersus*, and, though retaining the words in the *Annales*, I prefer to leave them here. If the words *quantum mutatus ab illo* belong to Ennius (as is quite possible, even probable, as Servius says *uersus* not *hemistichum*) the reference to Homer is quite impossible. The description must be of someone known in life to the speaker; it might very naturally refer to the dead body of Tarquin.

FR. 18. This famous simile is stated by Macrobius to be a reminiscence of *Il.* VI. 506 ff. = XV. 263 ff. In the Vergilian version, which is much closer to Homer than to Ennius, it is applied to Turnus going into battle (*Aen.* XI. 492 ff.).

caerula: = '(dark) green.' The word is applied by Propertius (V. ii. 43) to the colour of the cucumber, and by Ovid to that of the olive (*Ars Am.* II. 518) and the foliage of the oak (*Met.* XI. 183); cf. also Manil. V. 260 ff.

FR. 19. *detondit*: this form offered by the second hand in one MS. (B) of Priscian must be accepted; unless we assume such a tmesis as *deque totondit*, the reduplicated form of the other MSS. is impossible. Perhaps the fragment should be placed in Bk VI as describing the Roman raids on the territory of Tarentum (cf. especially *plurima expugnat oppida* of the consul Aemilius Barbula); or it may belong to the operations of Pyrrhus in Sicily (Bk VII).

FR. 20. This fragment is of very doubtful text. The *Cod. Neap.* of Charisius himself omits *Euax* and gives *Aquast aspersa Latinis*; the *Excerpta* offer *Euax aquas istas pensa lituus*. It seems dangerous to assume that the words *aquast aspersa* are a faulty version of the Plautus quotation which precedes the Ennius; they appear in both Charisius and the epitomiser (for *aquas istas pensa* is only a small corruption). Accepting them, we must read *Latinis* not *lituus*; we must further accept Bergk's suggestion that *ăqüast* is scanned as three syllables, but the whole matter is very uncertain. *Euax*: an interjection common in Plautus; cf. Varro, *L.L.* VII. 5.

FR. 21. The line is quoted for the superlative form which appears also in Cn. Matius *celerissimus aduolat Hector*.

Exin: for the form cf. Bk I. fr. 33 (*Exin candida*, etc.).

FR. 22. *concussa est turbine saeuo*: 'tossed round in a fierce whirl.' It is difficult to appreciate the force of *loci*, unless we regard it as depending on some word now lost. Vahlen rightly rejects the explanation that the genitive is constructed with *postquam*, but his own note ...*dicit abundanter sed non praue* is not helpful. It has been suggested that the line describes the burning of the camp of Syphax; but it might apply equally to many other incidents, among them the sack of Troy.

FR. 24. The connection of thought is not easy to guess. Baehrens' *tam quam* is very attractive and gives a most appropriate sense, but our authorities give *quamquam* without variant, and so I retain it with Merula's *sunt* which seems the simplest remedy. For the unusual rhythm cf. Bk VIII. frs. 1 (*Quoi par*, etc.) and 2 (*Spernitur*, etc.).

caelus: the rare masculine gender is to be noted. In Bk I. fr. 15 the word is a proper name.

FR. 25. *suas*: is an easy and certain correction of the MSS. *quas*.

latrones: 'mercenaries,' as often in Plautus; cf. Bk I. fr. 23.

FR. 26. Marius Victorinus' *efflant* is an obvious scribe's error due to a recollection of the Vergilian line (*Aen*. XII. 115). It is reasonable to assume that *Solis equi* stood at the beginning of the line.

FR. 27. The gender of *iubar* should be noted.

cursum; sometimes needlessly altered to *currum*, should be retained.

FR. 28. The gap is too great to make conjecture safe, though Ilberg's *circum quam caerula salsa ululabant* has been widely accepted. We know that the reference is to the island of Paros, but no more.

FR. 29. These words, applied by Ennius to marching elephants, were taken over by Accius to describe a band of

Indians. It seems better to leave them here than refer them conjecturally to any particular occasion.

FR. 30. The name of the authority quoted by Festus has disappeared, but his statement that *restat* bears the meaning of *distat* still survives.

impetus: cf. Bk XIV. fr. 3.

FR. 31. *cata* is stated by Varro to be Sabine for *acuta*; cf Bk X. fr. 3.

fere: this correction of *ferę* (*ferae*) seems simpler than either *fera* (O. Müller) or *fera e* (*e...dare* tmesis for *edere*—Baehrens).

FR. 32. The reference is to the revolution of the heavenly bodies as in Lucr. V. 644, and the line describes the return of Spring. *Aen.* VI. 748, where Servius remarks *est sermo Ennii*, however, is concerned with the Orphic-Pythagorean 'wheel of existence'; cf. Diog. Laert. VII. 12, etc.

patefecit: cf. Lucr. I. 11.

candida: 'bringing fair weather'; cf. Hor. *Od.* III. 7. 1. So *albus* is used by Horace of *Notus* (Gk λευκόνοτος) and *Iapyx* (*Od.* I. 7. 15, III. 27. 19), and *clarus* by Vergil of *Aquilo* (*Geo.* I. 406).

FR. 33. *Inde loci*: here clearly temporal; cf. Bk I. fr. 1.

lituus: the war bugle. Festus states that the word is derived from *lis*; its primary meaning, however, is 'crooked,' as is shown by its use to mean the augur's staff.

FR. 34. We can but regret the loss of the context of a phrase of such Biblical magnificence, though Servius, ad *Aen.* XII. 499, seems to consider the language over-violent.

FR. 35. Festus, in quoting this and Fr. 40 below, calls the form *termo* a Graecism for the usual *terminus*; cf. also Varro, *L.L.* V. 21. The forms *termen* and *termo* are, however, in reality old Latin, and the original *men* (*mon*) stem has been transferred to the ŏ declension in producing the later *ter-minus*. So *columen* has beside it *columna*.

FR. 36. *ueles*: for a description see Livy XXXVIII. 21.

uolgo: 'all together,' *i.e.* 'in mass formation'; cf. Caesar, *B.G.* v. 33.

siciles: *hastarum spicula lata* Paulus; the epithet *latis* is therefore strictly correct. The plural *sicilibus* is used because each man had more than one spear.

FR. 37. In this line I adopt the reading of Havet (*Rev. de Phil.* XIV. 27).

It equitatus: cf. Bk XVII. fr. 2.

celerissimus: cf. Fr. 21 above. We may compare *miserissimus*, found in inscriptions, and also *minerrimus* quoted by Paulus, *Epit.*

FR. 38. I leave this famous and beautiful fragment here, for, beyond the obvious fact that it describes the smile of Jove, we cannot fix the reference. The Vergilian reminiscence (1. 254 ff.) is well known; as Pascoli well remarks, the smile of universal nature does not follow the smile of Zeus in Homer.

tempestatesque serenae; cf. Fr. 91 below.

FR. 39. *Heia*: *militum properantium clamor* Servius; cf. the common *Heia age*. *Heiă*, as in the late Latin song, *Heia uiri, nostrum reboans echo sonat heia.* Plautus has *heiā* (*Merc.* 998). Vergil as a rule elides the last syllable.

FR. 40. *termo*: on the form cf. Fr. 35 above.

FR. 41. I follow Baehrens' restoration of the hexameter; the small changes in the word-order were doubtless deliberately made to break the verse form (*Hic...pes pede premitur armis teruntur arma*). The restoration is made practically certain by *Aen.* x. 361 and Furius Bibaculus, *Pressatur pede pes mucro mucrone uiro uir.* The common original of them all is *Il.* XIII. 130 f. Vahlen is clearly wrong in omitting *hic* as the parenthetic *ut ait Ennius* shows that it belongs to the quotation.

FR. 42. Again the parenthetic *ut ait Ennius* shows that *hic tum* should be retained.

parumper: 'for a short space of time,' as before. The fact that this and the last fragment are preserved in a military history written by one of Julius Caesar's subalterns is a remarkable testimony to the fact that a knowledge of Ennius was part of the common stock of every educated Roman, and that he was popular even among those who had no professional interest in literature.

FR. 43. I agree with Valmaggi that this line is best left here, rather than in any particular book, for, even granting the reference to M. Livius Salinator, we cannot be sure to which of his two triumphs the line alludes.

The verb *mactare* is from the root cognate to the Sanskrit *maha* (victim), and is therefore a different word from *macte*, with which Nonius (p. 540 Lind.) confuses it. Its double set of meanings is derived from 'to offer up in honour of the gods,' but the sense of *malo adficere* is much the more common of the two; cf. however, *mactant honoribus* from Cic. *de Rep.* I. 43. 67.

FR. 44. This line very closely resembles Bk XIV. fr. 3; cf. note ad loc.

celocis: the Greek κέλης, a specially light quick-moving bireme.

FR. 45. The reference is probably to the movements of light troops (*uelites*).

FR. 46. One of the most famous single lines preserved, stately alike in sound and sense. It would seem to belong to some interlude of general reflection, and may have been spoken by the conservative Cato.

FR. 47. A very doubtful line. I accept, though with hesitation, Valmaggi's *agoeae*, where *longa agoeae* = *longa agoea*, and resembles the Lucretian phrases *munita uiai, uera uiai*, etc. (III. 496, I. 659). *Agea*, which Vahlen retains, is almost impossible to explain metrically. There is no 'metrical' excuse for lengthening, and the quantity of *a* in ἄγυια is not certainly long. It nearly always occurs in the plural in the poets, but once at least the singular is ἄγυιᾰ (*Il.* xx. 254). *Ponĭt*, as before. *Agea* defined as *loca in naue per quae ad remiges hortator accedit*.

FR. 48. The reference may be to the *lateralis dolor*, which is called *certissimus nuntius mortis* by Lucilius (see below, *Spuria*, Fr. 19).

FR. 49. The remark of Servius—*Explebo est minuam*—is obviously a mere guess made because he did not understand the Vergilian *explebo numerum*, where the word is used in a sense totally different from that which it bears in our passage. In Vergil the meaning is 'I will complete the number' (of those due to the underworld); cf. the note of Norden ad loc. In Ennius *explebant sese* means *egrediebantur*. The *ex* has a privative force and is rhetorically and somewhat artificially contrasted with *re* in *replebant*, as if the object were to make an epigram of a simple statement of fact.

FR. 50. I accept, in the first line, Mommsen's *non si* for the *mŏn ĭ* of the Paris MS., and Vahlen's *quibus* for *at* (the error due to the form *q̄b*). The meaning is *Non si ora decem sint, quibus lingua loqui saperet*; the order, though strained, is not nearly so harsh as in Catullus' *Non, ita me diui, uera gemunt, iuuerint*. In the second line I accept Vahlen's *innumerum*, which is decidedly the best correction of the MS. *in metrum* yet proposed.

sint: in a 'contrary to fact supposition' in present time, the present subjunctive is the original construction. It is found so used not very uncommonly in Plautus. The collocation of tenses *sint*...*saperet* resembles that in Plautus, *Poen.* 1251; it is to be explained by the fact that *sint* is really equivalent in meaning to *esset*.

Fr. 51. I accept Mercier's reading; the phrase *freti uirtute* is natural and appropriate: cf. Lucr. v. 966, and the Homeric ἠνορέῃ πίσυνοι. Vahlen's *Ni metus ulla tenet uirtutem, rite quiescunt* is practically the version of Nonius. He does not, however, suggest a translation; and *rite* in particular is so difficult to explain as to appear almost certainly corrupt. It seems to be another case of unfortunate return to conservatism in Vahlen, for in his first edition he accepted Mercier's conjectures.

Fr. 52. Vahlen places this fragment in Bk iv, supposing it to belong to a speech of Cincinnatus when he was summoned from the plough to the Dictatorship. But the parallel he quotes from Dionysius (x. 24) is not close. On both occasions Nonius gives our line in company with one from the *Antiopa* of Pacuvius, in which the more ordinary feminine *propages* is used instead of our neuter *propagmen*.

Fr. 53. Augustine, who quotes the line twice, was troubled by its sentiment (*partim puto approbandum, partim cauendum*). In the letter he is evidently quoting from memory and offers *laudari exoptant*.

laudarier: the origin of such passive infinitive forms is doubtful. Even in the early period, however, they are used merely for metrical convenience, and are restricted to the last feet of iambics and trochaics by Plautus.

Fr. 54. *micant*: 'twitch'; the primary meaning of the word is 'to move rapidly.' Besides *Aen.* x. 396, we may compare the description of the dying Dido (*Aen.* iv. 691). Servius states that the second of the two lines was used by Varro Atacinus also.

Fr. 55. *cum pulchris animis*: the prepositional phrase takes the place of a genitive of quality as in the Terence passage, *Antipho...cum istoc animo*.

FR. 56. These lines are usually placed in Bk VI and referred to the preparations made on the outbreak of the war with Pyrrhus: cf. Orosius IV. 1. 2 ff. But though the arming of the proletariate agrees with that description, the last words suggest a crisis in which an immediate attack was expected on Rome itself. A possible occasion might be Hannibal's feint to draw off the army besieging Capua; but there is no evidence to enable us to assign the fragment to any particular book. The collocation *fero ferro* suggests the same word-play as that in Tibull. I. 10. 2.

FR. 57. *sultis*: a plural coined to suit *sis* (*si uis*). It is confined to the early period, while *sis* and *sodes* are common in the Latin of all ages. The persistence of the error in our texts suggests that Vahlen may, perhaps, be right in reading *sulti* for *sultis*, but there is no evidence that final *s* neglected in scansion (as here) was actually omitted in writing.

genas: used for *palpebras*, as Paulus says.

FR. 58. As Vahlen rightly insists, this and Fr. 12 above are not to be dismissed as imperfect forms of Bk VI. fr. 17, as such addresses may naturally be expected to have been common in the *Annales*.

FR. 59. Stated by Servius to belong to a description of cranes.

mollia: *flexibilia* Schol. Bern. ad *Geo*. III. 71.

FR. 60. Valmaggi, following Müller, joins our line to Fr. 64 below, and places them both in Bk II, supposing them to form part of a speech in the parley between Tullus Hostilius and the Alban dictator. But there is nothing to show that they belong to the same episode, and the present line might suit almost any battle piece in the *Annales*. Lucan's line (I. 6) seems a clear reminiscence of Ennius.

FR. 61. Vahlen, who regularly uses *cum* for both preposition and adverb, seems to have taken the first word as a preposition here. It is better, however, to read *quom* and take *saeuo obsidio* as a simple ablative of means.

Fr. 62. *exsiccat somno*: the phrase is based on the figure of 'the horn of sleep' used by Vergil in *Aen.* I. 691 and also by Furius, Lucretius (cf. Macrobius VI. 1. 44) and Statius (*Theb.* II. 27). In the note on the last passage it is stated that painters often represented Sleep as pouring down the contents of a horn.

FR. 63. The simile is the same as that in the scene of auspice-taking (Bk I. fr. 33). On the meaning of *carcer* cf. note ad loc.; the singular is unusual in this sense.

permittere: (cf. *emittere* l.c.) should be retained. Nonius (p. 238. 20 Lind.) defines the meaning of the word as *mittere, incitare uel praecipitare*; it is probably used reflexively, by an ellipse of *se*.

FR. 64. *Quianam*: 'wherefore,' as before. On the reference of the fragment cf. note on Fr. 60 above. I suggest that the present fragment may well belong to some mutinous soldier, and be concerned with the episodes at the beginning of the Second Macedonian war; cf. Bk X. fr. 8.

FR. 65. This line, which depends on a note in *Cod. Sangall.* 621 of Orosius, is introduced as if in comment on the fate of Minucia the Vestal. But this does not prove that its original reference was to the law regarding guilty Vestals; it might very naturally be concerned with the *lex horrendi carminis* of which Livy speaks (*horrendi* seems to recall *horridius*) and therefore find its place in Bk II (the trial of Horatius).

horridiūs: lengthened with 'metrical justification.'

FR. 66. For the sentiment cf. Livy XLII. 47. It is another form of Vergil's *Parcere subiectis et debellare superbos*.

FR. 68. *temere*: *subito* Servius. But the meaning 'rashly' or 'inconsiderately' would cover both this and *Haud temere est quod tu tristi cum corde gubernas* (placed by me among the *fragmenta incertorum librorum*), where Servius paraphrases *temere* by *sine causa*. The sense in our present passage is seemingly 'in inconsiderate haste.'

FR. 69. Evidently a description of Jove.

arcet: = *continet*; cf. Cic. *de Rep.* VI. 17. 17. I limit the second line of the fragment to *Omnia per sonitum arcet* which is all that Servius offers. Probus, however, quotes as from Lucretius a line *Omnia per sonitum arcet, terram mare caelum*; and the coincidence of the opening words has led Vahlen (following Bernays) to add *terram, mare, caelum* to our text. They assume that the name of Ennius has dropped out of the text of Probus, or else that the attribution to Lucretius is a simple mistake. Neither, however, is probable, and I prefer to suppose that Probus has really preserved a line of Lucretius which has disappeared from our texts (cf. Lachmann ad IV. 126). The reminiscence of Ennius is perfectly natural; cf. VI. 400 (where *sonitus* and *fulmen* appear exactly as in our fragment).

FR. 70. I follow Vahlen in assuming that *ueniunt* had its own subject, and *falarica* its own verb. His further suggestion, that the subject is a comparison of *fulmina* to missile weapons, as in Lucr. VI. 329, is highly probable; and we might restore *quae ueniunt, ualido contorta falarica missu*, which resembles the widely accepted reading of the *editio princeps* of Nonius, except for the retention of the MSS. *ueniunt*. But, strange as the phrase *ualide ueniunt* is, it is not necessarily corrupt. In *Aen.* IX. 702, which also seems to be a reminiscence of our line, the comparison is of a *falarica* to a *fulmen*, not *uice uersa* as in Lucretius.

FR. 71. *carmen*: of the note of a musical instrument,

seems practically to be confined to the *cithara* or *lyra*; but *canere* is used by Propertius of *tubae*, and it is the *uox propria* for army bugle calls, especially in the phrases *bellicum* and *classicum canere*.

raucus: this, the reading of *Cod. Par.* 8064, should be accepted. It was previously conjectured by Baehrens.

aere: the simple ablative of separation is very common with verbs in early Latin. We find various prepositional phrases also, however, and there seems to be no clear principle at work; cf. Frs. 49 and 62 above.

FR. 72. *fremebant*: *antiqui aquae sonitus fremitus dicebant* Servius. Ennius himself uses *fremitu* (in a tragic fragment) for the sound of rain; the same idea perhaps suggested the somewhat strange phrase *imber Neptuni* here. Both Vergil and Ovid, however, use *imber* of the sea.

FR. 73. *runata*: *proeliata* Paulus. This looks like a guess derived in reality from the meaning of *recedit*, for the more natural meaning would be 'armed with a *runa*' (a kind of spear). However, the meaning 'having used her *runa*' is not impossible, for the active *pilo* (as used by Hostius, *hastam pilans prae pondere fregit*, quoted by Servius ad *Aen.* XII. 121) implies the possibility of a 'middle' *pilatus = hastā pilatā* (this *pilata* is actually read in Paulus—and Festus—by Müller for *proeliata*). *Runata*, which seems to be a coinage of Ennius' own, may have been understood on this analogy.

FR. 74. *stant puluere*: 'are thick with dust.' There is no evidence to justify a specific reference to the battle of Cannae.

FR. 75. A famous but puzzling line which roused the wrath of Varro for its inaccuracy. It is to Varro himself that we owe the date 754 B.C. for the founding of Rome. 751 B.C. was also widely accepted (= 1183, Eratosthenes' date for the sack of Troy, less 432, the number of years which Cato the censor held to have elapsed between that date and the other); Cato himself seems to have given 745–4, Fabius Pictor 748–7, Cincius Alimentus 729–8. As Ennius held Romulus to be the grandson of Aeneas, he can hardly have supposed more than a century to have elapsed between the destruction of one city and the foundation of the other. Perhaps he took his information from some Greek source; Timaeus, for example, gave 814 B.C. ('thirty-eight years before the first Olympiad') as the date for both Rome and Carthage. But he was frankly without interest in chronology, and is hardly to be censured for refusing to accept Varro's date, still less for a lack of the accuracy which he expressly disclaimed. Further, the line is referred to the *Annales* conjecturally; if it belonged to the *Satires* and contained some personal reference to the later years of Ennius' own life, or even if it belonged to the prologue of *Ann.* XVI, it would not be flagrantly inaccurate if Ennius placed the foundation of Rome in the ninth century. A natural connection of thought in the latter case would be, 'In all the seven hundred years of Rome there has been no greater hero than the Tribune Aelius,' and the lines would mark the transition from the personal prologue (cf. notes ad loc.) to the actual narrative.

Augusto: a technical term of religion; cf. Paul. e Fest. p. 23 Lind. This religious association was, as Suetonius implies, the reason why Octavian adopted the title *Augustus*, and his quotation of our lines shows how 'the second Romulus' sought to associate himself in every way with the first and borrow antique dignity from the poet who celebrated him.

Fr. 76. *sola terrarum*: as *sola regni* in Bk III. fr. 5.

parumper: here bears the secondary meaning *cito et uelociter*.

Fr. 77. *succincti*: clearly a 'middle' use of the participle, though we should expect the accusative to be used of the weapon or garment as it is with *induor*, *e.g.* in Plautus, *Men.* 511. Ennius has two more instances of *succingor*, each time with an ablative of the thing as here, and Vergil follows his construction. Ovid (*Met.* X. 103) has *succincta comas*, though with a different meaning for the participle.

Fr. 78. *media regione*: simple ablative with locative force.

cracentes: *graciles* Paulus. The two words are connected etymologically. The interchange of *c* and *g* is familiar, and a special symbol for the *g* sound is said by Plutarch (*Quaest. Rom.* 54) to have been invented by Sp. Carvilius Ruga about 293 B.C., but the old usage survived in the abbreviations *C.* (*Gaius*) and *Cn.* (*Gnaeus*). Nonius quotes *cracilo* from Turpilius.

Fr. 79. It cannot be denied that *sĭcŭtĭ* must be a dactyl here. The metrical difficulty does not justify us in 'emending' to *sicut* as the editors do; and we have thus the only undoubted instance of Lindsay's 'cretic shortening' in the *Annales* (cf. notes on Bk I. frs. 5 and 38). But there is little doubt that in the vast majority of cases such scansions belong to 'popular' rather than 'artistic' prosody, so perhaps the homely nature of the metaphor has unconsciously influenced the style; or the line may well be the adaptation of a proverb. We know that Ennius did sometimes quote proverbs (cf. *Quaerunt in scirpo, soliti quod dicere, nodum*).

dimidiatum:...*ipsum quod diuisum est*...*dimidium*...*ex dimidiato pars altera* Gellius. This accuracy is praised by Gellius, quoting Varro; cf. note on Bk VII. fr. 14. It is another proof that Ennius really was *dicti studiosus*, and considered no matter too small for the artist's search for the *mot juste*.

Fr. 80. *spiras*: stated by our authorities to mean *multitudines hominum*. The word is probably a transliteration of σπεῖρα (which, as the editors point out, is often used by

NOTES: INCERTAE SEDIS FRAGMENTA   225

Polybius for *manipulus*), not the ordinary Latin *spira* which
means something twisted (as a rope, etc.).

Fr. 81. This obscure fragment is quoted by Nonius for
the use of *lapides* as a feminine which he declares is borrowed
from Homer (λίθος fem. is found). The reference cannot
be guessed, and the reading is very doubtful. Wakefield's
augmine has been widely accepted (cf. for the meaning Lucr.
III. 268); but the MSS. reading can be explained as 'so long
a column picks up stones' (and carries them forward).
Further no satisfactory ending has been proposed, and, as
the attribution to the *Annales* is merely conjectural, I suggest
that we might read *Tanto sunt sublatae agmine tunc lapides*
as a pentameter. Such an elision as *sublatae agmine* is by no
means impossible for Ennius and much worse examples are
found at a later date (*e.g.* Catull. LXXIII. 6); certainly the
difficulties of the early writers of elegiacs seem to have centred
in the pentameter. I have, however, left the words in the
MSS. order, and very doubtfully assigned the fragment to the
Annales.

Fr. 82. *trabalis*: seems to mean 'as thick and heavy as a
beam'; cf. (as well as *Aen.* XII. 294) Stat. *Theb.* IV. 4, where
the word is used with *hasta*.

Fr. 83. *tergus*: the masculine gender should be noted.

sagus: the word means properly a rough blanket or cloak,
but is used especially of the soldier's cloak (cf. *abolla*, worn
by soldiers and philosophers); metaphorically it can be used
for war, as *toga* for peace. The word is sometimes said to be
Gallic or Celtiberian, as both Gauls (Pol. II. 28. 7, etc.) and
Spaniards (App. *Hisp.* 42) wore the *sagus*.

pinguis: 'thick.'

Fr. 84. *terrai frugiferai*: despite his sneer, Martial could
not use these words as he does (XI. 90) had they not introduced
some specially famous or often quoted passage. Charisius

states that the case is dative; but as he is mistaken over Vergil's *aulai* (*Aen.* III. 354), he may be in error over our fragment also. Priscian (I. p. 291. 17 H.) states that both genitive and dative singular could have the disyllabic termination though nominative and vocative plural could not.

FR. 85. *in mundo*: *pro palam et in expedito ac cito.* It is found in Plautus also, but does not survive into the classical period.

FR. 86. I retain the *tonsillas apiunt* (*tonsillasapiunt*) of the best MSS., which is much superior to the widely accepted *rapiunt* of the inferior MSS. The verb *apio* is attested by Isid. XIX. 30, though there seems to be no other instance in literature of any other part of it except *aptus*. But its sense is perfectly clear: 'they tie the *tonsillae*' is merely a shortened form of 'they tie the cables to the *tonsillae*.' The order of the words, though harsh, is not impossible; cf. Fr. 50 above.

Tonsilla: a sharp-pointed iron-tipped stake to which ships were moored.

aduncas: Isidore defines *tonsilla* as *uncinus ferreus.*

FR. 87. *Vt*: local. The attribution to the *Annales* is conjectural; hence I place the fragment here rather than in Bk II (founding of the port of Ostia).

FR. 88. This line may describe the sufferings of Hannibal's elephants during the passage of the Alps; *hiems* can mean 'severe or bad weather' without reference to any particular season. However, the matter admits of no certainty.

FR. 89. The reading is that of Vahlen II which seems the simplest remedy, where both the order and the terminations of the words have been badly confused. The reference is to the stakes carried by the legionary for the fortification of the daily camp.

FR. 90. Vahlen does not include this fragment in the *Annales*, and indeed, short and vague as it is, it might find a place almost anywhere, even among the dramatic fragments. *Mucronem*, however, suggests a battle piece; hence I place it here.

FR. 91. *laeuum*: as before, a good omen. A possible reference might be to the miracle of the *Ancilia*, for in Ovid's account Jove thunders before the token is sent.

FR. 92. *uertunt*: *potantes exhauriunt* Servius.

craterās: the Greek inflection is somewhat unusually retained.

FR. 93. *momine*: = *momento*, 'impulse.' Apart from our fragment, the word is practically confined to Lucretius who has it several times. It is found, however, in late Latin.

FR. 94. A fragment of very doubtful text and interpretation, in which I follow Vahlen in retaining the MSS. *solum*: evidently the *cohum* is contrasted with the other parts of the heavenly sphere (cf. list in Isidore). The word is derived from the old form *couus* (= classical *cauus*), and its literal meaning is defined by Varro, *L.L.* v. 135. Paulus states that *poetae* used the word as a synonym for *caelum*, but it does not seem to be known outside Ennius.

FRAGMENTA DUBIA

These fragments, which are of very uneven merit and interest, are assigned to Ennius by conjecture only, except in a very few cases.

FR. 1. *Schol. Bern.* states that the commentator Gnipho, in a note *annalium libro decimo*, described the utility of the *acanthus* blossom as a dye. This probably is a trace of a genuine commentary on the *Annales* of Ennius by M. Antonius Gnipho, a contemporary of Cicero, who is mentioned by Quintilian (1. 6. 23). Even assuming this, however, it remains uncertain whether the text contained the name of the tree, or the presumably rare phrase *uestis acanthia* ('dyed garments') which *Schol. Bern.* mentions. Either of these is much more likely than Bücheler's suggestion, adopted by Vahlen, that the reference is to the Macedonian town of Acanthus captured during the war with Philip (Livy XXXI. 45. 15).

FR. 2. This line may well be genuine Ennius as the style seems worthy of him. But no authority gives the name of either author or poem; and it may therefore be a fragment from some other lost heroic poem. There seems to be no other instance of *gubernator* in the sense of *auriga*; the converse metaphor is found in Ov. *Trist.* 1. 4. 16.

FR. 3. These lines are quoted in close proximity to others of which Ennius is certainly the author, and are therefore probably genuine.

Corde suo: locatival.

FR. 4. The quotation is made from some *Annales*, but the form in which they appear (*Confricati oleo lentati paratique ad arma*) lead Müller and Valmaggi to suppose the work in question to have been in prose. The word *lentati*, however, is decidedly against this; the quotation must be older than Vergil, as Servius' note shows, and *lento* seems to be unknown in prose until the post-Augustan period. I therefore think it best to record the conjecture of Vahlen 1, which was admitted into Bk 1 (cf. the *testimonium* there quoted) with reference to the games celebrated by Romulus at the foundation of the temple of *Iuppiter Feretrius*, which were regarded as the origin of the ceremony called *Bellicrepa saltatio*.

FR. 5. This line, though obviously about an incident which would naturally be recorded by Ennius, has all the air of an example invented by the authority (pseudo-Censorinus) himself. Vahlen is doubtful of its authenticity; I should be inclined to believe that it is almost certainly spurious.

Valmaggi's argument in its favour is dangerously two-edged; he assumes that because the line comes between a quotation from Lucretius and one from Vergil, it cannot be an invented example. But we might argue that because the author's name is given in two cases, it would have been given in the third also had there been one to give.

FR. 6. The fragment is definitely assigned to Ennius by Festus, but the words are repeated exactly in Lucretius IV. 409. While no one would seek to deny that there are many reminiscences of Ennius in Lucretius, the borrowed phrases are always striking or beautiful in themselves, whereas our present phrase, though perfectly appropriate where it stands, is yet completely pedestrian in style. I therefore agree with those scholars who suppose that the quotation from *Annales* x has disappeared owing to the damaged condition of the text of Festus.

FR. 7. This description of the nod of Zeus and its effects (cf. *Il.* I. 528) cannot be definitely claimed for Ennius. Varro, who quotes it, without author's name, was familiar with the translation of the *Iliad* by Cn. Matius and quotes from it twice (*L.L.* VII. 95 and 96). There is a universal recognition of the high technical merit of Matius' fragments, and Gellius had an admiration for his learning and skill. Ninnius Crassus, too, who wrote at the beginning of the first century B.C., translated part of the *Iliad*. It is therefore possible that our line may belong to one or other of these two; the editors, however, assign it without hesitation to Ennius, as is apt to be done with any anonymous heroic fragment.

altitonantis: the Homeric ὑψιβρεμέτης. The long compound adjective of verbal form standing last in the line is certainly characteristic of the style of Ennius, but the attribution cannot be definitely made.

FR. 8. Servius states that the line belongs to a speech of

Jove, as it quite obviously does. The fragment, first referred
to Ennius by Baehrens, is not included in the text by any
recent editor except Pascoli; but the conjecture has no less
right to be recorded than many others.

mea membra: of the inferior deities is, perhaps, doubtful
for so early a writer as Ennius.

Officiis: for the ablative cf. note on Bk XVI. fr. 2.

FR. 9. This fragment may be genuine, but, even if so, it
would find an equally appropriate place in the *Scipio*.

Europa: as a geographical name, is found as early as the
Homeric Hymn to Aphrodite.

FR. 10. This line is certainly by Ennius, but I place it
here from my extreme uncertainty as to whether the correct
form has been recovered. I suggest:

(1) That Pliny's words *obsidionis famem exprimens* need
not, in fact probably do not, cover a definite historical allusion, for it is more than likely that Pliny would have mentioned the name of the town had it been Nesactum or any
other actually besieged by Rome.

(2) There is no record elsewhere in Roman history of the
incident described: Pascoli's quotation of Livy XLI. 11 does
not prove his point (...*in caedem coniugum ac liberorum
uersi*—a very different thing).

(3) Abandoning the definite historical allusion, we are no
longer tempted to change *liberis* to *pueris*, and can recognise
the metre as iambic.

(4) We may restore the fragment as *Offam eripuere liberis
plorantibus Patres*; this involves no real change except the
transposition of *plorantibus* and *liberis*. Pliny's alteration may
well have been deliberate, to avoid the complete *senarius*
which even his indirect quotation would have given. I therefore hold that the fragment should be placed among the
Scenica.

FR. 11. This fragment is so brief and indefinite that there is nothing to determine its authorship. The attribution to Ennius was made by Baehrens.

FR. 12. There may well be a reminiscence of Ennius in the passage of the *Bellum Hispaniense* from which this hexameter was produced by Wölfflin, but in the two cases where there is a definite quotation, the name of Ennius is given; further the conjecture *Accumulant* for MSS. *Exaggerabant* is arbitrary, and we can hardly accept the fragment as genuine.

FR. 13. It is almost impossible that this fragment can be correctly referred to the *Annales*. If the words are a quotation at all, they are most probably from some proverb suited to the colloquial *satura* tone of the *Apocolocyntosis*.

FR. 14. This fragment is quoted by Nonius from *Aen.* lib. II; the reference was corrected to Ennius lib. II in the Editio Princeps. The most probable theory is that of Ilberg, that there was a confusion between *Aen.* II. 252 (*fusi per moenia Teucri*) and Cic. *in Verr.* II. v. 28 ...*fusi sine mente ac sine ullo sensu iacerent*, and that the second passage has displaced the first, the name of Cicero being altogether omitted. It is quite possible however that there is a reminiscence of Ennius in both these, as also in Lucr. III. 113. This is the view of Pascal (*Riv. di fil. class.* XXVI. 27); but the whole question is one on which it is impossible to dogmatise.

FR. 15. This fragment, if genuine, may belong to the naval descriptions of Bk XIV.

FR. 16. In this fragmentary line I accept the additions of Vahlen. His *nare sagax* is admirably supported by his parallels, Sil. III. 296 and Claudian XXIV. 299. *Sagax* is the *uox propria* for the scent of a hunting dog; cf. Bk X. fr. 9 and Cic. *de Diu.* I. 31. 65.

FR. 17. This line seems to be assigned to Ennius by the *Explanator in Donatum* (*G.L.K.* IV. 565); but, as the other grammarians who quote it give no author's name, there is just enough doubt about the matter to make it best to leave the fragment here.

FR. 18. This line is obviously about Ennius, but Cicero does not state that it is by Ennius.

fūuimus: the quantity of *u* is noteworthy.

FR. 19. A line which very closely resembles the Homeric ὦ πάτερ ἡμέτερε Κρονίδη ὕπατε κρειόντων. The editors, as a rule, assign it to Ennius, and if genuine, it would most naturally be placed in the Council of the Gods in Bk 1.

FR. 20. Quoted as an example of the *hexameter minimus*, and assigned to Ennius by conjecture. On the possibility that it is the work of Censorinus cf. note on *Spuria*, Fr. 5.

crateris: Latin termination for a Greek noun.

FR. 21. The testimony of Barth, who quotes from a so-called '*Ms optimo*,' does not carry much weight, and the line is not likely to be genuine.

FR. 22. This line, which appears in a quotation from the *Antiquitates Rerum Humanarum*, may well be genuine. If so, it most probably forms part of the taunts of Remus, as Vahlen suggests.

FR. 23. Another line in which there is nothing to determine whether the attribution to Ennius is correct. The same remark applies to the next two fragments.

FR. 25. Quoted as an example of *soloecismus* in the use of the form *spoliantur*. Nonius (p. 770 Lind.) quotes a form *spolor* and gives examples from Afranius and Quadrigarius.

FR. 26. It is probable, as Varro quotes this line together with one that is certainly from Ennius, that it also is correctly assigned to him.

FR. 27. It is improbable that the attribution to Ennius is correct in this case, as the language of Varro clearly suggests that his illustrations of *una trabes* are derived from two sources as are those of *una canes*.

FR. 28. The *soloecismus per personas* found here is also found in Greek, *e.g. Il.* XVII. 248 ff.

FR. 29. Despite the arguments of Vahlen, I cannot feel sure that this fragment is genuine; the words of Varro, indeed, seem quite capable of meaning that Ennius is not the author, the quotation being introduced by *ut in his qui sunt uersibus plerique*. The extreme badness of the hexameters is against their Ennian authorship; on the other hand, it is very difficult to make a hexameter of any sort out of so many long proper names. We cannot, therefore, say with any certainty whether the fragment is or is not by Ennius.

FRAGMENTA SPURIA

FR. 1. A fragment which, like Fr. 4 below, is probably the work of the grammarian, invented to illustrate a particular type of line; cf. note on Fr. 5.

FR. 2. The unsupported authority of G. Barth cannot be accepted; and, as Müller points out, the word *pandam* is not elsewhere found before the Augustan age.

FR. 3. Quoted by *Auctor ad Herennium*, this line was attributed to Ennius by Naeke (*Rh. Mus.* III. 398), but it is impossible to suppose that both it and Fr. 10 can be genuine. If either is to be accepted, the present line has probably the better claim; but there would be no difficulty for a man of normal education and facility in handling his own language to produce such 'freak' lines for himself: in fact he would probably find it easier to do so than to search through the poets: cf. note on Fr. 5.

FR. 4. Probably invented by Victorinus himself; cf. Frs. 1 and 5.

FR. 5. This and the next two fragments cannot be better discussed than by a reference to the remarks of Hardie (*Res Metrica*, p. 4), especially the following: 'But it may be doubted whether Ennius really ever wrote such lines at all. They may have been fictitious examples of solecisms or eccentricities. We know (from Pompeius, p. 289. 10 K.) that Lucilius not merely *said* that there were 100 kinds of solecism each with its own appropriate name but actually described them; *e.g. tmesis*, as if we were to write—as if Ennius wrote—*Massili portabant iuuenes ad litora tanas*.' With this argument I cordially agree, and there is every likelihood that in some of the monstrosities included in our text we can trace the influence of Lucilius and his parodies. Some of these parodies may have been taken seriously by later grammarians, so that an attribution to Ennius in our authorities is no proof of authenticity. Accordingly I reject the following Frs. 5, 6, 7 , 12, 18 on the same grounds.

FR. 8. I cannot accept this line as genuine though Vahlen retains it. The point of Varro's note is entirely lost unless the form *Casmena* (*Carmena*) is retained; and Vahlen is obliged to read *Camenas*. There is no doubt that the line is a Saturnian. We might restore *Músas quas-mémorant* (one accent on the word-group), *nós* (emphatic and therefore accented) | *nóscimus Casménas*; but this is quite uncertain, and the authorship of the line is unknown.

FR. 9. Diomedes gives no author's name nor reference of any sort, and I suggest that the line does not belong to Ennius. Both it and Fr. 13 below are too like 'An Austrian army awfully arrayed' to be taken very seriously; cf. note on Fr. 13.

FR. 10. This line is certainly referred to Ennius by Diomedes, but the *Explanator in Donatum* attributes it to Plautus. This contradiction suggests that in such cases well-known early names were attached very much at random, and that the fragment is therefore not genuine.

Fr. 11. Attributed to Ennius by Müller *propter caesurae defectum*. But there is nothing in this argument, as the line is quoted as an example of another freak type in which each foot is a separate part of speech, and could, therefore, have no caesura whoever its author.

Fr. 13. This line is rightly called an example of *absurda et indecens uerborum structura* by Plotius Sacerdos. Further, not all the grammarians who quote it give the name of Ennius, and it is anonymous in the *Auctor ad Herennium*, our oldest and best authority. His words ...*hic nihil prohibet in uitiis alienis exemplis uti O Tite e.q.s.* suggest: (1) that he felt it to be unusual to *borrow* illustrations; (2) that in this instance his custom was different from what it was in other places. The suggestion that his two examples of excessive alliteration are borrowed does not therefore invalidate the other suggestion made on Fr. 3 above. I further suggest that the *poeta* from whom the lines are taken is Lucilius and that we are in the present fragment dealing with another of his hundred solecisms; cf. note on Fr. 5 above. The second fragment quoted by our authority could easily be from Lucilius, as its metre (trochaic tetrameter catalectic) seems to have been a favourite of his.

Fr. 14. This line is prefixed by Valmaggi to the oracle of Pyrrhus (following Stowasser). But I suggest that it cannot be genuine because:

(1) The changes introduced are arbitrary. In particular *poetae*, from which *Epirotae* is produced, is probably genuine, and is intended to introduce the quotation *Aio te e.q.s.*

(2) There is no authority for the name *P(h)emonoe* at a date anything like so early as that of Ennius. It does not occur elsewhere in Latin before Lucan; in Pliny and Isidore

the name is given as that of a particular priestess at Delphi.

(3) If the name be accepted, there is no proof that it is not the subject of the earlier *reddidit* (*per uersus hexametros reddidit responsa Phemonoe e.q.s.*); this is, indeed, the most natural supposition.

(4) The word *tamquam* is not accounted for.

(5) The scansion *cluŏ* is highly doubtful for Ennius.

(6) The form *cluo* is not attested for Ennius.

(7) There is no authority for the statement that *cluo* has the original meaning of the Greek κλύειν (= hear the voice of) and follows its construction.

(8) The phrase *purpurei Epirotae* is very strange in an address to the person himself and passages like Hor. *Od.* I. 35. 12, Ovid, *Met.* VII. 102 are no real parallel.

(9) No other among our authorities quotes such a line.

FR. 15. There is no trace elsewhere of any body of *scholia* on Statius different from that preserved under the name of Lactantius; and Colonna's unsupported testimony does not warrant a belief in its existence. The construction *perculsi pectora* (sometimes called *accusatiuus Graecus*) is unknown in the early period: neither Bennett nor Frobenius can quote any example of it except the present fragment which they both accept. Hence I do not consider the fragment genuine.

FR. 16. I cannot accept these lines, though none of the editors rejects them. In Orosius they run: *Qui antehac inuicti fuere uiri, pater optume Olumpi,* | *Hos ego in pugna uici uictusque sum ab isdem*; and in Paulus Diaconus: *Qui inuicti ante fuere uiri, pater optume Olumpi,* | *Hos et ego in pugna uici uictusque sum ab isdem*. The variants seem to be obvious corrections made to remove the metrical errors. As it stands in Orosius the first line is a foot too long, and we have to scan *fūere*, which, if not quite impossible, is rare in

Ennius. *Hōs ĕgŏ in* is also very doubtful. It can be regarded only as an instance of 'prosodic hiatus,' to be explained perhaps as a case in which the final syllable would in the dramatists be shortened by the law of *breues breuiantes*, and thus resembling the *Vale, uălĕ, inquit, Iolla* of Vergil. It is doubtful, however, whether Ennius would have recognised *egō*, and the passage which should be of great importance with regard to his admission of hiatus (Cic. *Orat.* xlv) is unfortunately of doubtful reading ...*at Ennius saepe* (sc. *hiabat*) *Scipio inuicte*.... *Saepe* is the reading of the *codices mutili*, while *semel* appears in the rest. *Semel* cannot be right in any case; and *saepe* seems, with our existing knowledge, an exaggeration, and is, moreover, inconsistent with the later words *Hoc idem nostri saepius non tulissent*. The only safe conclusion seems to be that we cannot introduce such a scansion as *Hos ĕgŏ in* by pure conjecture; cf. the remarks of Norden in *Ennius und Vergilius*, p. 85.

FR. 17. This fragment, asserted by Colonna to come from *anonymus quidam grammaticus*, who quotes it *expresse ex Ennio*, cannot be accepted. His error is due to ignorance of the genuine fragment referred to in Seneca (*Epp.* 108. 34), which makes it plain that *Quem super ingens | Porta tonat caeli* (Verg. *Geo.* iii. 260) owes nothing to Ennius but *porta caeli*, and that those words are not from the *Annales* but from the well-known epigram on Scipio: *Si fas endo plagas caelestum ascendere cuiquam est | Mi soli caeli maxima porta patet*.

FR. 19. In Marius Victorinus this fragment is assigned to Lucilius. It is, however, accompanied by another which is erroneously assigned to Ennius in place of Lucilius. But it is an entirely arbitrary assumption that we are dealing with a simple transposition of names. Most probably two quotations from Lucilius were given, one of which was misplaced and so ousted the genuine Ennius fragment.

INDEX TO THE NOTES

Isidore, 142, 190, 226, 227, 233
Isthmian Games, 191
Istria, 177, 199
It (final), quantity of, 188

Janus, 171
Jove, 121, 135, 148, 176, 215, 220,
   227, 230
Junis, 136, 171
Juno, 121, 122, 176, 177, 178
Juvenal, 161

Keil, 145
Koch, 120

Lachmann, 194, 205, 221
Lactantius, 186, 236
Lacte, 193
Lacus Timauus, 201
Laevinus, M. Valerius, 181
Laeuus, 118, 131, 227
Lambinus, 144
Lampadio, 150
Landgraf, 142
Larisa, 206
Latium, 106, 131
Lavinia, 107
Leucata, 181, 186
Lex Oppia, 192
Liba, 125
Lindsay, Prof. W. M., 99, 103, 116,
   127, 130, 134, 161, 164, 168,
   183, 210
Liris, 137
Lituus, 214
Livius Andronicus, 93, 119, 163,
   166, 168, 177, 207
   Hymn to Juno, 177, 178
   Odyssey, 163, 166, 168
Livy, 124, 133, 159, 174, 179, 203, 204
   I, 112, 124, 126, 128, 177; V, 132,
   133, 158; VII, 117, 137, 161,
   204; VIII, 146, 174; XX, 161;
   XXI, 134; XXII, 173, 179; XXIV,
   211; XXV, 151, 194; XXVI, 175,
   186; XXXI, 190; XXXII, 186,
   187; XXXIII, 188; XXXIV, 192;
   XXXV, 228; XXXVII, 195, 196,
   197; XXXVIII, 197, 199; XLI,
   201, 203, 205, 230
Lucan, 134, 219, 235

Lucania, 159
Lucian, 100
Lucilius, 108, 122, 123, 141, 143,
   157, 160, 192, 197, 208, 217,
   234, 235, 237
Lucretia, 134, 135
Lucretius, 97, 120, 124, 143, 157,
   182, 217, 220, 221, 227, 229
   I, 104, 200, 211; II, 119, 142,
   205; III, 132, 183, 206, 231;
   IV, 209; V, 142, 148, 161, 179,
   196, 214, 218; VI, 103
Luna, 95

Macedonia, wars with, 186, 189,
   206, 220, 228
Macer, C. Licinius, 204
Macrobius, 97, 98, 121, 134, 136,
   141, 149, 160, 171, 182, 190,
   191, 194, 203, 204, 212, 220
Mactare, 216
Madvig, 187
Magnesia, 197
Mähly, 197
Mamurius, 125
Manicata, 179
Manilius, 212
Marcius Vates, 127, 158
Mars, 121
Martial, 95, 157, 225
Matius, Cn., 212, 229
Mayllus, 109
Me, 126
Meddix, 175
Melos, 178
Mensae, 125
Mercier, 218
Merula, 104, 118, 127, 179, 188,
   206, 213
Messalla (augur), 114
Messapus, 100
Metapontum, 100
Mettius Fuffettius, 126, 128
Minerva, 170
Minturnae, 138
Minucia, 220
Minucius Felix, 160
Mis, 127
Moloch, 157
Mommsen, 114, 115, 217
Müller, C. O., 124, 188, 214, 228

For EU product safety concerns, contact us at Calle de José Abascal, 56–1°,
28003 Madrid, Spain or eugpsr@cambridge.org.

www.ingramcontent.com/pod-product-compliance
Ingram Content Group UK Ltd.
Pitfield, Milton Keynes, MK11 3LW, UK
UKHW012330130625
459647UK00009B/190